SUPERIOR NATIONAL FOREST

A Complete Recreation Guide
for Paddlers, Hikers, Anglers, Campers,
Mountain Bikers, and Skiers

D1091290

DISCARDED

Robert Beymer

THE MOUNTAINEERS/SEATTLE

The Mountaineers: Organized 1906 ". . . to explore, study, preserve, and enjoy the natural beauty of the Northwest."

3 2 1 0 9
5 4 3 2 1

Published by The Mountaineers
306 Second Avenue West, Seattle, Washington 98119

Published simultaneously in Canada by Douglas & McIntyre, Ltd.,
1615 Venables Street, Vancouver, B.C. V5L 2H1

Manufactured in the United States of America

Edited by Miriam Bulmer
Base maps courtesy U.S. Forest Service, modified by Chris Jansen
Cover photographs: Mountain Lake Overlook
   Insets: (top) Trout Creek, BWCAW; (bottom) Stuart Lake Campsite
All photos by the author unless otherwise noted
Cover design by Betty Watson
Book design by Nick Gregoric

Library of Congress Cataloging in Publication Data

Beymer, Robert.
   Superior National Forest : a complete recreation guide for
 paddlers, hikers, anglers, campers, mountain bikers, and skiers /
 Robert Beymer.
       p.   cm.
   Includes index.
   ISBN 0-89886-168-3
   1. Outdoor recreation--Minnesota--Superior National Forest--Guide
 -books.   2. Superior National Forest (Minn.)--Guide-books.
 I. Title.
 GV191.42.M6B49   1989
 917.76'771--dc19   89-3229
                                                                 CIP

CONTENTS

LIST OF TABLES

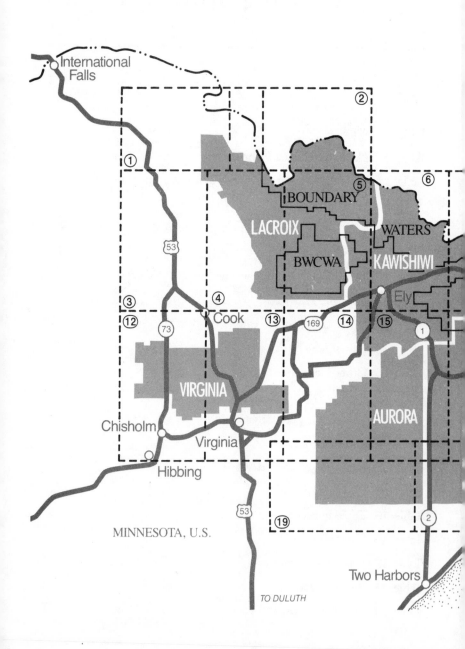

International
Falls

①

53

③ ②

BOUNDARY

⑤ ⑥

LACROIX

WATERS

KAWISHIWI

BWCWA

③
⑫

④

73

Cook

⑬

169

⑭

Ely

⑮

1

VIRGINIA

Chisholm

Virginia

Hibbing

53

AURORA

MINNESOTA, U.S.

⑲

②

TO DULUTH

Two Harbors

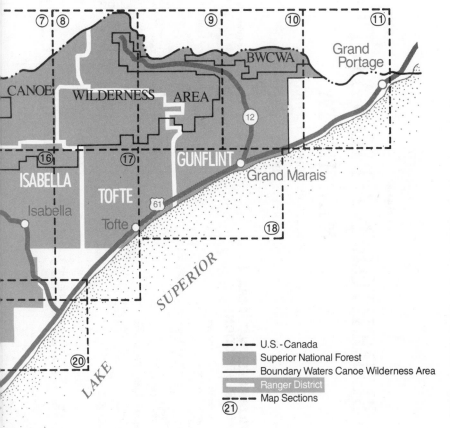

ONTARIO, CANADA

⑦ ⑧ ⑨ ⑩ ⑪

BWCWA

Grand
Portage

CANOE WILDERNESS AREA

⑫

⑯ ⑰ GUNFLINT

ISABELLA TOFTE Grand Marais

Isabella 61

Tofte ⑱

SUPERIOR

⑳

LAKE

—··— U.S.-Canada
Superior National Forest
Boundary Waters Canoe Wilderness Area
Ranger District
——— Map Sections
㉑

U. S. DEPARTMENT OF AGRICULTURE
FOREST SERVICE
R. MAX PETERSON, CHIEF

SUPERIOR NATIONAL FOREST

MINNESOTA

FOURTH PRINCIPAL MERIDIAN

1984

B.W.C.A. WILDERNESS WATERCRAFT HORSEPOWER RESTRICTIONS

No horsepower limit - Permanent

Little Vermilion Lake
Loon Lake
Lac LaCroix (that portion south of Snow Bay and east of Wilkins Bay)
Loon River
Sand Point Lake

2 10 horsepower limit - Permanent

Canoe Lake
Island River (east of Isabella Lake)
Clearwater Lake
South Fowl Lake
Alder Lake
North Fowl Lake
Seagull Lake (that portion generally east of Threemile Island)

10 horsepower limit - Temporary until January 1, 1994 or until termination of the resort adjacent to Brule Lake

10 horsepower limit - Temporary until January 1, 1999

Seagull Lake (that portion generally west of Threemile Island)

3 25 horsepower limit - Permanent

Fall Lake
Newton Lake
Moose Lake
Newfound Lake
Saganaga Lake (except that portion west of American Point)
Sucker Lake
Snowbank Lake
E. Bearskin Lake
South Farm Lake
Trout Lake
Basswood Lake (except that portion generally north of Jackfish Bay and Washington Island)

ALL OTHER LAKES OR PORTIONS OF LAKES WITHIN THE WILDERNESS ARE PADDLE ONLY.

Scale ¼" = 1 mile

0   1   2   3   4   5   6 miles

5 Kilometers

LEGEND

▬	National Forest Boundary	6 9	U. S. and State Highway
▭	National Forest Land	64	County Route
▬	Boundary Waters Canoe Area Wilderness Boundary	766	Forest Road, Trail or Portage
▬	Quetico Provincial Park Boundary	⌐	Interchange
▬	Main Highway	⊤	Landing Field
▬	Secondary Highway	⚒	Mine
▬	Good Road	F / R	Falls / Rapids
▬	Secondary Road	●	Boat Launching Site (Ramp)
====	Primitive Road Not maintained for public travel	▲	Boat Launching Site (Carry Down)
-----	Designated Trail or Portage	•••••	Designated Snowmobile Trails Inside B.W.C.A.
─┼─┼─	Railroad		Canoe Route
▬ ▬	Mining Protection Area Boundary	■	Archaeological/Historical Site
▬ ▬	Purchase Unit Boundary	⚔	Picnic Site

◣	Recreation Site Forest Service Camping allowed, minimal facilities
◭	Recreation Site, Forest Service With camping facilities
◮	Recreation Site, Forest Service Without camping facilities
△	Recreation Site, Other With camping facilities
✕	Campground, Other Water access only
△	Recreation Site, Other Without camping facilities
⚐	Winter Sports Area
✕	Customs
▪	Canadian Ranger Cabin
⚑	District Ranger Station
⊞	Trailhead for Hikers
⊙	Trailhead for Canoeists and Boaters
◆	Point of Interest
90	Canoeing BWCAW Entry Points
92	Hiking BWCAW Entry Points

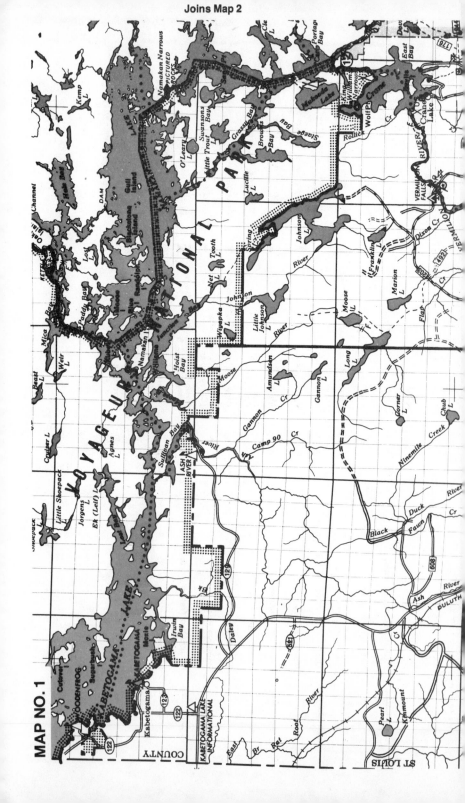

MAP NO. 1

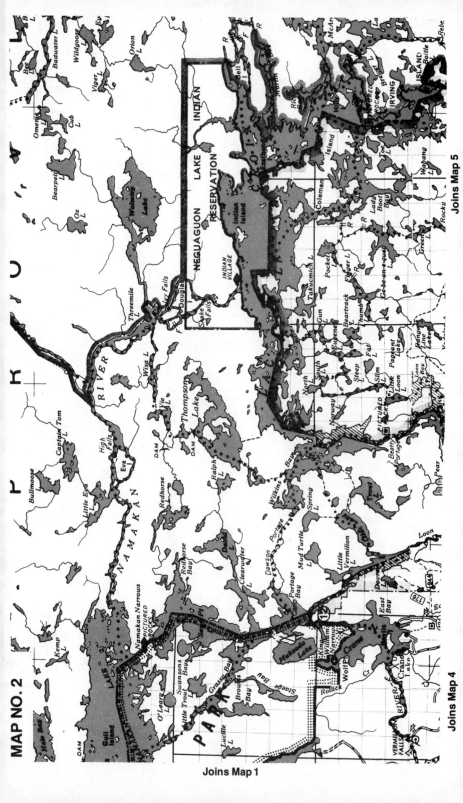

MAP NO. 2

Joins Map 1

Joins Map 4

Joins Map 5

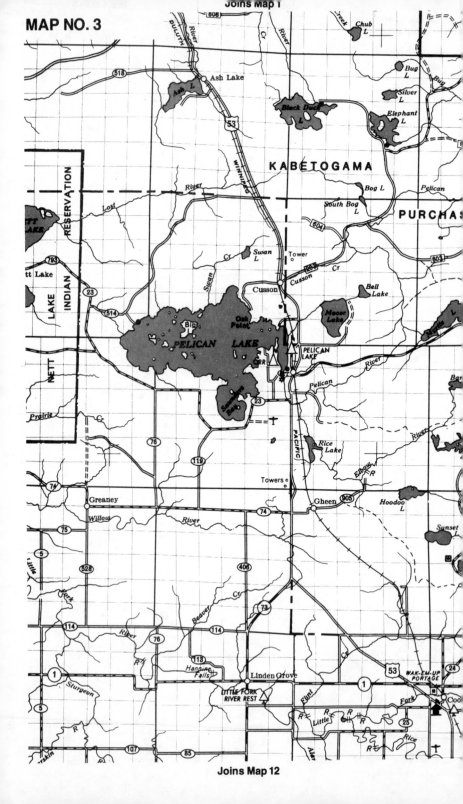

MAP NO. 3

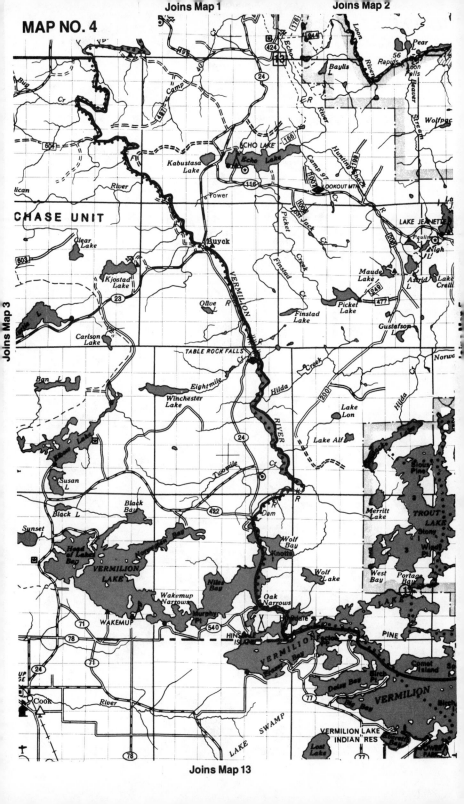

MAP NO. 4

Joins Map 3

Joins Map 13

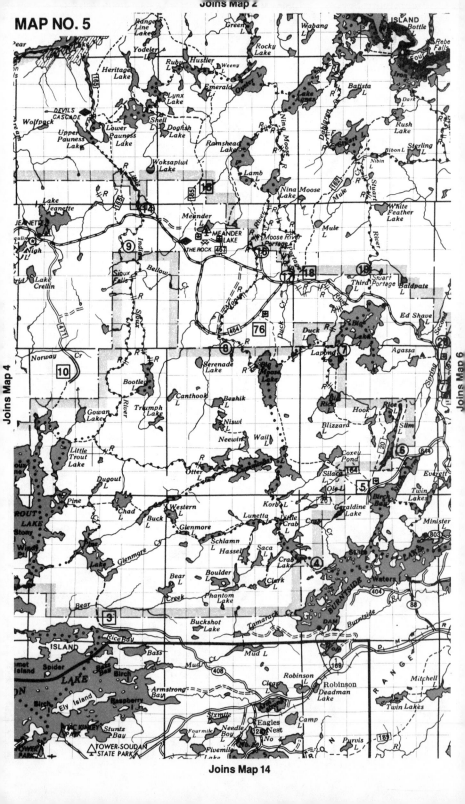

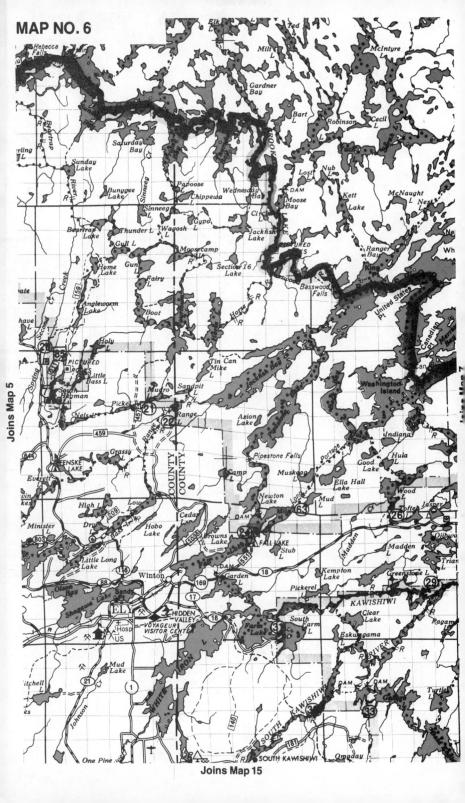

MAP NO. 6

Joins Map 5

Joins Map 15

P A R M

Black L

Kahshahpiwi Lake

Silence Lake

Dettburg L

Edge L

Rod L

Glacier Lake

Yum Yum

Summer Lake

Noon L

Isabella

East L

Dumas L

Fauquier L

Gamma

Other Ma

Goodier

Louisa Lake

No Man L

Tint Map L

Emerald Lake

Neil L

White I

Burke L

Meadows Lake

Fisher

Canadian

Bayley Bay

North Bay

Merriam Bay

L A K E

Poacher Lake

Polaris

K N I F E   L A K E

Spoon L

Pickle L

Se L

Inlet Bay

R I V E R

Knife L

Dix L

Skoota

Kekekabic

Rice Bay

Prairie Portage

Trident Lake

Vera L

Missionary

Manomin Lake

Sucker

Splash

Ashigan

Solitude L

Hatchet L

Wisini L

Gerund

Fraser

Newfound Lake

Boot L

Jordan

Vista L

Atworth

Sagus

Smite

25

Seagull

27

Disappointment Lake

Beaver L

Fisher L

Kiang L

Bow L

Jasper L

160

9

248

Benezie L

Starlight Lake

Jut L

Lake Carol

Amber L

Alice Lake

Ojibway

18

74

Delta

Museum Lake

Triangle L

30

Fire L

PICTURED ROCKS

Fishdance

29

R I V E R

Lake One

Lake Two

Lake Four

Hope L

South Hope

Maniwaki

Ragam

Rock Island

Lake Three

Hudson L

Ahmoo

Arrow L

Whittler

Cherry

Horseshoe Lake

South Wilder

Pose L

Turtle L

Kayoskh L

Path L

Fishdance

Gull L

Pang L

Cattoo L

Diana L

Pelt L

Perne L

Tomahawk L

Quadga L

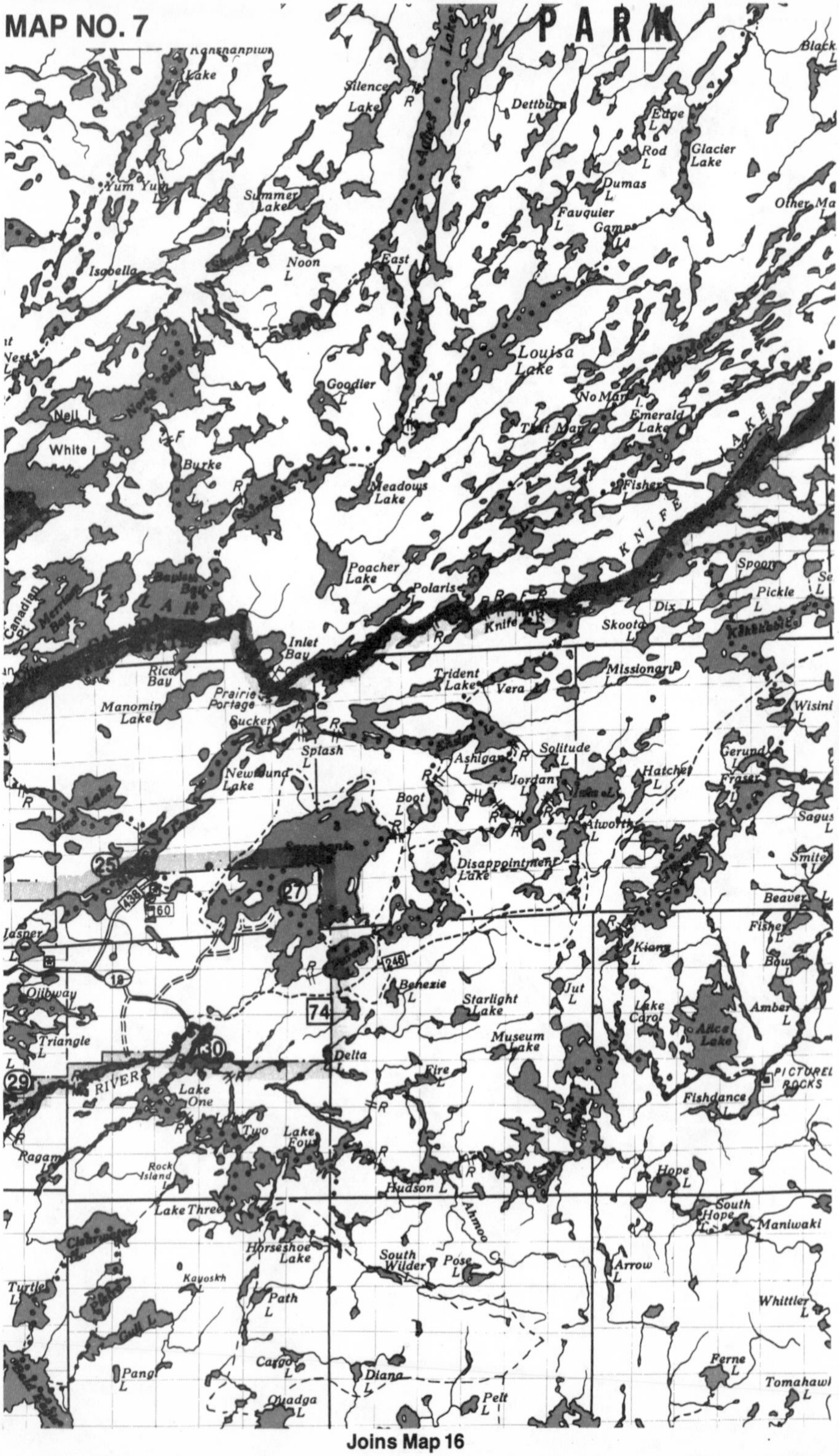

Joins Map 6

Joins Map 8

MAP NO. 8

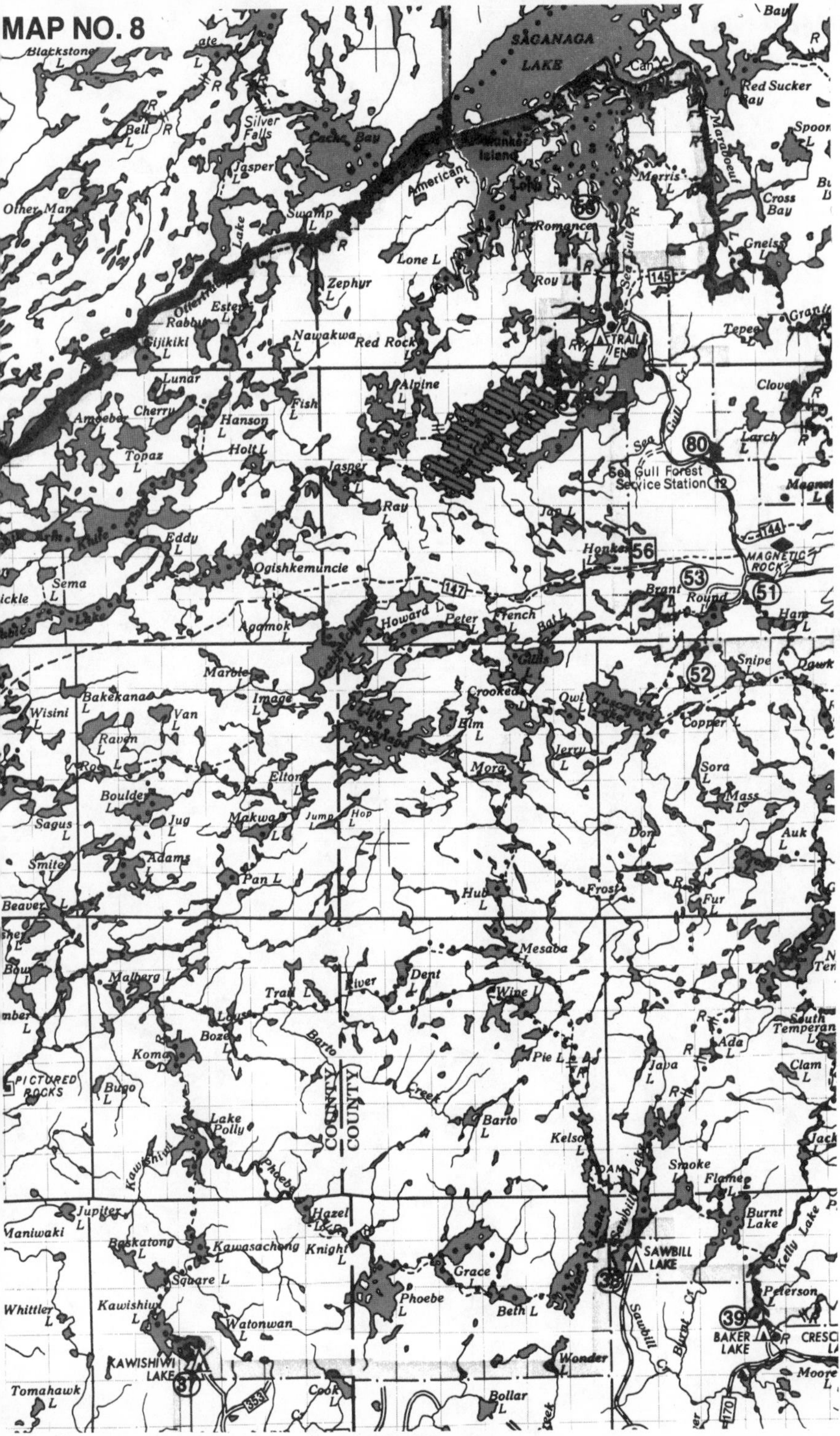

Blackstone L

ale

SAGANAGA LAKE

Bay

R

Silver Falls L

Cache Bay

Can

Red Sucker Bay

Bell L

R

Jasper L

Spoon L

Yankee Island

Merris L

Swamp L

American Pt

Cross Bay

Other Man

Lone L

L

Romance

Bu L

Gneiss L

Ottertrack Lake

R

Roy L

Zephyr L

145

Este L

R

Sijikiki

Nawakwa

Red Rock

TRAIL END

Tepee

Granit

R

Lunar L

Alpine L

Clove R

Amoeber

Cherry

Hanson L

Larch L

Topaz

Holt L

Jasper

Gull

Sea Gull Forest Service Station

Magnet L

Eddy

Ray L

Honker

56

MAGNETIC ROCK

Sema L

Ogishkemuncie

147

Brant L

Round

51

ickle

white

Agamok

Howard

Peter

French

Bat L

Ham L

Marble L

Image L

Gull

Crooked

Owl

Snipe

Dawk

52

Wisini L

Van L

Elm L

Jerry

Copper L

Bakekana L

Raven L

Sora L

Ros L

Elton L

Mora L

Mass L

Boulder L

Jug L

Makwa L

Jump Hop L

Auk L

Sagus L

Adams L

Pan L

Don L

Frost L

Fur L

Smite L

Hub L

Beaver L

she L

Mesaba L

Bou L

Ten

Malberg L

Trail

River

Dent

Wine L

South Temperan

Barto

Lous

Boze L

Ada L

umber L

Koma L

Pie L

Java L

Clam L

PICTURED ROCKS

Bugo L

Creek

Barto

Jack

Lake Polly

Kelso

Smoke

Flame L

Burnt Lake

Maniwaki

Jupiter L

Hazel L

Knight

Kawishiwi

Baskatong L

Kawasachong

Grace L

Peterson

Square L

Phoebe L

Beth L

SAWBILL LAKE

39

Whittler L

Kawishiu L

Watonwan L

BAKER LAKE

CRESC

Moore

KAWISHIWI LAKE

37

Wonder L

Tomahawk L

Cook L

Bollar L

170

COOK COUNTY

Joins Map 9

Joins Map 17

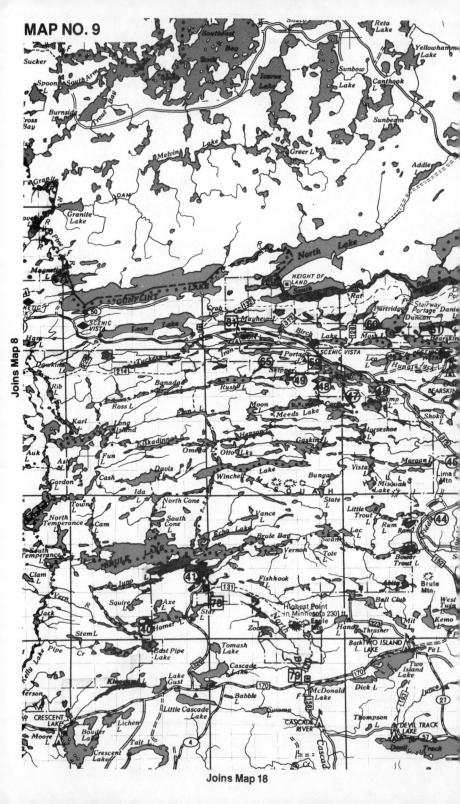

MAP NO. 9

Joins Map 8

MAP NO. 10

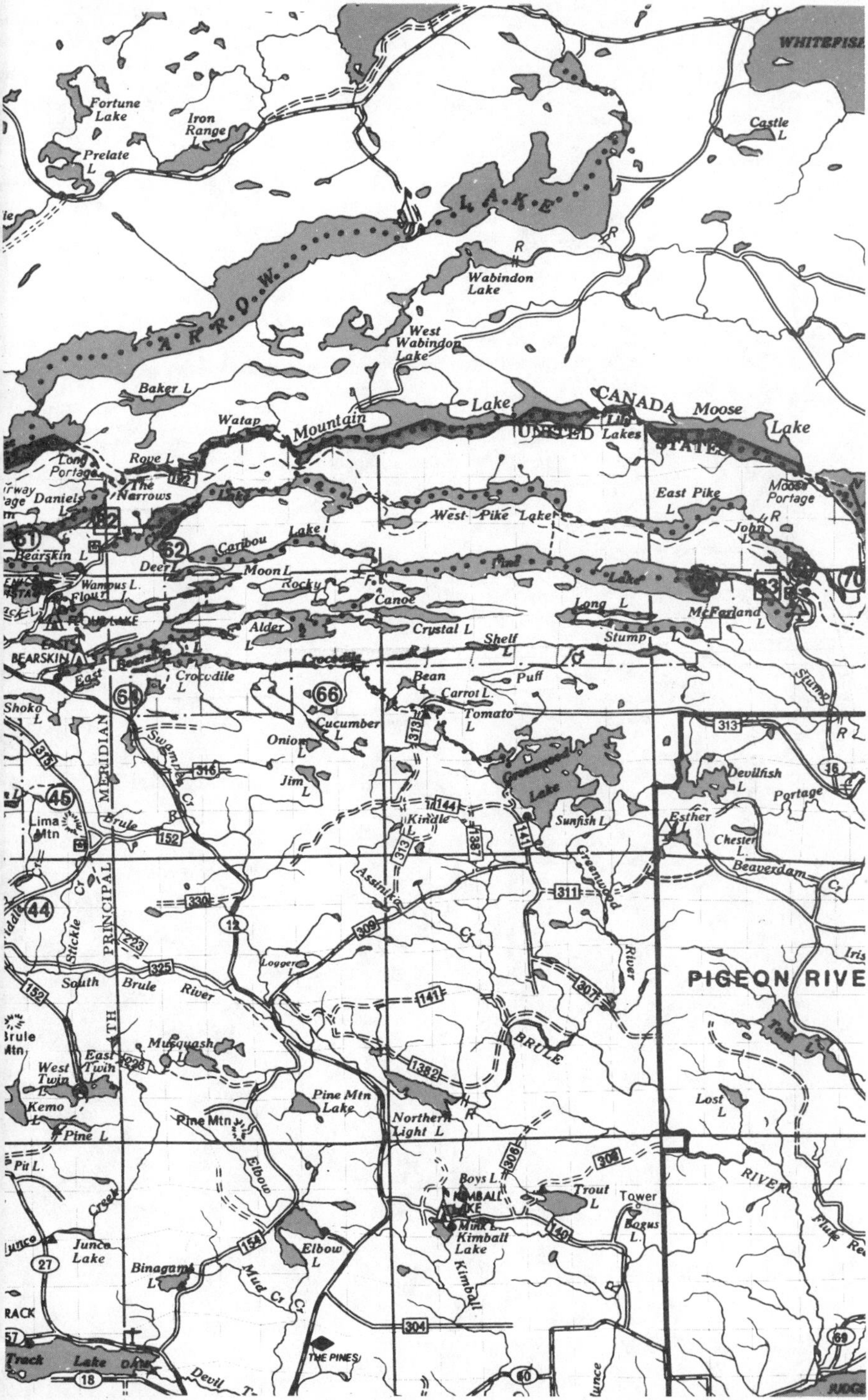

WHITEPINE

Fortune Lake

Iron Range

Prelate L

Castle L

A·R·R·O·W   L·A·K·E

Wabindon Lake

West Wabindon Lake

CANADA   Moose Lake

UNITED STATES

Baker L

Watap   Mountain   Lake   Lakes

Long Portage   Rove L   12

The Narrows   Daniels

Moose Portage

East Pike

John L   R

51   62   Bearskin L   Deer   Caribou Lake   Moon L   Rocky   West Pike Lake   Fine   Lake   83   70

McFarland L

Wampus L   Flour   Canoe

FLOUR LAKE   Alder   Crystal L   Shelf L   Long L   Stump

BEARSKIN   East   Crocodile   Crocodile   Bean   Puff   Stump

Shoko   60   66   Cucumber L   313   Carrot L   Tomato   313   Devilfish L   Portage   15

MERIDIAN   Onion L   Jim L   Green Lake   Esther

45   Swamp   316   144   Sunfish L   Chester L   Beaverdam Cr

Lima Mtn   Brule   152   Kindle   313   137   141   311

44   Stickle Cr   330   Assini   309   Greenwood River   PIGEON RIVER

South   Brule   River   12   223   325   Logger   141   307   Toad L

Brule Mtn   Musquash   328   138   BRULE   Lost L

West Twin Ls   East Twin   Pine Mtn Lake   Northern Light L   RIVER   Pike Rd

Kemo   Pine Mtn   Elbow   138   305   309

Pine L   154   Boys L   Trout L   Tower

Pit L   Junce Cr   KIMBALL LAKE   Mink L   149   Bagus

27   Junce Lake   Binagami L   Elbow L   Kimball Lake

RACK   Mud Cr   304

57   Track Lake   DAM   Devil Tr   THE PINES   60   69

Joins Map 18

Joins Map 11

Joins Map 10

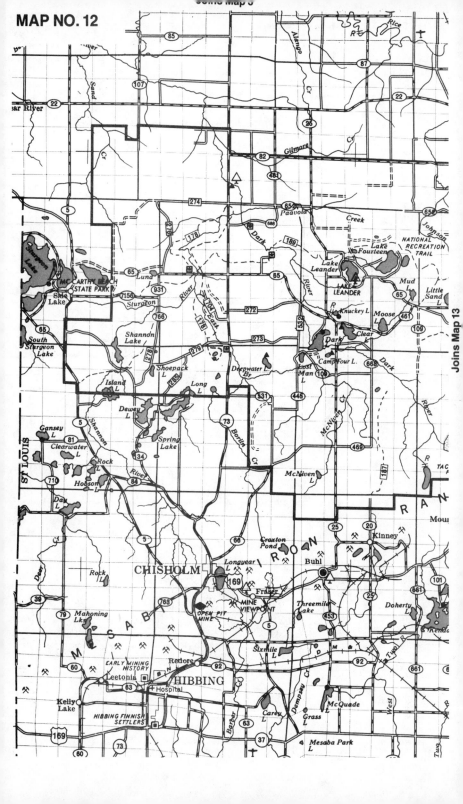

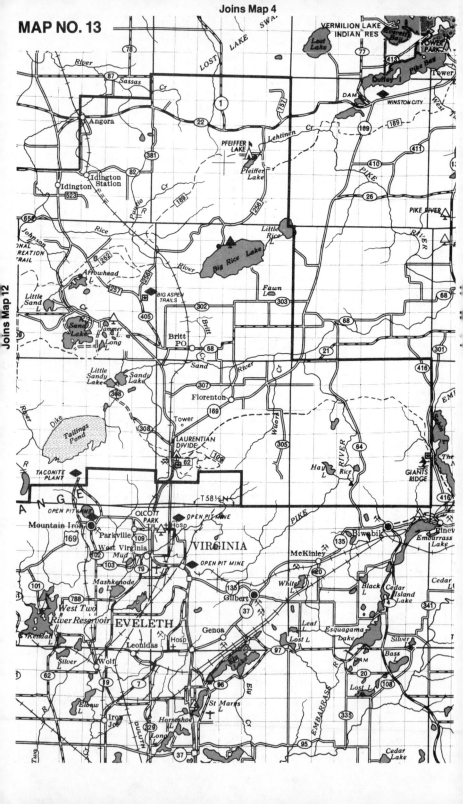

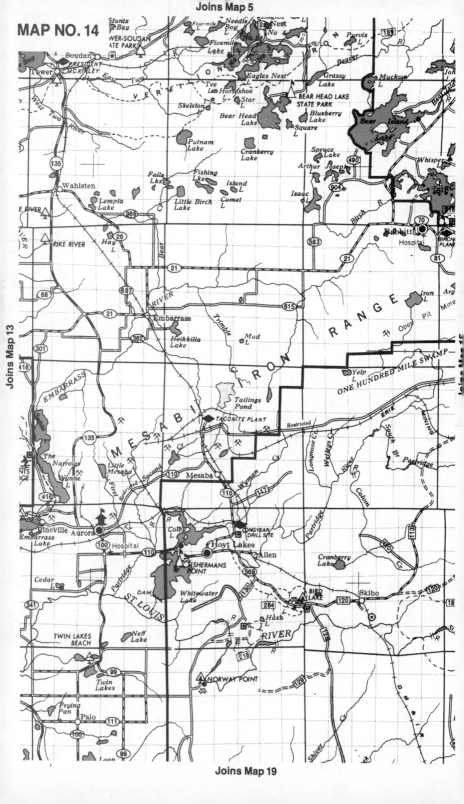

Stuntz Bay

Fourmile

Needle Boy

Eagles Nest No. 4

Purvis

181

WER-SOUDAN STATE PARK

Fivemile Lake

Soudan

PRESIDENT McKINLEY

Tower

VERMILION

East Two

Beaver

Muckwa

Grassy Lake

BEAR HEAD LAKE STATE PARK

Bear Island Lake

Joh

Eagles Nest

Tee L

Horseshoe

Star L

Skeleton

Bear Head Lake

Blueberry Lake

Square L

Whisper

West Two River

135

Wahlsten

Lempia Lake

969

26

Hay L

PIKE RIVER

Falls Lks

Fishing Lks

Island L

Little Birch Lake

Comet L

Spruce Lake

Arthur

Joseph

490

904

R

Isaac

R

Putnam Lake

Cranberry Lake

Babbitt

70

Hospital

BIRCH PLANT

81

583

21

68

527

21

362

RIVER

Embarrass

Heikkila Lake

Trimble Cr

Mud L

615

RANGE

Iron L

Arg

Mine

Opel Pit

301

416

EMBARRASS

Yelp L

ONE HUNDRED MILE SWAMP

MESABI

IRON

Tailings Pond

TACONITE PLANT

Restricted

ERIE

MINING

135

The Narrows

Wynne

Little Mesaba

Cr

110

Mesaba

Wyman

113

Longnose Cr

Wetleg Cr

River

Coluin

South By Partridge

416

First

Restricted Second

Pineville

Aurora

100

Hospital

Colby L

LONGYEAR DRILL SITE

Hoyt Lakes

Allen

Partridge

Cranberry Lake

LEO

113

110

569

Embarrass Lake

Cedar L

Partridge

FISHERMANS POINT

DAM

Whitewater Lake

1190

284

BIRD LAKE

120

Skibo

120

18

341

ST. LOUIS

Hush

RIVER

129

TWIN LAKES BEACH

Neff Lake

218

Shiver

99

NORWAY POINT

129

Twin Lakes

Frying Pan L

Palo

111

100

Loon

99

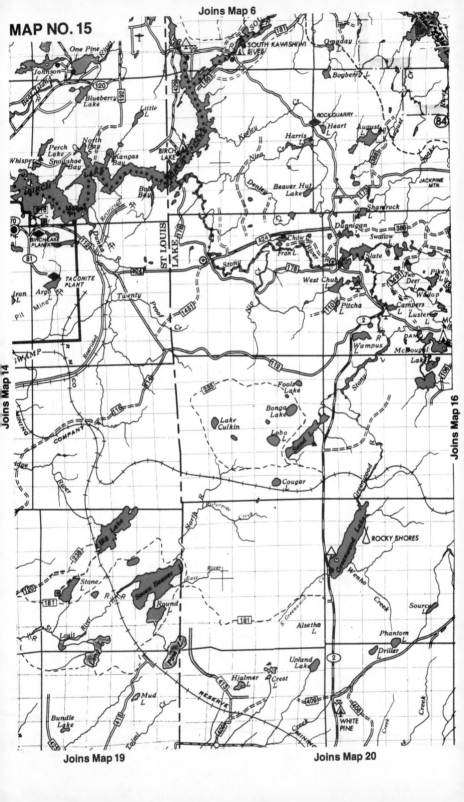

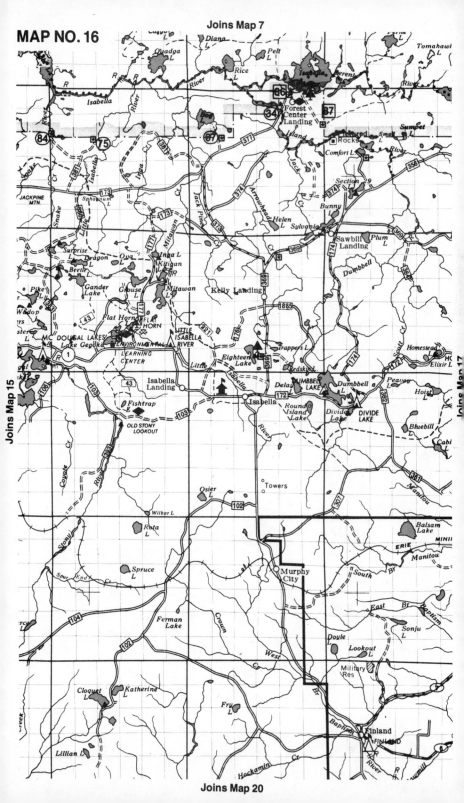

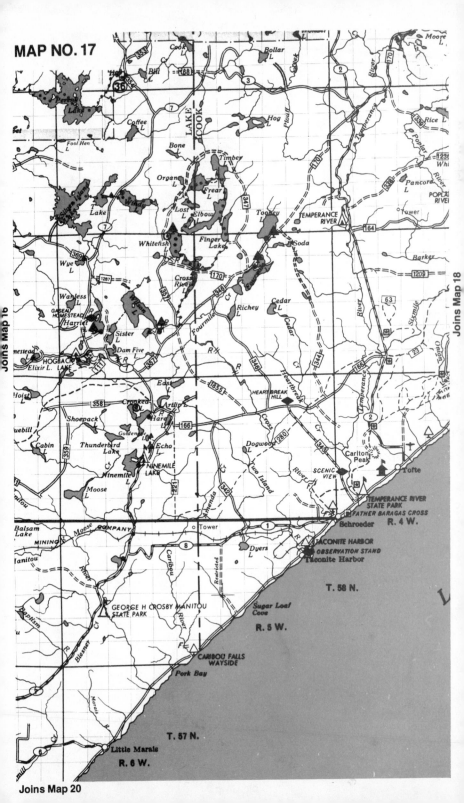

MAP NO. 17

Joins Map 1b

Joins Map 18

Joins Map 20

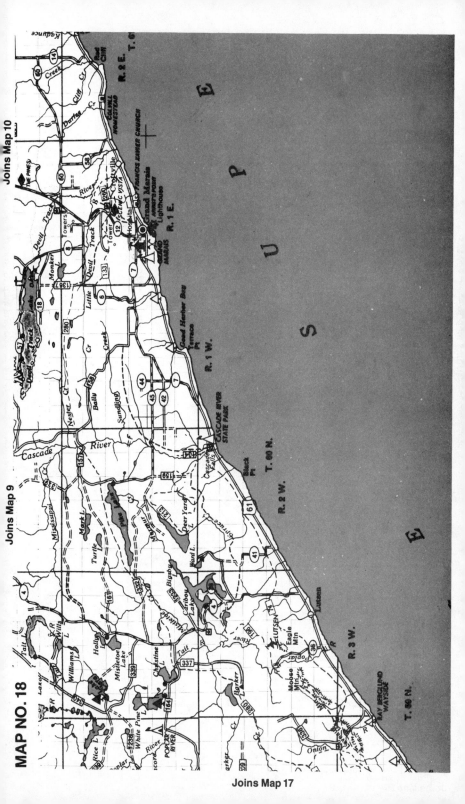

Joins Map 10

Joins Map 9

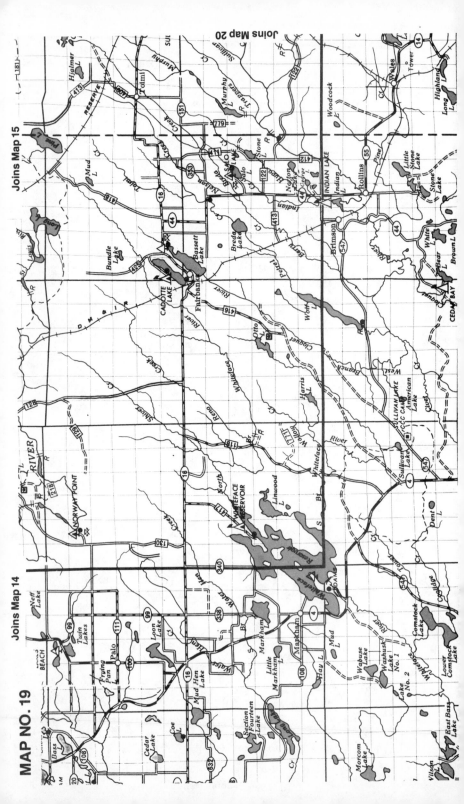

MAP NO. 19

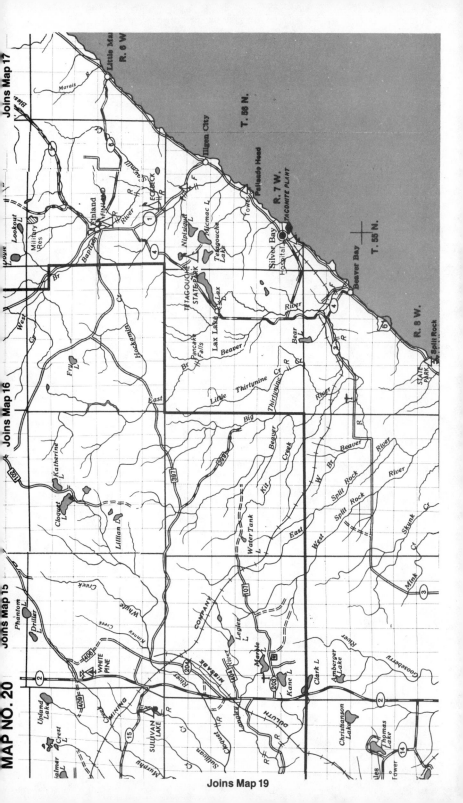

Joins Map 17
Joins Map 16
Joins Map 15
Joins Map 19

PREFACE

I was originally attracted to Superior National Forest because of the canoeing opportunities in the Boundary Waters Canoe Area Wilderness (BWCAW). Since 1967, I've paddled throughout the aquatic network of lakes and streams that lies along the Canadian border of northeastern Minnesota. In recent years, however, I've discovered many other recreational opportunities in the Forest. Since moving to Ely, I have hiked most of the trails, explored nearly all of the back roads and bicycled many of the "non-roads" in Superior National Forest. I've skied cross-country from December through March, gathered wild rice on a cool September morning and picked blueberries on a sun-drenched afternoon in July.

During those outings, I've heard wolves howling on moonlit nights and I've seen their tracks in the soft ground and fresh snow along my paths. I've observed dozens of moose browsing in bogs and along lakeshores and forest roads. I've seen bald eagles swoop low to snatch fish from a rapids in early spring, when the lakes were still covered by ice. Curious otters swimming across my path have hissed at my canoe, and black bears have entered my campsites in search of food.

During my travels around our beautiful nation, I've found no place more appealing than Superior National Forest. The Rocky Mountains may be more grand, more breathtaking; the fast-flowing streams of the Ozarks offer a more thrilling brand of canoeing; the wilderness backcountry of Alaska is, without a doubt, more isolated and more pristine. But nowhere in America is there a place more lovely, more tranquil, more wild and primitive and, at the same time, more *accessible* to its visitors than Superior National Forest. Merely a long day's drive from Chicago, Kansas City and St. Louis, the Forest is readily available to literally millions of Midwesterners with no more than a week's vacation to spare. And the recreational opportunities are virtually unlimited: canoeing, backpacking and hiking, mountain biking, fishing, cross-country and alpine skiing, car camping, horseback riding, berry picking, picnicking, sea kayaking and more.

Nevertheless, I feel compelled to make two confessions. Confession number one: The original idea for this book is not my own. A couple of years ago, Steve Hoecker, assistant forest ranger in the La Croix District, called me to discuss the idea of promoting recreation in Superior National Forest outside the BWCAW. Steve thought I might be interested in doing a guidebook. He was right.

During the two years of research, the project grew as I discovered more and more recreational potential that I hadn't previously known about. There is a whole lot more to Superior National Forest than the BWCAW. And you don't

Echo River rapids near Crane Lake

have to be a canoeist to enjoy it. For instance, I learned about mountain bikes and the tremendous resource that the Forest is for bikers. I discovered accesses to lakes that I had never heard of. And I took a different approach to the BWCAW, considering canoe routes that could be enjoyed easily in one day or less by visitors who preferred to camp outside the Wilderness. The project has been exhausting at times, but a learning experience, and always a labor of love.

Confession number two: Most of the information contained in this book is already available to you at no charge. The USFS distributes "Recreational Opportunity Guides" (ROGs) to visitors seeking information about Superior National Forest. A ROG is usually a one-page handout that describes one particular activity in one particular location. Each of the six districts distributes ROGs that pertain to the opportunities in its own part of the Forest. In addition, I gathered information from the Minnesota Department of Natural Resources, from the Minnesota Office of Tourism and from various private and quasi-public organizations that, in one way or another, contribute to the topic of recreation in Superior National Forest. This was necessary because, contained within the overall Forest boundaries, are state, county and private lands that are not under the jurisdiction of the Forest Service and are, therefore, not dealt with by ROGs.

This information formed the basis for my research. To all who contributed to the publication of those ROGs and other literature in the public domain, I offer my sincere appreciation. Besides drawing from those unknown authors, I interviewed many public officials who are largely responsible for the outstanding recreational facilities in Superior National Forest. I found them all to be cooperative and some to be genuinely enthusiastic about the project. At the risk of overlooking someone, I want to publicly thank those who made the most significant contributions: Barb Soderberg, SNF recreation specialist, whose cooperation, assistance and encouragement on this project, as on past projects, has been invaluable. Jack Blackwell, Dave Tucci, Ron Krupa, Gary Lidholm, Judy Ness, Gordon Peters and Walt Okstad at the SNF central headquarters in Duluth. Darrell Richards, Dave Worshek, Jerry Rustad and Bill Raida in the Laurentian District. Steve Hoecker, Mark Toot, Yvonne Schmidt, John Wolf, August Carstens, Don Potter and John Kuyava in the La Croix District. Mike Manlove, Jerry Jussila, Jim Hines, Gil Knight and Brenda Madden in the Kawishiwi District. John Dorio, Terry Olson and Kay Getting in the Isabella District. Terrence Eggum and Wayne Russ in the Tofte District. Tom Brady, Becci Spears, Tim Norman, Duane Cihlar, Leroy Pratt and Jeff Larson in the Gunflint District. James K. Hane, district forester, Minnesota Division of Forestry. Tom Pederson, Superior Hiking Trail Association coordinator. Paul Radomski, assistant fisheries manager, Minnesota DNR. Ed Solstad, Minnesota Rovers Outing Club.

I'm also fortunate to have some patient friends who were willing to pose motionless with 40-pound packs on their backs or to repeat an uphill ride on a mountain bike while I pointed a camera. Special thanks to my friends and outdoor models: Kathleen Anderson, Steve Ashe, Scott Beattie, Lynn Brasgala, Barb Gecas, Sharlene Gecas, Lloyd Gilbertson, Ann and Kevin Hubbard, Steve Johnson, Natalie McFaul, Kathy McIntosh, Marcia Ready, Steve and Ann Schon, Paul Smith, Mark and Melinda Spinler, Rolf and Linda Swanson, Check Tiffany and the Voyageur Outward Bound School.

As always, I owe a special debt of gratitude to my loving wife, Cheryl, for her patience, encouragement and assistance with this project.

This book is written for you, the Forest visitor. I've tried to make it informative, interesting and as accurate as possible. But believe it or not, the Forest does change. Foot trails are rerouted, old roads are closed and new roads are constructed, old accesses to lakes and streams are replaced by new ones, and even some of the lakes and streams change their appearance from one season to another, or from year to year. Any corrections that you feel are important for future editions of this book will be appreciated. Please write me in care of the publisher. I'd love to hear from you!

R.H.B.
March, 1989

A NOTE ABOUT SAFETY

Travel in many parts of Superior National Forest entails unavoidable risks that every traveler assumes and must be aware of and respect. The fact that an area is described in this book is not a representation that it will be safe for you. Trips vary greatly in difficulty and in the amount and kind of preparation needed to enjoy them safely. Some routes may have changed, or conditions on them may have deteriorated since this book was written. Also, of course, conditions can change even from day to day, owing to weather and other factors. A trip that is safe in good weather or for a highly conditioned, properly equipped traveler may be completely unsafe for someone else or unsafe under adverse weather conditions.

You can minimize your risks by being knowledgeable, prepared, and alert. There is not space in this book for a general treatise on wilderness safety, but there are a number of good books and public courses on the subject, and you should take advantage of them to increase your knowledge. Just as important, you should always be aware of your own limitations and conditions existing when and where you are traveling. If conditions are dangerous, or if you are not prepared to deal with them safely, change your plans! It is better to have wasted a few days than to be the subject of a wilderness rescue.

These warnings are not intended to keep you out of the backcountry. Many people enjoy safe trips through the backcountry every year. However, one element of the beauty, freedom, and excitement of the wilderness is the presence of risks that do not confront us at home. When you travel in the backcountry, you assume those risks. They can be met safely, but only if you exercise your own independent judgment and common sense.

HOW TO USE THIS BOOK

This book is organized into chapters on the basis of specific activities that can be enjoyed in the Forest. Chapter 3 is devoted to canoeing, Chapter 4 to hiking and backpacking, Chapter 5 to cross-country skiing and other winter sports, Chapter 6 to camping, picnicking and sightseeing outside the BWCA Wilderness, Chapter 7 to bicycling and Chapter 8 to fishing. Chapter 1 is a general introduction to the Forest, including information about the geologic and human history of the region, its wildlife, and the climate. Chapter 2 tells you how to best enjoy Superior National Forest. The Appendix in the back of this book contains addresses and phone numbers for more information.

Each chapter is organized by District. After a general introduction to each topic, you are given specific route descriptions and/or suggestions about where to enjoy the activity in each of six Forest Districts, starting in the southwest corner of the Forest (Laurentian District) and proceeding toward the northeast through the La Croix, Kawishiwi, Isabella and Tofte districts to the northeast corner (Gunflint District). Each District is administered from an office (sometimes referred to as a ranger station), and directions to the various activity areas are given from the District office, unless otherwise specified. The locations of these district offices are described in Chapter 2.

The book is organized to help you find the information you need easily. If, for instance, your primary interests are canoeing and fishing, you'll find what you need to know in Chapters 3 and 8. If, on the other hand, you are interested in a variety of activities, but only in the Ely area (Kawishiwi District), for instance, you can turn to any chapter and find the discussion of the Kawishiwi District in the same place in each chapter (third, after the Laurentian and La Croix districts are discussed). Cross-referencing is used throughout the book to call your attention to related discussions, driving directions and other pertinent information.

Photographs are generously distributed throughout the book to show what you will soon be able to experience yourself. Tables also supplement the text in most chapters, affording an opportunity to see at a glance the many recreational opportunities awaiting your visit. Twenty pages of maps that collectively cover all of the Forest are included in the front of the book. Every subject discussed in the text is referenced to one or more of the maps so that you can find its precise location in the Forest. The maps can be used to locate trails, lakes, rivers, campgrounds, dispersed campsites and Forest roads. They are *not* intended for navigational use, however. Instead, detailed topographic maps are recommended for all trails and routes discussed in this book.

Skiers along the Lonely Lake Trail near Gunflint Lake

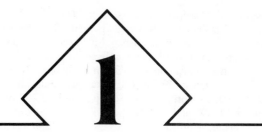

SUPERIOR NATIONAL FOREST

Superior—a more appropriate name could not have been given to this extraordinary National Forest. Located in the northeastern corner of Minnesota, sandwiched between Lake Superior and the Canadian border, this vast wooded region harbors bald eagles and ospreys, moose and whitetailed deer, timber wolves and black bear. Administered by the United States Forest Service, with headquarters in Duluth, it is the largest federal forest in the contiguous 48 states.

Superior National Forest represents many different things to many different people. To those who live and work in the nation's metropolitan areas, it is a peaceful place for respite from the hustle and bustle of urban living—a remnant of the great North Woods that was known to the Sioux and Chippewas, the French-Canadian voyageurs and the independent trappers and explorers of the 18th and 19th centuries. To many, the Forest is their recreational playground—an area set aside for canoeing, hiking, biking, cross-country skiing and fishing, or for simply communing with nature. They conjure up images of canoes gliding silently across sky-blue lakes, or the soft swish of skis on a snowy trail, or the haunting cry of a loon at dusk. Many more people who have never visited the Forest are content to simply *know* that these scenes exist. Still other people live within its boundaries and rely on its resources for their very existence. For them, a load of logs on its way to a local mill is a reassuring scene that better represents the Forest. Birch and aspen trees are fuel woods used for heating their homes during the long winters. Whitetailed deer and fish are valuable food sources. Motorboats and snowmobiles are essential for transportation, not merely forms of recreation.

For those who prefer silent forms of recreation, the Boundary Waters Canoe Area Wilderness (BWCAW), which constitutes nearly one-third of the Forest, is a refuge. The BWCAW is largely restricted to visitors who paddle canoes or travel on foot. Logging and mining are prohibited, and planes flying *over* the million-acre preserve cannot drop below 4,000 feet. Outside the Wilderness, there are also many places where the human-powered recreationalist can find solitude. Motors, however, are not restricted in the Forest outside the BWCAW, and people who use them have just as much right to be there as quiet visitors.

Superior National Forest contains over 2,000 lakes. Yet only 12 percent of the Forest's 3.9 million acres is covered by water. The rest is blanketed by dense northern forests of pine, spruce, aspen, birch, cedar and tamarack, or saturated by vast bogs and impenetrable swamps. In addition to 1,500 miles of canoe routes through the nation's most popular Wilderness, Superior National Forest includes 27 United States Forest Service (USFS) campgrounds, nine Minnesota Department of Natural Resources (DNR) campgrounds, 2,200 developed campsites within the BWCAW and 254 "dispersed" campsites outside the Wilderness. These camping areas provide quick access to 354 fishing lakes, 162 public boat landings, 29 picnic areas, 400 miles of designated hiking trails and 450 miles of groomed cross-country ski trails. In addition, the Forest has over 2,700 miles of roads.

THE LAND

The geologic history of Superior National Forest is long and complicated—far too complex to detail in this book. It is a story of volcanic eruptions, giant rifts in the earth's surface, settling seas, massive upheavals and glacial scouring.

Northeastern Minnesota lies on the southern edge of a massive bedrock formation called the Canadian Shield. The Precambrian rocks that constitute this continental foundation are known to be older than 2.6 billion years. At one time, a vast inland sea covered what we now call the North Woods, resulting in sediments in the southwestern part of the Forest that became the world's most productive iron ore range. The geologic struggle to reclaim the continent continued when a period of mountain building occurred about 1.6 billion years ago, followed by extensive volcanic activity along what is now the North Shore of Lake Superior. That ancient mountain range, the only one in the state, now accounts for both the highest point (Eagle Mountain) and lowest point (Lake Superior) in Minnesota.

Perhaps the most significant alteration of the landscape resulted from a changing climate. The rocky terrain received successive geologic "face-lifts" during four major periods of glaciation, which lasted until about 10,000 years ago. The great ice sheets plowed up whole forests, leveled rock outcroppings, stripped the land of soil and quarried massive blocks of bedrock. Evidence of this invasion is scattered across northeastern Minnesota—parallel grooves (striations) on outcrops, large stranded boulders (erratics) left behind by the retreating ice, and ridges of deposited rock debris (moraines) that mark points of glacial retreat.

Included within the Forest are nearly 450,000 lake-covered acres. Today, most of the Forest features exposed bedrock, with only a thin veneer of glacial deposits. Topography within the Forest varies from steep ridges with sheer cliffs at the northeastern end to a flat, sandy landscape in the southwest. Boggy lowlands dominate the Forest's south-central part, while low ridges of exposed granite are common in the rolling hills of the northwestern section.

HISTORY

The first residents of Superior National Forest were hunters and plant gatherers, who moved into the region after the last glaciers retreated. Through the

One catches a glimpse of the past at an old trestle across Elephant Lake.

18th century, the Sioux were the dominant Indians in the area. Because of competition over the fur trade, however, the Chippewa moved in from the east and, in the process, drove the Sioux out of this area and onto the plains. By the 1860s, this region was controlled by the Chippewa, or Ojibway.

While the earliest people in the area left no written records, evidence of their presence is found buried beneath the earth's surface. This unwritten record includes fragments of bones from the animals—including arctic caribou, moose, hare and deer—they killed for food, fur and hides. Charred bits of wild rice and other seeds reveal the plants they gathered, while charred wood from campfires identifies the types of forest that were present in their time. Pieces of broken clay pots, spearpoints, arrowheads, knives and scraping tools of stone and copper represent a "tool kit" from the past. Evidence of Laurel Culture settlements, dating back to the birth of Christ (500 B.C.–A.D. 500), has been discovered at several locations in the Forest, including a ricing camp in the Laurentian District. Further archaeological findings place other Indian cultures in the Arrowhead region, including the Blackduck Culture (A.D. 500–1300), the Sandy Lake Culture (A.D. 60–1600) and the Ojibwe (Anishinaabe) Culture (A.D. 1640).

Not all evidence of prehistoric habitation is beneath the surface. Mounds of earth along the Vermilion River were built for burying the dead or for places of worship. Astute observers may also see small pits used for threshing wild rice on terraces adjacent to some of the Forest's wild rice lakes. The keen eye will also find arrowheads, scraping tools and bits of ancient pottery at countless locations, as well as pictographs on rock bluffs in the Forest.

In 1688, Jacques de Noyons probably became the first white man to visit the Superior National Forest region, and he ushered in a new and exciting era in the history of northern Minnesota. European demand for beaver pelts brought economic importance to the "hinterlands" west of Lake Superior and the fur trade era was underway.

Free-spirited voyageurs were the backbone of the fur trade. They were small, powerful men who provided "horsepower" for the large canoes that traveled the aquatic highways of the lake country. Up before dawn, they paddled their birch bark canoes 12 hours each day—with one paddle stroke per second. The goods or furs that they carried were packed in 90-pound bales, and each voyageur was required to carry at least two bales.

Many of the lakes and streams on which you will paddle, the portages that you will cross and the campsites where you will spend your nights, are the same ones used for decades by hardy voyageurs, who, in turn, used the same routes and campsites established by the Indians.

As the beaver disappeared from the north country under the pressure of intensive trapping, so did the fur trade and the voyageurs. By the start of the 1900s, the fur trade as it once existed had totally vanished from this area, giving way to the more lucrative ventures of lumbering and mining.

One hundred fifty years ago, northeastern Minnesota was covered by a forest of giant pines. Logging operations began in the 1830s and continue to the present day, although most of the giant pines are now gone. With the invention of the railroad came the ability to log large tracts of land. Some of the larger lumber companies built railroads into the timbered areas for the sole purpose of hauling out logs and moving in men and supplies to the lumber camps. At the industry's peak, during the first three decades of this century, a maze of railroads crisscrossed northeastern Minnesota from Duluth to the Canadian border.

Just as the trappers of the 18th and 19th centuries nearly decimated the beaver population of northeastern Minnesota, loggers destroyed the region's great pine forests. They felled 38 million acres of timber, without replanting. It was only after the magnificent white pines were almost gone that people took the first small steps to protect what was left. Today only scattered pockets of virgin timber remain in Superior National Forest, most in the remote interior parts of the BWCA Wilderness and along the high, steep ridges of the Tip of the Arrowhead region—areas that were too much trouble for lumberjacks with more limited means than are available today.

Ironically, the Great Depression may have done more to restore the forests of northeastern Minnesota than any other factor. In 1933, President Franklin D. Roosevelt was given the authority to enact the Emergency Conservation Work Act, which resulted in the creation of the Civilian Conservation Corps (CCC). During its short existence, the CCC was responsible for planting hundreds of acres of pine trees, constructing roads, buildings and portage trails, and doing other public works projects.

While the logging companies found a wealth of timber in northern Minnesota, mining companies found wealth beneath the surface. A "false alarm" initiated the mining boom in the Arrowhead region. In 1865, high-grade gold ore was discovered along the south shore of Lake Vermilion by the state's chief geologist. His first assays indicated that the lode might be wealthier than California's, and the announcement spawned the Vermilion Gold Rush, which brought 300 people to the south shore of Lake Vermilion by the spring of 1866. Very little

A voyageur greets visitors to the Crane Lake area.

gold was actually found, however, and within a year wild-eyed enthusiasm had turned to despair.

Those dejected prospectors didn't realize that they were walking away from an even greater source of wealth for northeastern Minnesota—iron. The first pit in the Mesabe Range was completed in 1872, and by 1884 the highest-grade iron ore in the world was being mined at Soudan in the Vermilion Range, 20 miles west of Ely.

The high-grade ore was depleted by the middle of the 20th century, and the industry turned to a lower grade called taconite. Now millions of tons of taconite pellets are extracted each year.

By 1986, nearly 15 percent of Superior National Forest had been inventoried by USFS personnel for the presence of "cultural resource properties." Seven hundred twelve historic sites and 453 buried prehistoric properties were identified. Exploring the Forest for evidence of these sites can provide an exciting and educational experience. Most of these sites are very fragile, however, and cannot be replaced, once destroyed. If a site *is* destroyed, the information contained in it is lost forever—like tearing pages from a history book. Help preserve America's heritage by leaving archaeological and historic remains undisturbed, by encouraging others to do the same and by reporting information about these remains to USFS personnel. Historic materials and sites on National Forest lands are protected by law. Violations can result in a maximum penalty of $100,000 and 20 years in prison. So enjoy, but don't destroy!

WILDLIFE

Lying on an ecological "crossroads," Superior National Forest embraces elements of three major ecological systems: the prairie, the eastern deciduous forest and the boreal forest. Accordingly, visitors have an opportunity to see not only a wide variety of species but also some unusual ones as well. Two hundred twenty types of birds are common in the Forest, 155 of which normally breed there. Fifty-two species of mammals, seven types of reptile and 12 kinds of amphibian also live there. In 1987, there were 75 known breeding areas for bald eagles in the Forest, including 50 active nests where 59 young were produced. About 20,000 whitetailed deer, 1,500 black bears, 6,500 moose and 300 timber wolves have their homes here. Boreal owls, martens, fishers, wolverines and even cougars can be found in the Forest, in addition to peregrine falcons, otters, mink, great blue herons, pileated woodpeckers, lynx, porcupines and a variety of ducks.

One of the keys to observing any particular wildlife species is to search in the proper habitat. Some species are common along highways and forest routes, some are found only on high ridges, while others inhabit lowland swamps and bogs. Certain kinds of wildlife prefer mature forests, while others require open areas or young forests with considerable new growth. A few, like the timber wolf, are seldom seen at all, but you'll see evidence of their activities all around you.

A special environment exists along the edge of Lake Superior, nestled in the shadows of the Sawtooth Mountains. The lake's average water temperature changes only about 10°F throughout the year, from approximately 35° to 45°F. The cool summer air off the lake greatly affects the local weather, which, in turn, influences the type and amount of vegetation that grows near the lake. This, of course, also determines the animal wildlife in the area.

Lightning-caused fires are another force that shapes the environment. For most of this century, forest fires were suppressed as quickly as possible. Beginning in 1987, however, the Forest Service adopted a policy of allowing lightning fires in the BWCA Wilderness to burn, as long as human lives and property are not endangered. Periodic fires not only enhance wildlife habitat by spawning new growth in areas that had been virtually devoid of underbrush, they also reduce fuel accumulations that could eventually result in a massive, devastating fire.

Human intervention also affects wildlife habitats. Thousands of Forest acres are involved each year in both wildlife and fisheries programs, and logging operations create different types of wildlife habitat. Different management "zones" have been designated throughout the Forest, and each type of zone is managed to accomplish the overall objectives of that zone. Young forests provide the variety of openings and browse that moose, whitetailed deer, grouse and other forms of wildlife need in order to thrive. High populations of moose and deer cannot exist within the same area, however, because deer carry a parasite that is fatal for moose. Some zones are now managed to encourage large timber cut areas (100 acres or more), which facilitate moose populations. Others are managed for whitetailed deer, which require smaller cut-over areas (5 to 25 acres). Although you may see both animals in nearly all parts of Superior National Forest, moose are more prevalent in the eastern half of the Forest, while deer are more common in the western half. Both are prey for the gray wolf, an endangered species ("threatened" in Minnesota) that thrives in Superior National Forest—the last substantial population in the Lower 48.

Tables 1 and 2 summarize the major animals and habitats found in Superior National Forest.

◁ Table 1 ▷ Wildlife

Wildlife	Habitat	Dist.	Recommended Viewing Areas	Notes
Bald eagle	Tall pines near water with good fish population.	LC	Vermilion, Echo, Maude & Astrid lakes	Wing spread up to 7 feet across; wings held horizontal in flight; eats fish and small animals
		K	Bald Eagle & Gabbro lakes	
		I	Isabella, Perent & Silver Island lakes	
		T	Crescent, Brule & Timber-Frear area lakes	
		G	Greenwood Lake, Seagull River in spring	
Osprey	Tall dead trees near water with good fish population	LC	Pelican Lake, Vermilion & Echo rivers	Wing spread up to 6 feet across; wings angled in flight; eats fish
		T	White Pine, Brule, Crooked & Four Mile lakes.	

Table 1 cont'd — Wildlife

Wildlife	Habitat	Dist.	Recommended Viewing Areas	Notes
Beaver	Slow-moving creeks & small ponds	A	Anywhere in forest—watch for dome-shaped lodges & dams made of sticks and mud	Most often seen after sunset
Black bear	Throughout the forest	A	Garbage dumpsters, landfill sites, popular campsites & campgrounds; most often around dusk or during the night	Eats nuts, berries, insects, plants; seldom exceeds 3 ft. high, 300 lbs., 6 ft. long
Great blue heron	Shallow water along the shores of lakes	LC	Vermilion Lake (rookery w/150 nests)	Flies with a very slow, steady wing motion
Moose	Large clear-cuts (over 25 acres); shallow lakes and boggy areas; most common in the eastern part of the forest	LC	Along the Echo Trail, esp. near Indian Sioux Fire area	About 1,000 to 1,200 lbs.; up to 10 ft. long, 7 ft. high at the shoulders; antlers shed annually: Population increased past 30 yrs
		K	Along Highway 1	
		I	Highway 1 between Isabella & Murphy City	
		T	Perent River region & Timber-Frear lakes area Along Forest Routes 165, 170 & 340	
		G	Greenwood Lake, Brule River and BWCAW west of Poplar Lake	
White-tailed deer	Second-growth forests of mixed species, edges of forests, and small clear-cuts (up to 5 acres)	T,G	Along the North Shore of Lake Superior	Up to 4 ft. high at shoulder, 6 ft. long; congregate in "yards" in winter
		LC	Forest management favors deer habitat in the western half of the forest	
		K,L		
Gray wolf	Where deer & moose predominate, throughout the forest	L	Watch for evidence along forest roads & highways, especially at intersections. Best times to listen for howling in March & August	Eats beavers and aged, sick or young deer and moose; seldom seen, sometimes heard, tracks & scat everywhere; 1 wolf per 11 sq. miles

Abbreviations: LC = La Croix, K = Kawishiwi, I = Isabella, T = Tofte, G = Gunflint, L = Laurentian, A = All districts

Table
2

Plant and Animal Habitats

Habitat	Special Features	Typical Plants and Animals	Districts
Lake Superior shoreline	Climate influenced by the moderating effects of a large body of water that seldom freezes: cooler temperatures in summer, warmer in winter.	White-tailed deer are the dominant large game. Sloping hillsides are covered largely by aspen and birch, with some spruce and balsam fir.	Gunflint, Tofte
Elevated ridges	Warmer, drier crests of high ridges in western part of the Forest support certain types of wildlife not otherwise common in the North Woods.	Open ledge rock supports little wildlife. Sparse tree cover includes scrub oaks, some maples and birch. Used as travelways by wolves.	La Croix, Kawishiwi
Lowland bogs	Found in some degree in all parts of the Forest, bogs are rich sources of sustenance for a variety of plants and animals.	Black spruce, tamarack and white cedar are the most common tree species. Unusual plants include pitcher plants.	Most common in Isabella & Laurentian
Sawtooth Mountain highlands	The most elevated peaks in Minnesota, with climate affected by nearby Lake Superior, these highlands afford the most dramatic topographic relief in Superior National Forest.	Flaming red maples in September.	Gunflint, Tofte

FORAGING

Wild berries can be found throughout Superior National Forest. Once a necessity for the survival of Native Americans and white settlers, today berry picking is enjoyed as a recreational activity. People come from all parts of the nation to collect the bountiful resources that Mother Nature has provided. Most plentiful are blueberries, raspberries, strawberries, rose hips, and pin cherries. Thimbleberries, Juneberries, chokecherries and cranberries are also found in the Forest.

Factors such as elevation, ripening seasons and climate contribute to the location of fertile berry-producing sites. Because abundant sunlight enhances berry production, the best sites are found in a variety of sunny areas. "Waste places"— pockets of land that have been disturbed but not developed, such as gravel pits— are good sites; the absence of trees and the freshly turned earth allow an abundance of new growth. The long, sloped sides of newly constructed roads provide good berry-picking sites, as do abandoned logging roads. Burned-over regions are especially good for blueberries, but watch for raspberries and strawberries too. Many islands offer sunny berry patches.

Gathering wild rice on a Wilderness lake

Much more than a recreational activity, collecting wild rice is an investment in your culinary future and a spiritual reunion with the region's past. Wild "rice" is a nutritious, annual cereal *grass* that can be boiled, eaten green, parched or stuffed into game. A tall grass (six feet) that's rooted in mud, it is found in shallow lakes and slow-moving streams or in the shallow back bays of rivers and lakes. Wild rice is spread by ducks and is found in some degree in nearly all parts of Superior National Forest, although it is most common in the southern and western parts of the Forest.

Harvesting wild rice is a marvelous combination of cultural enrichment, communing with nature and good physical exercise. Those who take the harvest seriously should be in reasonably good shape. Normally, a pole-pusher sits or stands in the stern of a clean, dry, empty canoe while a collector kneels directly in front, in the beam, holding two sticks. The collector bends the tall grass over the canoe with one stick and, with the other stick, gently knocks the "rice" into the boat. Only the ripe kernels will fall; the green ones will remain for a later harvest by some hungry duck or eventually fall into the water to replenish next year's supply.

The annual Minnesota wild rice harvest is carefully regulated by the state Commissioner of Natural Resources, and only Minnesota residents are eligible for a permit, which costs about as much as a fishing license. It is important that you carefully read the state regulations pamphlet before striking out. For example, to prevent damage to the wild rice, laws dictate that the sticks used to collect it shall be no longer than 30 inches and weigh no more than one pound.

SEASONS

Superior National Forest is truly a land of four distinct seasons, each very special in its own way. The following chart, taken from *Climates of the States, volume II* (U.S. Department of Commerce, 1974), shows you the average high and low temperatures for each month of the year at two locations that approximate the northwest and southeast corners of Superior National Forest. Duluth statistics were taken at the airport, well away from the lakeshore. Temperatures along the coast of Lake Superior may vary considerably from these inland averages. While the coast is blanketed with a cool, misty fog, two or three miles inland ("just over the hill"), the landscape may be drenched with warm sunshine.

Table 3	Daily Air Temperatures in Duluth and International Falls, Minnesota (°F)		
	Duluth		International Falls	

Month	Daily Maximum	Daily Minimum	Daily Maximum	Daily Minimum
January	17.9	−0.6	14.2	−8.1
February	21.4	0.1	19.2	−5.0
March	31.1	11.4	30.9	7.9
April	47.1	26.9	48.5	26.3
May	60.6	37.7	63.3	38.1
June	70.3	47.3	72.2	47.5
July	77.1	53.9	78.4	52.8
August	74.6	52.9	75.2	51.0
September	64.7	43.7	64.4	41.3
October	54.5	34.6	52.9	31.8
November	35.1	19.5	31.4	16.2
December	22.3	5.7	19.0	−0.2

| Average Snowfall: | 78 inches | | 58.6 inches | |

Chapter 2 includes a discussion of the relationship between the seasons and the recreational opportunities that exist in the Forest because of variations in climate (see "When To Go" section of that chapter).

FOR MORE INFORMATION

Daniel, Glenda and Jerry Sullivan, *Naturalist's Guide to the Northwoods of Michigan, Wisconsin, Minnesota & Southern Ontario.* San Francisco: Sierra Club Books, 1981.

Fridley, Russell W., *Where Two Worlds Meet: the Great Lakes Fur Trade.* St. Paul: Minnesota Historical Society, Education Division, 1982.

Green, Janet C., and Gerald J. Niemi, *Birds of the Superior National Forest.* Duluth: Superior National Forest, USDA, 1980.

Loegering, W.Q., and E.P. DuCharme, *Plants of the Canoe Country,* 1978.

Morse, Eric W., *Fur Trade Canoe Routes of Canada / Then and Now.* Toronto: University of Toronto Press, 1969 (2nd edition, 1979).

Nute, Grace Lee, *The Voyageur.* St. Paul: Minnesota Historical Society, 1931 and 1955 (1st paperback printing, 1987).

———, *The Voyageur's Highway.* St. Paul: Minnesota Historical Society, 1941 (10th printing, 1983).

Ojakangas, Richard W., Charles L. Matsch, *Minnesota's Geology.* Minneapolis: University of Minnesota Press, 1982.

Ryan, J.C., *Early Loggers in Minnesota.* Duluth: Minnesota Timber Producers Association, 1975 & 1976.

Sansome, Constance J., *Minnesota Underfoot.* Stillwater, MN: Voyageur Press, 1983.

Searle, R. Newell, *Saving Quetico-Superior: A Land Set Apart.* St. Paul: Minnesota Historical Society Press, 1977.

Siderits, Karl, *Mammals of the Superior National Forest.* Duluth: Superior National Forest, USDA, 1981.

Walshe, Shan, *Plants of Quetico and the Ontario Shield.* Toronto: University of Toronto Press, 1984.

PLANNING A VISIT

As any seasoned veteran knows, a wilderness trek begins long before you ever set foot on the trail or dip your paddle into the lake. Memorable experiences don't just happen; they are the result of careful planning.

Vacationing with a group of people creates a particular challenge, because of the variations in skills, interests and physical strengths of the participants. When the group is assembled ahead of the trip, decide as a group where to go, when to go, what equipment to take along, what can be shared, and what to eat. But first decide as a group exactly what kind of experience is appropriate. Do you want to enter the BWCA Wilderness, where there are no modern amenities for campers, where cans and bottles are not allowed, and where you will be isolated from the rest of the world? Or would your group be happier at the campgrounds or dispersed campsites outside the Wilderness? Do you prefer to move to a different campsite every night, or would you prefer camping at one site and exploring the area around your "base camp?" Make sure you aren't overly ambitious. Whether hiking, biking, skiing or canoeing, consider all the members of your group and plan to travel at the speed of the least experienced and/or weakest member.

If at all possible, keep your group small. Even outside the Boundary Waters, where there is no group size restriction, few campsites have tent pads for more than two or three small tents. Some are barely large enough for only one tent. A small group has much less impact on the environment and on other visitors. And you'll have a much better chance of seeing wildlife and feeling a "part" of the woodland environment.

WHERE TO GO

Planning a destination is often as much fun as taking the trip itself. Forest visitors who don't camp in the BWCA Wilderness do not need permits or reservations for any type of travel or camping. BWCAW visitors, on the other hand, are subject to a number of special regulations, including the necessity for overnight camping permits, which are regulated by a quota system. There is no charge for camping at any dispersed campsite in Superior National Forest, either inside or outside the Wilderness, although fees *are* assessed at the developed campgrounds. The only activities for which fees are charged are cross-country and downhill skiing, but only on trails where special use permits are granted by the Forest Service to private enterprises (such as Lutsen Mountain and Giants Ridge ski areas).

The maps in this book illustrate the vast network of roads that are available to visitors, affording relatively easy access to all parts of the Forest outside the BWCAW. Not all roads are created equal, however, and many of them are not suitable for passenger cars. An explanation of the road system is included in Chapter 7. Even if you're not interested in biking, you should read the section about roads and "non-roads" if you plan to drive a car into the back country.

LAURENTIAN DISTRICT (Maps 12–15, 19, 20)

The Laurentian District is unique among the six districts in Superior National Forest. Not only is it the most populated region, it actually *looks* different than all other districts. Until 1988, this region was divided into two districts, with headquarters for one in the town of Virginia, Minnesota, and the other in Aurora. For the most part, the landscape in the western part is flat, with sandy soil and little, if any, exposed bedrock. Extensively logged over in the past, the woodlands are now dominated by plantations of young pines and a preponderance of aspens. There are many areas without forest cover where ranching and farming are practiced. The eastern part of the district is also quite flat, covered extensively by bogs and wet lowlands. Iron mining has been the district mainstay for the past century. Ten "Iron Range" towns in and around the Laurentian District (northern St. Louis County) account for more than 50,000 residents. That's a greater population than is found in all of the rest of Superior National Forest, as well as all of Lake and Cook counties combined!

Headquarters for the Laurentian District is in the small town of Aurora (population approximately 2,500). A mining-based community that lies off the beaten paths of northeastern Minnesota, it offers visitors everything you'd expect in a small, self-sufficient town, including a supermarket, several convenience stores, restaurants, motels and plenty of gas stations to accommodate the limited flow of traffic.

The ranger station is located at the southeast edge of town. From the downtown business district, drive 0.25 mile south on Highway 100 to County Road 130. Turn left there and drive 0.4 mile east to the district office. The largest town in the district (and in all of Superior National Forest, with a population of approximately 10,500) is Virginia, about 15 miles west of Aurora. Because of the split nature of this district, distances to points of interest in the western part are measured from Virginia, while distances to points of interest in the eastern part are measured from Aurora.

For more information, contact the Laurentian Ranger District, USFS, Box 391, Aurora, MN 55705. Or call (218) 229-3371.

LA CROIX DISTRICT (Maps 1–5)

The La Croix District occupies the sparsely populated northwestern corner of St. Louis County. It is bordered on the north by Voyageurs National Park and

Campsite along the Hogback Lake Trail

the Canadian border and on the west by the Nett Lake Indian Reservation. The eastern part of the district contains the western end of the BWCA Wilderness. A rolling, rocky landscape, covered by pine, spruce, aspen and other northern tree species, characterizes the region.

Headquarters for the La Croix District is in the little town of Cook (population approximately 800), on Highway 53, 25 miles north of Virginia. Cook has a supermarket, several restaurants, motels, service stations, convenience stores and most incidentals that might be needed for your trip.

For more information, contact the La Croix Ranger District, USFS, Box 1085, Cook, MN 55723. Or call (218) 666-5251.

KAWISHIWI DISTRICT (Maps 5–7, 14–16)

The Kawishiwi District administers the north-central part of Superior National Forest, which occupies the northeast corner of St. Louis County and the northern part of Lake County. Situated in the heart of canoe country, characterized by a rolling landscape with many rock outcrops this is truly the land of glacial lakes. The BWCA Wilderness occupies much of the district, except for the populated Ely-Winton area.

The Visitor Center for the District is found 0.5 mile east of the junction of Highway 1 and Highway 169 in the bustling little town of Ely (population approximately 4,000). A former mining community that has turned to tourism for its economic vitality, Ely offers a full range of commercial services to visitors, including two supermarkets, several convenience stores, restaurants, motels, laundromats, service stations, clothing stores, camping supply stores and, surely, more canoe trip outfitters per capita than any other town in America. You could literally drive to Ely with nothing but a dream, and everything you need for a wilderness canoe trip could be bought or rented there.

For more information, contact the Kawishiwi Ranger District, USFS, 118 South Fourth Avenue East, Ely, MN 55731. Or call (218) 365-6185.

ISABELLA DISTRICT (Maps 7–8, 16–17, 20)

The Isabella District occupies the north-central part of Lake County and the south-central portion of Superior National Forest. Containing no incorporated towns and only one small population center, it is, by far, the least populated of the six districts. The southern half of the district is covered by mostly level, low wetlands, while the northern half is characterized by rolling landscape with mixed forest vegetation. The extreme north end of the district contains the south-central part of the BWCA Wilderness. The Laurentian Divide slices right through the middle.

Headquarters for the Isabella District is the ranger station on Highway 1, one mile west of "downtown" Isabella, which is little more than a couple of gas pumps, a restaurant, a bar and a tackle shop. The closest bona fide commercial center is Ely, 40 miles to the northwest, although there is a grocery store, a gas station and restaurants at Finland, 16 miles southeast of Isabella.

For more information, contact the Isabella Ranger District, USFS, 2759 Highway 1, Isabella, MN 55607. Or call (218) 323-7722.

TOFTE DISTRICT (Maps 8–9, 17–18)

Bordering the north shore of Lake Superior, the Tofte District occupies the southeastern corner of Superior National Forest and the southwestern corner of Cook County. The landscape varies from rolling hills in the northern part of the district, which holds part of the BWCA Wilderness, to the rugged Sawtooth Mountain highlands bordering Lake Superior at the district's south end. The only towns and population centers are found along the North Shore, on Federal Highway 61.

The headquarters for the Tofte District is the ranger station on Highway 61, one mile southwest of Tofte. The tiny village of Tofte consists of little more than a couple of gas pumps, a restaurant and a bar. The closest full-service commercial centers are Silver Bay, 31 miles to the southwest, and Grand Marais, 27 miles to the northeast—both on Highway 61.

For more information, contact the Tofte Ranger District, USFS, Tofte, MN 55615. Or call (218) 663-7981.

GUNFLINT DISTRICT (Maps 8–11, 18)

Located in the northeastern corner of Cook County, bordered on the north by Canada and on the south by Lake Superior, the Gunflint District occupies the northeast end of Superior National Forest. Like the Tofte District, this is a hilly region that includes the Sawtooth Mountains, the Misquah Hills and the Laurentian highlands. The northern part contains the east end of the BWCA Wilderness, including the highest point in Minnesota (Eagle Mountain, elevation 2,301 feet). Most of the population (approximately 4,000 in the whole county, which includes the Tofte District) is found along Lake Superior.

Headquarters for the Gunflint District is in the prosperous little town of Grand Marais (population approximately 1,500) on the north shore of Lake Superior, 45 miles south of the Canadian border. There you'll find supermarkets, convenience stores, restaurants, motels, laundromats, service stations, clothing stores and canoe trip outfitters. And after your trip, you'll surely enjoy a visit to the municipal pool, where a shower, sauna and whirlpool bath can be had for a reasonable fee.

For more information, contact the Gunflint Ranger District, USFS, Box 308, Grand Marais, MN 55604. Or call (218) 387-1750.

WHEN TO GO

When is the best time to visit Superior National Forest? That depends, in large part, on your choice of activities.

The longest season of the year is winter. The ground is usually covered with a deep blanket of snow from early December through the end of March, and some-

Skiers break for lunch beside the North Star Trail near Gunflint Lake.

times well into April. That four-month period is ideal for cross-country skiing and other winter sports. Although northern Minnesota has a national reputation for bitterly cold temperatures, average winter temperatures are not at all uncomfortable for winter activities (see "Seasons" in Chapter 1), and they maintain ideal snow conditions. Snow depths vary from about 60 inches to over 100 inches, and are greatest in the Sawtooth Mountains and the Laurentian highlands. Seldom is there a sufficient base of snow for skiing in the woods prior to Thanksgiving. Ski touring across frozen lakes is often ideal in November, however, before the weight of accumulated snow creates slush on the thick ice.

Spring is a relatively short transition period in Superior National Forest. It's a lovely time of year, with mild daytime temperatures and crisp nights, no biting insects and very few people to contend with. For outdoor sports enthusiasts, however, early spring (April) is a somewhat frustrating season. There is usually not enough snow in the woods for skiing, but there is still ice on the lakes, which defers water sports. The temperatures are ideal for hiking and backpacking, but the trails are often wet and muddy. Streams are running full, which makes fording difficult at best, often treacherous and sometimes impossible. Nevertheless, for anyone who prefers to be in the woods alone, it's a pleasant time to be outdoors. And as soon as the ice melts, it's a wonderful time to be in a canoe, affording opportunities to explore tiny creeks that may be too dry for navigation later in the summer.

For all practical purposes, summer extends from Memorial Day weekend to Labor Day weekend. High temperatures average in the mid- to upper 70s, while average lows dip to the low 50s. But then, "average" means very little. It's entirely possible (though rare) to have week-long stretches in June when temperatures rise to the 90s, or morning frost or even snow on the ground in late August. Be prepared for any type of weather. Seventy-five percent of all BWCAW visitors enter the Wilderness during these three months. Fishing is usually best and the wildlife most visible in the early part of summer, but biting insects are a nuisance then. August is the most popular month among Forest visitors, because, normally, that's when the water is the warmest for swimming, biting insects are the least bothersome and good weather is the most predictable (although 20 inches of rain fell in August of 1988).

If it weren't for school schedules, autumn would surely be the most popular season in Superior National Forest. Mild days are followed by crisp nights. Biting insects have virtually disappeared. The golden leaves of aspen and birch mingle with the brilliant red maples, and the colorful array is enhanced by the deep green hues of spruce and pine. Framed by blue skies mirrored in crystalline lakes, it's a lovely setting that more and more people are discovering each year—ideal for backpacking, mountain biking, horseback riding and canoeing. It's also a peaceful season in the backcountry, since most autumn visitors are content to see the Forest from their cars and campgrounds. While the Sawtooth Mountains and the North Shore attract the most attention, visitors will find appealing destinations in all parts of the Forest. It's an unpredictable season, however, so be prepared for anything! October can have delightfully warm temperatures one week, followed by bitterly cold windchills the next. Seldom does a September pass without at least *some* snowfall, and an early blizzard can invade the northland, as one did in September of 1986, dumping eight inches of wet snow on many surprised campers.

If avoiding other people is high on your priority list, or if you must contend with the BWCAW quota system, it's wise to to avoid the peak visitation periods. Throughout the year, Friday, Saturday, Sunday and Monday are the busiest days in Superior National Forest. Planning a visit for Tuesday through Thursday will result in fewer encounters. Canoeists seeking solitude should also avoid the summer holidays and the last week in July through the third week in August. Ski trails (and resorts) are busiest on the winter holidays—Christmas to New Year's Day, Martin Luther King Day and Presidents' Day. Skiing in March is rewarded by warmer temperatures, longer daylight hours and far fewer people on the trails. Along the North Shore, when fall colors are at their peak, so is visitation in the Tofte and Gunflint districts.

If these peak periods are the only times that fit into your vacation schedule, don't worry. You can still avoid the crowds by choosing a destination carefully. There are many appealing entry points in the BWCAW that entertain very few visitors. And even during the busiest summer periods, when the entire Wilderness is filled to capacity, visitors can still find many interesting destinations *outside* the BWCAW that are seldom visited. Hikers and bikers can nearly always escape from the crowds, and campers can find solitude by avoiding the developed campgrounds in favor of the many dispersed campsites that are scattered across the Forest.

Presently, the capacity of existing recreational facilities in the Forest far exceeds actual use. Although the BWCA Wilderness is rapidly approaching the "saturation point," most areas outside the Wilderness entertain relatively few visitors. By planning carefully where and when to go, you will have no problem finding a quality outdoor experience in Superior National Forest.

WHAT TO TAKE

The types of gear and clothing that accompany your Forest visit will depend, of course, on your choice of activities, the length of your visit, whether or not you plan to camp and where, the season, and the amount of comfort you desire. Obviously, people who visit the Forest only during daytime hours need not be as well equipped as those who camp overnight. Folks who come to fish have a different set of requirements than those who come only to pick blueberries.

This book is not a "how-to" primer. You should already have enough knowledge and resourcefulness to enjoy a wilderness experience. A novice should seek the advice of experienced friends and/or respected camping store salespersons. In addition, at the end of each chapter (except Chapter 2), is a list of books that provide you with valuable background information about the type of recreation discussed in that chapter.

Nevertheless, a few important points should be emphasized. Above all else, visitors must remember that Superior National Forest is truly a wild region, and you should always BE PREPARED—for anything from normal wilderness chores to sudden emergencies.

CHECKLISTS

One good way to make certain that you are prepared is to get in the habit of using checklists while packing for any Forest outing. Believe it or not, there are people who forget to take rainwear along. Even more incredible, some people ac-

CHECKLIST FOR OVERNIGHT OUTINGS

Gear

_____ Pack with rain cover or liner
_____ Map case with map and compass
_____ Matches, whistle and pocket knife
_____ Folding saw in sheath
_____ Stove and fuel
_____ Two 50-foot cords
_____ Candle lantern &/or flashlight
_____ Cooking kit with cold handles
_____ Cup, spoon and plate
_____ Water bottle & filter
_____ Dish soap, scrubber & drying net
_____ Toilet paper in plastic bag
_____ Wash cloth and towel
_____ Night kit: toothbrush and paste, soap, comb, mirror, lotion, etc.
_____ First aid kit for emergencies
_____ Tent with ground cloth
_____ Sleeping bag with liner
_____ Air mattress or foam pad
_____ Food

Clothing

_____ Wool trousers
_____ Long underwear
_____ Wool socks (2 pair)
_____ Liner socks
_____ Wool sweater
_____ Cotton T-shirt
_____ Wool cap & mittens
_____ Handkerchief
_____ Down vest, stuff sack
_____ Rainwear
_____ Nylon wind jacket
_____ Camp shoes
_____ Hiking shoes/boots
_____ Sweat suit (sleeping)

Optional Gear and Clothing

_____ Rain tarp (extra rope)
_____ Fire gloves
_____ Camera with film
_____ Fishing gear
_____ Entertainment: book, harmonica, etc.
_____ Extra underwear
_____ Shorts/swim suit
_____ Wool jacket
_____ Sunglasses
_____ Hatchet
_____ Inflatable pillow
_____ Pen and paper
_____ Insect repellent
_____ Sun block and glasses

CHECKLIST FOR DAY OUTINGS

_____ Day pack (for shoulders or waist)
_____ Matches, whistle & pocket knife
_____ Rainwear
_____ Spare wool sweater or down vest
_____ Toilet paper
_____ Insect repellent
_____ Map and compass
_____ Water bottle and filter
_____ Sun lotion
_____ First aid kit
_____ Trail snacks
_____ Gloves

tually *decide* not to include it, because the forecast is for fair weather. A canoe trip guide for an outfit near Ely once began a week-long expedition into the BWCA Wilderness with everything but the food pack. Not until lunchtime, after several portages and miles of paddling, was the omission discovered. His feeling of late afternoon hunger was exceeded only by his sensation of embarrassment when the oversight was acknowledged to his group.

Get in the habit of using a checklist while packing for any wilderness trip, regardless of its intended duration. A "simple" oversight while packing could result in a good deal of discomfort—even danger—when you run into a thunderstorm deep in the woods without rainwear, for instance.

EMERGENCIES

An emergency kit of *some* kind should always accompany a Forest outing, regardless of the activity. While in the woods, think in terms of the distance away from towns, highways and other sources of potential assistance should you need it, rather than the time that you plan to be away. There is a critical difference! Many people understand why they need to plan for possible emergencies while on canoe trips or treks into the backcountry. They know that when they are 10 to 15 miles (or more) from their car or from the nearest source of help they must be prepared to take care of themselves. (On foot or in a canoe, "10 to 15 miles" translates into a full day of travel.) Those same people, however, might begin a mountain-bike journey that follows an abandoned logging road 15 miles into an isolated part of the Forest with little more than a bottle of water. They say to themselves, "We'll only be gone two or three hours," and they think it's not necessary to prepare for a longer, unexpected stay. They fail to understand that if a mechanical failure or accident renders a bike useless, they are no better off than the proverbial canoeist who is up a creek without a paddle, miles from the nearest help, with no protection from a potentially harsh environment. And the canoeist probably has a better chance of being found by another canoeist. The old, abandoned logging roads see very little traffic. Regardless of the activity you're enjoying, always be prepared for the possibility of finding yourself stranded in the woods. That applies to canoeing, hiking, biking, skiing, horseback riding, and even flying *over* the wilderness. Even when simply driving on the back roads of Superior National Forest, it is a good idea to carry a few emergency provisions, including a saw to remove windfalls across the road, a knife and matches to build a warming fire, drinking water and a few high-energy snacks in case of an unexpected layover, rain gear and some extra warm clothing.

If, in spite of your efforts, someone in your group becomes ill or injured, assess the seriousness of the situation. The standard SOS call is a series of three signals of any kind, audible or visible. If there are more than two people in the party, or if another group is in the area, send for help. All messages should be written with the name of the injured person and the location pinpointed exactly. Explain precisely what is wrong and what type of assistance is needed. If you are in the BWCAW, evacuation by plane or other motorized means is approved only when no other alternatives are available and the victim needs the immediate services of a doctor. Otherwise, you are responsible for transporting the victim to the nearest medical facility. All emergency searches, rescues and evacuations are authorized by the local county sheriff, and if an evacuation is necessary, the beneficiary will be billed for the expenses incurred.

CLOTHING

The varying degrees of energy required for different activities combined with a wide range of temperature extremes in northern Minnesota make layering of clothing imperative. You should be ready for any kind of weather, regardless of the date. Snowstorms occur as late as April and as early as September. "Average" temperature means little. Even in midsummer, the nights can be quite chilly.

Hypothermia occurs when a person's body temperature drops below normal, and can result in uncontrolled shivering, slurred speech, lack of coordination, poor concentration and, in some cases, death. It most often strikes during the relatively mild months in autumn and spring, not during the cold weeks of midwinter. Why? Because during the winter, outdoor recreationalists are usually prepared for the worst. That's not always the case the rest of the year.

Layering permits people to stay comfortably cool while active, warm and dry while resting. Even on a brisk autumn day, when temperatures hover near the freezing point, an active person has no trouble keeping warm. The problem is *over*heating. When the body heats up too much during a skier's long, gradual ascent or a hiker's short, steep climb or a canoeist's portage, perspiration increases. Excessive perspiration is absorbed by clothing. When the exercise stops, chilling starts, because wet clothing is not a good insulator. It is ironic, indeed, that overheating can cause chilling, and the threat of hypothermia.

The concept of layering is the same for every person and for every situation. What the layers are, however, varies from person to person and depends on a number of factors, including temperature and wind velocity. Three different kinds of layers are required to keep dry and comfortable at any time of year: an inner layer that wicks moisture away from the body; a middle layer (or layers) that traps "dead" air to insulate the body; and an outer layer that keeps out wind and moisture (the two key ingredients for hypothermia) while permitting dissipation of the water vapor created from perspiration.

WATER

In spite of the fact that this is canoe country, potable water is not always readily available. Hikers and bikers, in particular, should carry enough water (one quart or more) with them, since access to lakes and streams on many trails is limited. And canoeists should be aware that, even though the water in lakes and streams often *looks* pure enough to drink, it may not be.

One of the hidden hazards that you should take steps to avoid is a disease that may be contracted from drinking untreated water. Giardiasis is a severe intestinal disorder that can be incapacitating, though usually not life-threatening. It is caused by a microscopic organism called *Giardia lamblia,* usually referred to simply as *Giardia.* Beavers are most often blamed for transmitting the organism, but *Giardia* can also be readily transmitted between humans and other animals.

The most dependable water treatment to destroy *Giardia* (and other biological contaminants) is to boil water for 5 to 10 minutes. There are also some good filters on the market that are specifically designed to remove *Giardia.* The Forest Service advises that chemical disinfectants such as iodine or chlorine tablets or drops are not yet considered as reliable as heat in killing *Giardia,* although these products work well against most waterborne bacteria and viruses that cause diseases. Iodine, nevertheless, is considered more effective than chlorine. If boiling is

A high ledge overlooks a small beaver pond along the Angleworm Trail.

not possible, filter the water first and then allow the iodine to work at least 30 minutes before you drink the water. If the water is exceptionally cold or cloudy, allow the iodine to work at least an hour.

Boiling is considered a nuisance by many campers, and it requires a considerable amount of fuel. In cool weather, however, you can derive another benefit from the process. Boil your water at night for the next day, fill your bottles with hot water just before retiring for the night and take them to bed. You'll enjoy the warmth throughout much of the night and by morning, the water will be cool enough to drink.

MAPS

There are very few signs along the hiking trails, bike routes, back roads and canoe routes of Superior National Forest, and current, accurate maps are essential to finding your way. With a good map, a compass and knowledge of how to use both, there is no reason to fear getting lost—misplaced on occasion, perhaps, but not hopelessly lost! The maps in this book were accurate when published, but new Forest roads are constantly being constructed and old roads are periodically closed. For the most current road map, contact any SNF district office for an official Superior National Forest map, which at the time of this publication sold for only $1, or contact the central office in Duluth (see the Appendix).

United States Geological Survey (USGS) 7.5-minute topographic maps are available for the entire Forest. USGS maps are particularly useful for wilderness travel because they show topographic relief by means of contour lines. They also show roads, trails, and settlements, as well as forest areas, lakes, streams, open areas, and other natural features. Unfortunately, many of the maps are out of date and therefore may not show recent changes in roads and trails. USGS "topo" maps can be ordered from: Denver Distribution Center, USGS, Denver Federal Center, Building 41, Denver, CO 80225.

For information on the map or maps best suited for particular activities, see the appropriate chapters.

PESTS

Were it not for flying pests and a long winter, the Minnesota Arrowhead region would surely be perceived by the world as Eden and overrun by tourists and locals alike. But throughout the year, bugs or wind-chills dominate the scene and, fortunately, that discourages the invasion of civilization. If you intend to visit the Forest sometime between May and September, planning for pests should be part of your pre-trip preparations.

Mosquitos are a nuisance during much of the summer, from Memorial Day to Labor Day, but they are generally most bothersome during the first half of summer. That's also when biting gnats (sand flies) and no-see-ums (tiny flying insects whose entire anatomy is simply teeth and wings) plague the North Woods visitor. As the temperature rises and the ground dries, mosquitos, sand flies and no-see-ums diminish. Alas, then the black flies usually emerge to make the lives of human beings as miserable as possible.

Some kind of insect repellent is a must during the summer season. So is a tent with insectproof netting small enough to keep out the no-see-ums. Wearing lightweight, long-sleeved, loose-fitting shirts and long pants with socks pulled over the outside of the pant legs will also discourage the little beasts.

If these tiny pests aren't nasty enough to deter you, consider the larger ones. Mice, chipmunks, scavenging birds and, of course, the infamous black bears. Unlike the insects, these curious critters are no threat to you personally. They simply want your food. At campsites, gray jays (also called Canadian jays or whiskey jacks) may swoop down and pick food right off a plate if it is left unattended. Mice, chipmunks and bears, on the other hand, are normally patient enough to wait until you retire for the night. If your food is not suspended above the ground, it's a mighty susceptible target.

Nevertheless, don't let the many woodland noises keep you awake at night. It often takes North Woods neophytes several nights in a tent before they can relax enough to sleep soundly. Perhaps it will help to remember that the loudest noises heard in the woods at night are caused by the smallest critters. A horde of mosquitos at dusk sounds like a squadron of jet fighters. Mice and chipmunks rustle the leaves so much you expect to see a moose outside your tent. (A moose, by the way, is one exception to this rule. It crashes through the woods like a tank on maneuvers.) One of the quietest animals in the woods, on the other hand, is the black bear. If there's one outside your tent, you aren't likely to hear it walking

Black bears are fairly common in Superior National Forest.

around—until he knocks over the dirty pots and pans you were too lazy to wash after the last meal.

Don't worry, though. The careful camper has little, if anything, to fear from a visit by a black bear. The bears that inhabit Superior National Forest are usually quite timid. Seldom exceeding five feet in length and 300 pounds in weight (and normally much smaller), black bears feed mostly on nuts, berries, insects and various plants. Like any wild animal, however, when wounded, cornered, teased or protecting their young, they may be aggressive.

In Superior National Forest, bears cause the most problems in areas that are the most heavily visited by campers—some campgrounds outside the BWCAW and the most popular routes within the Wilderness. Some are perennial problem areas. Other problem locations vary from year to year. How aggressive the bears are depends on how accustomed they are to finding food at areas of human habitation and on how good a supply of natural foods there is.

There are no hard and fast rules to ensure protection from a bear, but if you carefully consider the following tips, there's a good chance that there won't be any trouble during your visit.

• Bears have an excellent sense of smell and are attracted by food odors. Avoid odoriferous foods and don't leave your food where bears can get to it. While car camping, keep your food in the trunk of your car at night and when you are away from the campsite.

• While camping in the backcountry, suspend your food pack between trees or over a large limb at least 10 feet above the ground and six feet from any tree trunks or limbs large enough to support the weight of a bear.

• Keep a clean campsite. Thoroughly burn all food scraps and leftover grease. Don't dispose of leftovers in the camp latrine.

• Never store food—even the smallest snack—in your tent.

• If you leave your campsite, tie your tent flaps open. Bears are naturally inquisitive and may want to tour your temporary home. If the tent is closed, a new doorway could be slashed.

• Never stand between a sow and her cub. Female bears are extremely protective of their young.

• If a bear does wander into your campsite, don't panic. They are usually frightened off by loud noises. Try yelling or banging some cooking pots together.

• In the event that a bear refuses to leave or demonstrates unusual hostility, you should yield to the beast and move to another campsite. Discretion is the better part of valor.

HOW TO BEHAVE

As more and more people escape to the woods each year, their combined impact on the environment has increased. The question is no longer "Can you survive a visit to Superior National Forest?" but "Can the Forest survive you?" You can minimize your impact on both this wonderful area and other visitors by observing the following suggestions and reminders:

• Keep your group small. In the BWCAW, groups cannot exceed 10 people. Outside the Wilderness, there is no limit, but you will increase your enjoyment and decrease your impact on both the environment and other visitors by keeping your group small. Besides, most campsites are not large enough to adequately accommodate more than two or three small tents.

Pets are welcome on National Forest trails, but they should be kept on leashes for their own protection as well as a courtesy to other hikers.

- Travel and camp quietly. You will increase your chances of seeing wildlife and enhance the Forest experience for yourself and others. Most campsites are on lakes, and noise carries a great distance across water.
- Make camp early enough in the day to ensure finding an available campsite. In the heavily traveled parts of the BWCA Wilderness, sites off the main routes and in back bays provide more privacy and solitude than those along the beaten path.
- Bring a small camp stove. It cooks quicker and cleaner than a wood fire, and it may come in handy during rainy weather when dry wood is hard to find. If you must have a campfire, burn only dead wood found lying on the ground. Don't cut live trees or peel bark to start fires. In fact, leave your axe at home. Axes scar trees, are dangerous in the hands of inexperienced users, and also add

unnecessary weight to your pack. Cutting, carving, or peeling bark off live trees is not only unsightly, but also causes damage to the forest. And it's illegal.

• Put all campfires dead out when you are finished with them. Douse them with water and stir the ashes until they are cold enough to touch with a bare hand.

• Keep your drinking water clean. Before heading for the lake or stream to wash dishes, think about what you're doing. The water for tomorrow morning's coffee will come from the same place. All soaps pollute water. Bathe and wash dishes well away from lakes and streams.

• Burn leftover food in a hot fire. If you must bury leftovers or fish entrails, bury it at least 150 feet from the water in six to eight inches of soil. Never dump leftovers into a latrine. Bears may tear it apart to get to the food scraps. And remember, it's against Minnesota state law to dispose of fish remains in the water.

• If you bring a dog, please respect other visitors' rights. Keep your dog on a leash while on portages, and do your best to prevent excessive barking. And if the little beast leaves a "calling card" along a trail, remove it immediately!

• Leave natural and cultural resources as you found them. Avoid removing rocks, flowers or moss. Help preserve America's cultural heritage by leaving archaeological and historical sites undisturbed.

• When breaking camp, leave absolutely no trace of your presence there. With regard to leftovers, if you can't eat it or burn it, then pack it out. After a fire is dead out, sift through the ashes for twist ties, foil and other debris that was not completely burned. Pack it out in your litter bag, along with any cigarette butts and other trash. Add to that any litter found along portages and at landings. As any good Boy Scout knows, you should always leave an area cleaner than you found it.

THE BOUNDARY WATERS CANOE AREA WILDERNESS

Many of the trails included in this guide penetrate the Boundary Waters Canoe Area Wilderness, which includes over one million acres of federally protected lakes, streams and forests. The BWCAW Act of 1978 established the boundaries of this canoeing wilderness and the regulations that govern it. The BWCAW has no piped water, no prepared shelters and no signs to point the way. There are no cabins, no resorts and no permanent residents except for the large populations of moose, whitetailed deer, timber wolves, black bear and other native creatures. Motorboats are prohibited from all but a few of the larger border lakes. The only roads are old, abandoned logging roads that are quickly reverting back to their natural state, and a sizable part of the Wilderness has never been logged. This is a land set apart from the rest of the world, a special place reserved for people who are willing to explore it only by foot or in a canoe.

Over the years the BWCAW has become the most popular wilderness in America, receiving 180,000 visitors—10 percent of all wilderness users in the nation. These visitors are now putting pressure on the ecology of this region. Because of the BWCAW's popularity, the Forest Service was compelled to implement a User Distribution System in 1976. Three fourths of the visitors were using only 10 percent of the 83 designated Wilderness entry points, places where one may enter the BWCAW, leading to congestion along some of the most popular routes and causing environmental stress at many campsites. Consequently, quotas

Paddling down the Cross River from the Ham Lake entry point

were established for the entry points. Now only a certain number of groups may enter the Wilderness on any given day at any given entry point between May 1 and September 30, the distribution period.

In recent years, canoeists have found their favorite entry points filled up during the busiest parts of the summer. Those who have carefully studied the situation, however, have also found four good ways to beat the system. One method is to enter the BWCAW at entry points that traditionally receive the least use. Another option is to enter the Wilderness during the least busy parts of the distribution period: early May, late June through early July, after Labor Day, or on a Tuesday, Wednesday or Thursday during the peak summer periods. Yet another tactic is to plan a trip in Superior National Forest *outside* the BWCA Wilderness. Finally, more and more people are discovering that you don't have to actually *camp* in the BWCAW to enjoy it. By camping outside the Wilderness and paddling into it during the day, you can enjoy the best of both worlds. Wilderness permits are not required for day use. (See Chapter 3 for more information.)

Like all federal parks, the Wilderness is governed by special regulations that were designed to preserve its wild and scenic appeal for generations to come. Most of the rules are common sense and should be adhered to while using *any* public lands, whether or not they fall within the BWCAW. Some regulations, however, apply only to the Boundary Waters. For instance, permits are needed from May 1 through September 30, group size is limited to 10 people, fires may be built only in fire grates, camping is allowed only at designated sites, food may not be carried in cans or bottles, motorized or mechanical equipment is banned (except motorboats on certain designated routes). For a complete list of all regulations, contact the Forest Supervisor in Duluth or any of the district rangers (see "Where To Go" in this chapter).

In order to reduce competition for the lmited number of developed campsites and to avoid too much "user pressure" on the Wilderness, entry quotas have been established for all canoeing entry points and many of the foot trails in the BWCA Wilderness. The daily limits range from as few as one at many entry points to as many as 35 at Moose Lake. They are in effect only during the distribution period. The quotas do not apply to day visitors, for whom there is no established limit. Some of the foot trails that receive very little use at any time have not been assigned quotas, simply because there is no need for them. If user pressure starts to build, the Forest Service will, no doubt, assign quotas to these trails, too.

All permits are available through advance reservations, for a non-refundable fee of $5 per reservation. You do not *have* to make a reservation before arriving at the BWCAW, and it is seldom necessary for most of the foot trails and many of the canoeing entry points. Nevertheless, many entry points do fill up during the busiest parts of the year, and if you have your heart set on a particular destination for a particular evening (like camping at the base of Eagle Mountain during the most colorful autumn weekend), a reservation is advisable. It assures you that a permit to enter the Wilderness on a specific day and at a certain entry point is guaranteed. (It does *not* guarantee, however, that your favorite campsite will be vacant when you arrive there. Campsites cannot be reserved.)

Reservations for the following summer may be made after February 1 by writing to BWCA Reservations, Superior National Forest, P.O. Box 338, Duluth, MN 55801. Or call (218) 720-5440. Phone reservations will be accepted only with the use of a valid MasterCard or VISA during normal business hours. Prior to mid-May and after mid-September, the office is open from 8:00 A.M. to 4:30 P.M. weekdays. During the summer season, reservations will be taken from 7:00 A.M. to 6:00 P.M. daily.

Reservation requests must include: (1) the name, address and phone number of the party leader; (2) the desired entry point; (3) the desired entry date; (4) the planned exit point; (5) the planned exit date; (6) the party size; (7) the method of travel (canoeing, hiking, etc.); (8) the name of at least one other group member, if applicable; and (9) payment (check, money order or charge card with expiration date). List alternate starting dates and entry points on the application, in case your first choices are not available.

Permits will be mailed to people who make their reservations at least one week before their departure dates. Reservations made less than a week before departure will be processed, but no confirmation will be sent to the applicant. These permits will have to be picked up at any Forest Service office or cooperating business (for instance, an outfitter or a resort). Only the party leader or alternate whose name appears on the reservation may pick up the permit. Identification is required, and periodic checks may take place in the Wilderness.

If you have not made a reservation for a permit in advance of your trip, simply drop by the appropriate district office or a cooperating business within 48 hours of your departure date. If the quota for your desired entry point has not been filled, you'll be issued a permit on the spot, free of charge.

The Forest Service personnel at the reservation office are available only for making reservations. For information about the BWCAW, contact the district office that has jurisdiction over the entry point and area that you will be visiting.

(Chapters 3 and 4 identify the trails and entry points by district.) The local personnel can do a better job answering questions about the specific details (water levels, trail conditions, bear problems) of your route. They cannot, however, process your reservation.

If you are planning your first trip to the BWCAW, first take a long moment to consider whether or not you really want *that* kind of experience. The Boundary Waters are not for everyone. In the Wilderness, everything you need for an enjoyable camping trip must be carried in your canoe and/or on your back. You're on your own, and the extent to which you enjoy the experience will depend on your own resourcefulness.

ACTIVITIES FOR THE DISABLED

Superior National Forest is a place for everyone, and so is the Boundary Waters Canoe Area Wilderness. Wilderness travel is physically demanding, but it need not be a test of endurance. Wilderness activities offer great opportunities for personal growth, and the best wilderness trip is usually one that is tailored to your own interests and abilities. Prerequisites are few, and being "able-bodied" is not one of them.

Physically impaired individuals can and do enjoy the Forest as much as able-bodied persons. Each and every form of recreation discussed in this book need not be restricted to people who are free of disabilities. People who use wheelchairs, folks who have sensory impairments and those with other types of disabilities can fully enjoy and appreciate the canoe routes, woodland trails, bicycle paths, Wilderness campsites and fishing opportunities in Superior National Forest *without* the use of motors.

Whereas the Wilderness may be intimidating to any first-time visitor, it may be even more so to those with physical impairments. To help out, the Forest Service has published a pamphlet entitled *Disabled Visitors' Guide to the Boundary Waters Canoe Area Wilderness.* Included are some planning and safety tips and six maps that illustrate parts of the Wilderness where campsites and portages are more "user-friendly" to the disabled. The maps identify the campsites that are located on the easiest terrain and are, therefore, the best for use by individuals with physical impairments.

The pamphlet was prepared in cooperation with Wilderness Inquiry II, a non-profit organization based in Minneapolis that brings people of all ages and varying levels of physical ability together for outdoor experiences. These experiences include BWCAW canoe trips, bicycle tours, sea kayak expeditions and other ventures to exotic locations. All trips involve muscle-powered modes of travel. Some are designed specifically for youths, some are for families. A typical trip includes one or two people who use wheelchairs, two or three people who are sensory impaired, one person with some other type of disability, and four or five non-disabled people. For more information, contact Wilderness Inquiry II, 1313 Fifth Street Southeast, Suite 327, Minneapolis, MN 55414. Or call (612) 379-3858, voice or TTY.

Voyageur Outward Bound School also sponsors a program for disabled and able-bodied people. As in all of its programs, the emphasis is for participants to discover the true limits of their capabilities—focusing on abilities, rather than disabilities. And, like the standard courses, this program involves wilderness camp-

Vermilion Falls

ing, cooking over fires, canoeing and portaging. Other activities may include kayaking and rock climbing. For more information about this program, contact Voyageur Outward Bound School, 10900 Cedar Lake Road, Minnetonka, MN 55343. Or call (612) 542-9255 or (800) 328-2943.

The Forest Service suggests contacting three other organizations that can help individuals with physical impairments to experience the Forest. They are Camp Northland (475 Cedar Street, St. Paul, MN 55101; (612) 292-4128), Wilderness Canoe Base (P.O. Box 130, Grand Marais, MN 55604; (218) 388-2241, voice or TTY) and Vinland National Center (3675 Ihduhapi Road, Loretto, MN 55357; (612) 479-3555, voice or TTY).

A FINAL COMMENT

Planning a wilderness trek can be exciting. It can be challenging, and it can be rewarding. To some, it's nearly as much fun as the expedition itself. You are in total control, and the success of your vacation rests, in large part, on your ability to plan it effectively. The more thorough you are in this process, the more likely you are to have an enjoyable trip without bitter disappointments and without surprises.

But once you set foot on a trail, or launch your canoe from a landing, or pedal off onto a lonely back road, you are no longer in total control. It's entirely possible that, while paddling across a large lake, a strong gale may render your canoe windbound. You could be helplessly stranded on a lonely island for hours—even days—before the wind subsides enough to permit safe passage. Likewise, while hiking along a trail, a violent summer storm may litter the trail with windfalls that could slow your progress to a virtual crawl. Or a premature winter storm could blanket your bicycle path with six inches of heavy, wet snow. The January ski weekend that you've been anxiously awaiting for months could be chilled to an unbearable -40°F. Or the mosquitos, sand flies and ticks could be so bothersome in June that your family reunion at a favorite campground is nearly ruined.

It's important for you to accept Mother Nature on her own terms. For some visitors, that's hard to do. Some folks need to be in control at all times—in control of the weather, the insects and everything else that influences the "success" of a Forest outing. The sooner you can learn to relax, lay back and accept what comes, the sooner you will become "one" with nature, and the more enjoyable your visit to Superior National Forest will be, regardless of the challenges that confront you.

Log stairs provide an easier path from Flying Lake to Gotter Lake.

CANOEING

The greatest concentration of lakes in Minnesota is found in the northeastern corner of the state. Superior National Forest alone contains more than 2,000 crystal-clear glacial lakes that look pure enough to drink. Interconnected to form hundreds of miles of canoe routes, they've been attracting boaters, anglers and canoeists for most of this century. Before that, they were used as "highways" for centuries by Indians, white trappers and fur traders.

This chapter will introduce you to the many canoeing options available in Superior National Forest, starting with a look at all the BWCAW entry points, which are described by district. Only day trips are suggested—routes short enough to explore the Wilderness from the comfort and security of your campground, cabin or base camp. (If you want additional information about longer routes for overnight trips into the BWCAW or adjacent Quetico Provincial Park, refer to the "For More Information" section at the end of this chapter.) Canoe routes found in Superior National Forest *outside* the Boundary Waters—canoe trails that attract few people outside the local area—and tables summarizing the solitary lakes and streams that have public boat landings, have also been included.

Before launching your canoe, refer to Chapter 2 for some helpful tips on planning your excursion.

Visitors need not concern themselves with whitewater primers before visiting the Forest. Most of the canoeing waters in Superior National Forest are lakes or placid, slow-moving streams. The lakes are often separated by rapids, but anything greater than a riffle is accompanied by a portage.

Some knowledgeable whitewater enthusiasts choose to run rapids deemed "safe" by their standards. Others—even those with a great deal of canoeing experience—always choose to avoid the rapids by walking the portages. The latter choice is recommended. Part of the fun of running rapids is the element of risk. In a wilderness setting, however, the prudent paddler avoids opportunities for risk whenever possible. A minor accident on a frequently used stream in a populated region may result in little more than an inconvenience—a few minutes' wait, until more paddlers happen by for a rescue. In the Wilderness, on the other hand, a "minor" accident could be a life-threatening catastrophe. A person stranded along an isolated, seldom-used stream, many miles from the nearest road, could get mighty hungry before help arrives.

Many books have been written about canoe camping (see "For More Information" at the end of this chapter). You can read to your heart's content, but, frankly, nothing is better than actual hands-on experience. If at all possible, take your first Wilderness canoe trip with a trusted friend who has been there before and who "knows the ropes."

If that's not possible, you can "hire a friend." In canoe country, these friends are called outfitters, and they have been introducing novices to canoe country for years. They'll supply the most suitable, tested equipment. They'll pack the food— food that is lightweight, easy to prepare and *legal* in the BWCA Wilderness. They'll review the route, advising where the best campsites are located, where the fish are hiding and where the bears have been the greatest nuisance. You'll pay a premium price for that "friendship," but for a first-time Wilderness visitor, it is well worth the expense (see Appendix for addresses and more information).

FISHING

If your number-one reason for paddling a canoe is to sneak up on some un-suspecting fish, skip directly to Chapter 8 before reading the rest of this chapter. It includes an index of the lakes and streams mentioned in this and other chapters, along with the fish species that are found in each of those lakes and streams. It might save you time deciding which lakes are "worth the effort."

Fishing in Little Gabbro Lake

The Vermilion River provides some whitewater opportunities.

WHITEWATER CANOEING AND KAYAKING

Not known for its white water, the area, nevertheless, does contain a number of exciting streams for whitewater canoeing and kayaking. They are not formally identified as "whitewater canoe routes," and their respective difficulties vary with the water levels, which vary with the seasons. Before attempting any of them, consult with local district officials first. They can advise you on the current condition of the streams, as well as the best places to put in and take out. Use extreme caution! Scout the entire rapids first. Blind corners can hide potentially dangerous cascades and obstacles.

The Stony River begins in the northern part of the Laurentian District and flows into the Kawishiwi District. It offers some challenging rapids that should be approached only by an expert. The Vermilion River in the La Croix District provides some whitewater opportunities for skilled canoeists, as well as some falls that should not be attempted even by experts. In the Kawishiwi District, the South Kawishiwi River from the Lake One Landing down to the South Kawishiwi River Campground has a number of relatively safe rapids when the water level is appropriate. Some of the Knife River rapids can also be shot. The Basswood River attracts whitewater enthusiasts, but there have been accidents and injuries there. They are difficult rapids, remotely located, and are not recommended by district officials. Some kayakers enjoy the rapids between Fall and Newton lakes. The upper reaches of the Temperance River are enjoyed by some whitewater enthusiasts in the Tofte District. One of the most popular river routes in the Gunflint District is the Granite River. Most paddlers portage around the scenic rapids, but experienced whitewater canoeists and kayakers can run many of them. It is the historic border route from Gunflint Lake north to Saganaga Lake.

SEA KAYAKING

Sea kayaking, a sport that seems to be growing throughout the nation, is not yet common in Superior National Forest. Nevertheless, these overgrown kayaks are well suited to some of the big water that's found here. Frequent portaging is awkward, though not impossible, so the most ideal routes are those with the fewest overland carries.

The most appealing lake in the La Croix District is island-studded Lac La Croix, a Canadian border lake that stretches more than 25 miles from end to beautiful end. Part of the BWCA Wilderness, you can access it from Crane Lake with only two short portages. Or you can eliminate the necessity of unloading the vessel at all by using the two railroad transport systems at both portages (see "12—Little Vermilion Lake" in this chapter). Basswood Lake, in the Kawishiwi District, can also be accessed with mechanized portages (see "25—Moose Lake" and "63—Four Mile Portage" in this chapter). Basswood is a big lake with several large bays and a reputation for big waves when there's any wind at all. That causes problems for canoeists, excitement for sea kayakers.

The popularity of sea kayaking is increasing most rapidly in the Tofte and Gunflint districts, where the North Shore waters of Lake Superior provide a splendid course for kayaking. With some fine state parks distributed along the coast, it's possible to paddle from park to park, spending your nights at the state campgrounds (see Table of Campgrounds in Chapter 6).

BOAT LICENSES

All watercraft on Minnesota waters must be registered. Canoes registered in another state do not have to be registered in Minnesota. If you bring an unregistered canoe, however, you must register it in Minnesota, even if your state does not require registration.

An application for a license can be mailed to the Minnesota Department of Natural Resources License Center, 625 North Robert Street, St. Paul, MN 55101. Include the following information: length of craft, manufacturer, year, serial number, hull material, whether or not motors may be used with it and primary use of the craft (pleasure/commercial). You may also register your canoe at any one of several locations in the Superior National Forest region, including the deputy registrar's offices in Ely, Grand Marais and Virginia. The licensing fee was $7.50 in 1988, with the license good for three years.

PADDLING THE BOUNDARY WATERS

The Boundary Waters Canoe Area Wilderness (BWCAW), with 1,175 lakes, is a canoeist's paradise, where you can paddle for days without encountering a motorboat, passing under a bridge, or seeing a resort or cabin.

Resting on the portage trail to Little Gabbro Lake.

Access to the BWCAW is restricted to designated *entry* points. Often, entry points are water-trailheads where canoeists can park their cars and actually start paddling or portaging. Sometimes, however, a considerable amount of paddling is necessary to reach an official entry point.

Of the 80 designated entry points in the BWCAW (83 if you include those from Canada), 60 are practical for canoeists and are described in this chapter. The remainder, suitable only for hikers, are described in Chapter 4.

The entry point descriptions that follow are grouped by district. The numbers used to identify the entry points are those assigned by the Forest Service and do not follow numerical order. Although the numbers generally increase in value from west to east, they do not always follow this sequence.

MAPS

The map numbers following the entry point names refer to the maps in Chapter 2 on which their locations are shown. These maps, however, are not meant to be used for route finding. For that purpose detailed canoeing maps are required. They are not included in this book because they are readily available from two sources:

W.A. Fisher Company, Box 1107, Virginia, MN 55792.
The Fisher "F" maps are topographic maps in a scale of 1.5 inches = 1 mile. When ordering, ask for the F-series maps.

Creative Consultants, 27 Board of Trade Building, Duluth, MN 55802. The Creative Consultant maps are topographic maps in a scale of 2 inches = 1 mile. When ordering, ask for the McKenzie Maps.

The Forest Service annually reviews the maps for accuracy. They may be purchased at many camping supply stores and outfitters in the Arrowhead region (as well as in the Twin cities and many other communities in Minnesota) or directly from the publishers.

Some of the water routes located outside the BWCAW are not shown on the above maps. In such cases, USGS maps are recommended. See page 58 for more information.

View from the Herriman Lake Trail

Gotter Lake

DRIVING DIRECTIONS

General driving directions for reaching the entry points in each district immediately follow each district name; readers are referred back to this information as
needed. Additional driving directions may be included in individual entry point
descriptions.

OTHER INFORMATION

The information provided for each entry point pertains only to its immediate
vicinity, including the kind of wilderness experience that the area affords,
whether motorboats are permitted, scenic and historic highlights, and the difficulty of routes originating there. Routes short enough not to require overnight
camping are also mentioned. Portage distances are given in rods (one rod equals
16.5 feet or 5.5 yards), the traditional measure for this purpose.

LA CROIX DISTRICT

Driving Directions. The trailheads for all but two canoeing entry points are located along the Echo Trail (St. Louis County Road 116), which connects the Ely
area with the Crane Lake area. To reach the Echo Trail from Cook, drive 16 miles
north on Highway 53 to the little town of Orr. Turn right onto County Road 23
and drive 17 miles northeast to its junction with County Road 24 at Buyck. The
Echo Trail intersects County Road 24 3.5 miles north of Buyck. Entry Point 12 is

accessible from County Road 24 near Crane Lake, while Entry Point 1 is located north of Tower, accessible from State Highways 1 and 169.

1—Trout Lake (Maps 4–5)

Canoeing Maps: Fisher—F-1, F-8
McKenzie—15

Busy Trout Lake has many fine picnic sites on scenic points along its shoreline, but is used by very few canoeists. Motors (25-horsepower limit) are allowed on the lake, and most of the boats are filled with anglers in search of the fish that lurk beneath the surface.

The trailhead is located at Moccasin Point on Lake Vermilion. To get there from Cook, drive 5 miles south on Highway 53 to County Road 22 at Angora. Turn left and proceed 8 miles east on County Road 22 to Highway 1, which continues straight ahead 6½ more miles to its junction with Highway 169. Turn left onto Highway 1/169 and then immediately left again onto County Road 77. Drive

Paddlers follow the lazy meanders of Pine Creek, just east of Trout Lake.

north for 11.8 miles to the road's end. The boat access is public, but the parking lot next to it belongs to Moccasin Point Resort, which charges a small parking fee.

Access to Trout Lake is across Lake Vermilion, a big, beautiful lake fringed by resorts, summer cabins and year-round homes. From the north shore of the lake, two portages (a short distance apart) lead to Trout Lake's Portage Bay and the BWCA Wilderness. The eastern route is a "truck portage" for motorboats. Just to the west is a shorter portage (60 rods) in a small bay fed by a creek draining Trout Lake.

For most folks, just getting into Trout Lake is plenty of paddling for one day—8 miles round-trip from Moccasin Point to the portage. If you get an early start, you might consider pushing yourself all the way to Norway Point, a beautiful pine-covered campsite on the east shore of Trout, about midway up the lake. A beautiful sand beach ("Waikiki") near the north end of the lake is another worthy destination. Or, if you have no aversion to long portages, consider the 260-rod portage to Pine Lake to escape the sound of motorboats. Regardless of your intended route, postpone your trip if there is a gale across the lakes. Vermilion and Trout are best enjoyed by canoeists on days with little or no breeze.

8—Moose River, South (Map 5)

Canoeing Maps: Fisher—F-9
McKenzie—12, 16

The Moose River meanders south (upstream) from County Road 116 to Big Moose Lake. With only two portages (160 rods and 60 rods) between the trailhead and Big Moose Lake, this is a good route to escape quickly from civilization into wilderness solitude.

The trailhead is located 60 miles northeast of Cook. Follow directions to the Echo Trail (see La Croix District driving directions in this chapter). From County Road 24, drive east on the Echo Trail for 20.1 miles to the junction of Forest Route 464. Turn right and proceed another 3.7 miles to the Moose River bridge. There is a small parking space next to the river access.

Five campsites are scattered along the shore of Big Moose Lake, four of which are within 5 miles of the trailhead. Moose are common in this area. For the hikers in your group, a 2-mile trail connects the north end of the lake with Forest Route 464 (see "Big Moose Trail" in Chapter 4). Likewise, a 1.8-mile portage trail connects the south shore of the lake with Cummings Lake, and a 1.5-mile path leads northeast to Duck Lake from the east side of Big Moose Lake. These trails offer ample diversion for the kids when they grow tired of fishing or swimming at the nice sand beach on the east side of the lake.

9—Little Indian Sioux River, South (Map 5)

Canoeing Maps: Fisher—F-8
McKenzie—12, 16

The Little Indian Sioux River, leading south from the Echo Trail, is a slow-moving, shallow stream that winds through a wide marshy valley teeming with wildlife, including a plethora of birds, beavers, muskrats, deer and moose. Though you'll be paddling upstream, current is seldom the retarding factor that a strong south wind can be.

This is the fifth least used canoeing entry point in all of the BWCA Wilderness, and one of the quickest ways to "feel" the Wilderness, with little effort required.

The trailhead is located at the Echo Trail bridge. Follow directions to the Echo Trail (see La Croix District driving directions in this chapter). From Country Road 24, drive 16.4 miles east on the Echo Trail to Little Indian Sioux River. The boat landing is on the south side of the road, and a small parking lot is on the north side of the Echo Trail.

Novice paddlers looking for an easy outing might want to turn around at the beginning of the second portage, 3 miles from the trailhead, just before the confluence of the Little Pony River. By stopping *before* the second portage, only one short (8-rod) portage is necessary to get around Sioux Falls. Seasoned paddlers who get an early start can make it all the way up the Little Pony River to Bootleg Lake, where there is a campsite at the north end of the lake, 8 miles from the trailhead. That trip includes four portages (each way), the longest 120 rods.

12—Little Vermilion Lake (Map 2)

Canoeing Maps: Fisher—F-15, F-22
McKenzie—14

Little Vermilion Lake is the westernmost entry point for the BWCA Wilderness. More popular with motorists than with canoeists, the trailhead at Crane Lake is also shared by fishermen and boaters heading for Voyageurs National Park and canoeists en route to Quetico Provincial Park.

The trailhead is located at Crane Lake, 45 miles northeast of Cook. From Highway 53 at Orr, it is 29 miles via County Roads 23 and 24, blacktop all the way, to the trailhead at Crane Lake. Here, there is a public boat ramp, but only private parking lots.

If you're in search of solitude, look elsewhere. For day trips, it's not realistic for most folks to consider paddling any farther than the south end of Little Vermilion Lake. The two southernmost campsites on the U.S. shore of the lake rest on a lovely sand beach 10 miles from the trailhead. From there, you can also hike on the Herriman Lake Trails (see Chapter 4).

14—Little Indian Sioux River, North (Map 5)

Canoeing Maps: Fisher—F-16
McKenzie—14

This is the second most popular entry point along the Echo Trail, used by campers and day-trippers alike. It's an 8-mile trek to the Canadian border at Loon Lake, and along the way is Devil's Cascade, a scenic 75-foot drop in the Little Indian Sioux River through a 200-foot-deep granite gorge.

The trailhead is located 53 miles northeast of Cook. Follow directions to the Echo Trail (see La Croix District driving directions in this chapter). From County Road 24, drive east on the Echo Trail for 16.3 miles to Forest Route 1873. The parking lot and beginning of the 40-rod portage to the river is 0.25 mile north of (left from) the Echo Trail.

Only 5 miles from the parking lot, the gorge is a popular destination for canoeists who want a relatively easy and interesting day trip. Only three portages (40, 60 and 40 rods) are necessary. Allow at least two hours for paddling each way. A spacious campsite overlooks the gorge at a point near the middle of the 0.5-mile portage around the falls.

16—Moose River, North (Map 5)

Canoeing Maps: Fisher—F-16
McKenzie—12

The Moose River is a narrow, shallow, meandering stream that is barely wide enough for two canoes (sometimes only one!). In midsummer, a dense growth of alder hangs over the canoe as you negotiate the tight turns.

Black bears are best enjoyed from a distance.

The trailhead is located 60 miles northeast of Cook. Follow directions to the Echo Trail (see La Croix District driving directions in this chapter). From County Road 24, drive 22.7 miles east to Forest Route 206. Turn left and drive 1 mile north to the parking lot at the road's end.

Although the portage north from the parking lot is 0.5 mile long, it's a good, nearly level path to the river. Along the east side of the stream, you'll see a user-developed trail that leads from the muddy bank up to an overlook that sits high above the river, affording a fine view of the river valley. Beyond it are only two short carries (20 and 25 rods) before reaching Nina-Moose Lake, a reasonable day trip destination even for a group with little canoeing experience. There is a good swimming hole at a nice sand beach (when the water level is low) at the base of a pine-covered slope. Formerly a campsite, it was closed to campers because of excessive erosion. Please confine your activities to the beach. While on Nina-Moose Lake, make sure your food is not left unattended. Bears are often a nuisance in this area.

17—Portage River (Map 5)

Canoeing Maps: Fisher—F-9, F-16
McKenzie—12

The Portage River is not recommended for the weak-hearted. Because it is a rugged route to Nina-Moose Lake, which is also served by the Moose River (a much easier entry point), virtually no one uses the Portage except those who like to explore, and the Forest Service crews who have to maintain the portages.

The trailhead is located 62 miles northeast of Cook. Follow directions to the Echo Trail (see La Croix District driving directions in this chapter). Drive 25.5 miles east from County Road 24 to the Portage River bridge. There is a small parking space on the south side of the road, near the bridge. Put in and paddle under the bridge to enter the BWCA Wilderness.

If you're intrigued by the prospect of a new challenge, you may not want to return via the same route. A "nice" day loop can be created by lunching at Nina-Moose Lake and then returning to the Echo Trail by way of the Moose River. Of course, you'll have to make prior arrangements to have a vehicle waiting at the Moose River parking lot or walk 3.7 miles back to the Portage River parking area. Good luck!

KAWISHIWI DISTRICT

Driving Directions. The trailheads for six of the 18 canoeing entry points are accessible from the Echo Trail (County Road 116). To get there from the Ely Chamber of Commerce, drive 1 mile east on Highway 169 to its junction with County Road 88 (Grant McMahan Boulevard). Turn left and drive 2.3 miles along the north shore of Shagawa Lake to the beginning of the Echo Trail, which is blacktop for the first 10 miles and gravel beyond. Seven other entry points are accessible from Fernberg Road (County Road 18), which is a blacktop continuation of State Highway 169 east of Ely. Three entry points are accessible from Highway 169, the final two from State Highway 1 south of Ely.

Pine Lake campsite

4—Crab Lake (Map 5)

Canoeing Maps: Fisher—F-9
McKenzie—16

Crab Lake is a favorite among canoeists who seek the thrill of catching bass in a wilderness environment (i.e. without motors). Access requires 3.5 miles of paddling across big Burntside Lake and a 1-mile portage that is occasionally flooded by beaver dams and climbs over a 130-foot hill. The long carry discourages all but the most dedicated canoeists.

To reach the trailhead at Burntside Lake, find the Ely Chamber of Commerce and drive 4.4 miles west (through town) on Highway 1/169 to the junction of County Road 88. Turn right and proceed 2.6 miles north on County Road 88 to County Road 489. The boat landing is 0.2 mile north of County Road 88, next to Burntside Lodge. A small parking lot accommodates about a dozen vehicles. Do not park on the lodge's private property.

September ricing on a Wilderness lake near Ely

Burntside Lake, located outside the BWCA Wilderness, has no motor restrictions and is dotted with private cabins and several resorts. It is also blessed with more than a hundred islands, making it one of the most beautiful lakes in Minnesota.

Few canoeists penetrate the region west of Crab Lake, a good place to quickly escape from the crowds on busy weekends. Ambitious day-trippers might also enjoy the 8-mile journey (each way) to Korb Lake via Little Crab Lake and Korb Creek. Others might prefer to explore the "back door" into Crab Lake by paddling and portaging up Crab Creek. This requires some bushwhacking, however, since it is not a maintained route. Believe it or not, the portage is easier.

6—Slim Lake (Map 5)

Canoeing Maps: Fisher—F-9
McKenzie—16

Slim is a long, lovely, narrow lake that stretches 3 miles from end to end, and a good destination for novices who wish to experience the "essence" of wilderness.

The trailhead is located west of the Echo Trail, 15 miles northwest of Ely. For directions to the Echo Trail, see Kawishiwi District driving directions in this chapter. From County Road 88, drive north on the Echo Trail for 8.8 miles. Turn left onto County Road 644 (North Arm Road) and drive 2.3 miles to a small boat landing on the left for Burntside Lake's North Arm. A narrow, unimproved forest road across from the boat landing leads northwest (right) 0.25 mile to a small parking area at the road's end. From there, an 80-rod portage trail crosses a beaver pond and proceeds northwest along the path of the old road to Slim Lake.

At the southernmost campsite on the lake, a trail leads inland to a high rock outcropping called Old Baldy, which affords a panoramic view across the North Arm of Burntside Lake. Beyond it are trails across ridges that lead as far as Coxey Pond and Cummings Lake (see "North Arm Trails" in Chapter 5).

7—Big Lake (Map 5)

Canoeing Maps: Fisher—F-9
McKenzie—12, 16

There are two resorts and some private cabins along the north shore of Big Lake, and no motorboat restrictions. Only the extreme southwest shore is part of the Boundary Waters; travel beyond that point is restricted to paddlers. Nevertheless, because of its remoteness, Big Lake is far from crowded and can accommodate, without conflict, the few motorboats and canoes that share its surface.

The trailhead is located south of the Echo Trail, 21 miles northwest of Ely. For directions to the Echo Trail, see Kawishiwi District driving directions in this chapter. From County Road 88 drive 17.2 miles on the Echo Trail to its junction with Forest Route 1027. Turn left and drive 0.3 mile to the end of the road at Big Lake, where there is a parking lot near the boat landing.

Beyond Big Lake, paddlers will find solitude, northern pike and, in the fall, wild rice. But there is little else. A small creek connects the lake with the Portage River, which leads either west (one 140-rod portage) to Duck Lake or south to Lapond and Big Rice lakes. Only an ambitious, seasoned canoeist should venture any farther, because the region is penned in by two very long and rugged portages (1.5 miles from Duck Lake to Big Moose Lake, and 1.7 miles from Big Rice Lake to Hook Lake).

19—Stuart River (Map 5)

Canoeing Maps: Fisher—F-9, F-16
McKenzie—12

The Stuart River is a shallow, winding, slow-moving North Woods stream that flows into Stuart Lake, 12 miles north of the Echo Trail. The wide river valley is boggy, and beaver dams spring up occasionally. As in most river valleys of this sort, wildlife abounds, but you'll have to paddle very quietly to see it. The river's sluggish current won't have much of an effect on a paddler's progress, but a low water level will.

During a dry year and near the end of any normal summer, the water level may be low enough to inhibit canoe travel, particularly at the north end of the river, where a canoe may scrape the rocky river bottom at almost any time of the year. Spring and early summer, when water levels are usually at their highest, are normally the best times to assault this entry point.

The trailhead is located north of the Echo Trail, 21 miles northwest of Ely. For directions to the Echo Trail, see Kawishiwi District driving directions in this chapter. From County Road 88, drive 17.3 miles on the Echo Trail to a small parking lot on the right (north) side of the road. A 1.6-mile portage trail leads from the parking lot north to the river.

Day trips are not popular on the Stuart River, because they mean crossing the 1.6-mile portage twice in one day. Dedicated explorers might want to consider the 15-mile round trip outing to White Feather Lake. A campsite there is accessible via a small creek connecting the midpoint of Stuart River with the lake.

20—Angleworm Lake (Map 6)

Canoeing Maps: Fisher—F-9
McKenzie—11

This long, narrow, beautiful body of water has eight campsites dispersed along its shoreline. Those sites are used far more often by hikers than by canoeists; few paddlers are willing to challenge the long portage, even for such a splendid reward.

The trailhead is located along the Echo Trail, 16 miles northwest of Ely. For directions to the Echo Trail, see Kawishiwi District driving directions in this chapter. From County Road 88, drive 13 miles on the Echo Trail to the trailhead and a small parking lot on the right. A portage trail leads east 2.25 miles to the south shore of Angleworm Lake.

It's not likely that a visitor will want to carry a canoe to Angleworm Lake for just one day—portaging would leave little time for anything more than a quick lunch. Nevertheless, Angleworm is a good destination for strong, seasoned campers who want to achieve the ultimate wilderness experience in a short amount of time. For an overnight outing, you probably won't want to go farther than Home Lake, 40 rods north of Angleworm.

A 10-mile hiking trail circles Angleworm, Home and Whiskey Jack lakes (see "Angleworm Trail" in Chapter 4). Four of the eight campsites are more suitable for backpackers than for canoeists, but two sites are accessible only to paddlers. The three nicest sites are along the east shore of the lake.

77—South Hegman Lake (Map 6)

Canoeing Maps: Fisher—F-9
McKenzie—11

South Hegman is one of the prettiest lakes in the BWCA Wilderness, but that's not why most folks visit it. Less than 2 miles from the parking lot is one of the clearest and most easily accessible displays of ancient Indian rock paintings (pictographs) in all of the Quetico-Superior region.

The trailhead is located east of the Echo Trail, 14 miles northwest of Ely. For directions to the Echo Trail, see Kawishiwi District driving directions in this chapter. From County Road 88, drive north on the Echo Trail for 10.8 miles to the parking lot on the right. An 80-rod portage leads downhill to South Hegman Lake.

The pictographs are located in the narrow channel between North Hegman Lake and Trease Lake, and require only 3 miles of paddling (round trip) and crossing two short portages (each twice). The beautiful, rocky scenery along the way is simply a bonus. Though the trip should take no more than a couple of hours, you might enjoy spending the whole day exploring North and South Hegman lakes and maybe even venturing across a 180-rod portage to Little Bass Lake.

21—Mudro Lake (Map 6)

Canoeing Maps: Fisher—F-9
McKenzie—11

Mudro Lake has long been a popular entry point among anglers en route to Fourtown Lake. Access to Mudro itself is quite easy—only a 30-rod portage and a 0.5-mile stretch on a small creek separate your car from the lake—but it's a small lake with little there to warrant a day of exploration.

The trailhead is located east of the Echo Trail, 14 miles north of Ely. For directions to the Echo Trail, see Kawishiwi District driving directions in this chapter. From County Road 88, drive 8.4 miles north on the Echo Trail to the junction with Forest Route 459. Turn right and proceed on this narrow, rough gravel road 4.3 miles to its T intersection with Forest Route 457. Turn left and drive 1.3 miles to the Picket Creek bridge. On the north side of the bridge is a private parking lot and the beginning of a 30-rod portage to Mudro Lake. Owners of the lot charge fees for parking and for launching canoes. If you'd rather not pay the fee, you can launch your canoe at a public landing on Picket Lake 0.25 mile south of the private access. Parking is not allowed there, however. About the only way to avoid any fee is to have a friend drop you off and pick you up at the public access.

Once on Mudro, most folks proceed north to Fourtown Lake, necessitating three more portages (the longest is 140 rods). There are more than a dozen nice campsites on Fourtown Lake where an afternoon shore lunch could be enjoyed.

Strong paddlers might consider the 10-mile loop through Fourtown to Horse Lake and then back to Mudro by way of Tin Can and Sandpit lakes. This route offers canoeists a good blend of large and small lakes, small creeks and an assortment of portages ranging in length from 10 rods to 140 rods.

22—Range Lake (Map 6)

Canoeing Maps: Fisher—F-9, F-10
McKenzie—11

The trailhead is located east of County Road 88, 13 miles north of Ely. From the Ely Chamber of Commerce, drive 1 mile east on Highway 169 to its junction with County Road 88. Turn left and proceed 1 mile north to the junction with County Road 781. Turn right and drive 0.5 mile to township road TM-4575. Turn left there and follow this gravel road as it bends sharply to the right (0.5 mile) and then sharply left (0.2 mile) to join the old Cloquet Road. Continue driving north on this former railroad line 10 miles to its end. This road starts out as a good gravel road, but gets rougher and narrower, and may be underwater occasionally, the farther north you get. Four-wheel-drive should not be necessary, but high-clearance vehicles are recommended. A gate blocks the road at the edge of the BWCA Wilderness. From the small parking lot there, you must walk the final 200 rods to Range Lake.

Range Lake from the access portage trail

The most frequent and logical destinations for short trips from Range Lake are Horse Lake, 3 miles to the north, and Jackfish Bay of Basswood Lake, 2 miles to the east. A trek to Horse Lake involves four portages totaling 1.6 miles—no problem for a seasoned tripper, but a novice might prefer the somewhat easier route to Jackfish Bay (three portages totaling 1 mile). Stream buffs will surely find the short stretch of the Range River appealing, and they might also want to explore Spawn Creek, which feeds the south end of Jackfish Bay. Beware of potentially strong winds on Jackfish Bay, however, where 25-horsepower motors are permitted.

Ambitious day-trippers will appreciate the 10-mile loop from Range Lake through Horse, Fourtown and Mudro lakes. Horse Lake was the site of an early 20th-century logging camp owned by Swallow & Hopkins Company, and astute observers may still see evidence of its operation there.

24—Fall Lake (Map 6)

Canoeing Maps: Fisher—F-10
McKenzie—17

For anyone visiting Ely, Fall Lake is, by far, the most convenient entry point for the BWCAW. It is not, however, for those who want to escape from the mid-summer crowds. The southwest three quarters of Fall Lake—not part of the BWCAW—is dotted with cabins, resorts and outfitters, as well as popular Fall Lake Campground and an environmental studies branch of Vermilion Community College. The route leading north to Pipestone Bay of Basswood Lake through Newton Lake is designated for motorboats of up to 25 horsepower. And although the route across narrow, winding Newton Lake is lovely, you're not likely to feel the sense of remote wilderness isolation you can at non-motor-designated entry points. But for the novice, Fall Lake offers an easy introduction to the BWCA Wilderness.

The trailhead is at the Fall Lake campground. To get there, drive 5 miles east of Ely on Highway 169 and the Fernberg Road. Turn left onto the Fall Lake Road, and proceed 1 mile north to the road's end at the Fall Lake Campground.

From the north end of the lake, you can portage 0.25 mile north to Newton Lake and observe Newton Falls at its south end and Pipestone Falls at its north end. It's a 4-mile journey (each way) from the Fall Lake landing to Pipestone Falls.

Fall Lake is rich in history, from prehistoric times (Indian burial sites and lithic scatter have been reported along the shoreline) to the logging era (a mill operated from 1900 to 1914 at the southwest end of the lake).

63—Four Mile Portage (Map 6)

Canoeing Maps: Fisher—F-10
McKenzie—17

The 4-mile trek from the northeast end of Fall Lake to Hoist Bay of Basswood Lake would be a rugged start to any trip. Virtually no one carries canoes across the portage, however: this is one of the few mechanized portages allowed in the BWCAW. A truck transports boats from one lake to the other for a fee. This is the only feasible way to get heavy motorboats from Fall Lake to Basswood Lake, where they are allowed only on the American side of this border lake. For those who paddle and carry their own canoes, if the destination is Basswood Lake, Entry Point 24 is a more practical access and shares the same trailhead (see Entry Point 24).

For a one-day outing, however, you might consider using part of the Four Mile Portage to access Ella Hall Lake, 1.5 miles northeast of Fall Lake. You can either employ the services of the truck and portage 45 rods directly from the road, or you can use your own power all the way by portaging 0.75 mile from Fall Lake to Mud Lake and then another 0.25 mile to Ella Hall.

25—Moose Lake (Map 7)

Canoeing Maps: Fisher—F-10
McKenzie—9

Moose Lake is the most popular of all BWCAW entry points. Thirty-five *groups* of campers may enter the BWCA Wilderness there each day. That number does not include the many daytime motorboaters, the hundreds of canoeists who paddle through the Boundary Waters to camp in Canada's Quetico Provincial Park, or residents of the many private cabins and resorts located at the southwest end of Moose Lake.

The trailhead is located 19 miles east of Ely. To reach it, leave the Chamber of Commerce in Ely and drive 16.9 miles east on Highway 169 and County Road 18 to Forest Route 438 (the Moose Lake Road). Turn left there and drive 3 miles on a good gravel road to the public landing and large parking lot at the road's end.

You don't have to paddle far to escape the sound of motors. One popular and easy destination is Ensign Lake, requiring only one very short portage (35 rods to Splash Lake) and a paddling distance of barely more than 6 miles across Moose, Newfound and Splash lakes. The rewards are ample; the drawback: you won't be alone!

Even closer is an often overlooked lake almost within hollering distance of the parking lot. Straight north of the Moose Lake landing, on the other side of the lake, a 0.5-mile portage leads to Wind Lake. Tucked away in two large bays are four campsites where you can spend a whole day in seclusion. The lake was the site of a logging camp from 1900 to 1914. (It is rumored that at the bottom of Wind Lake is a whole season's timber cut, which was stranded in low water and then sank after it became waterlogged.)

Trout anglers may be attracted to two small lakes just off the Moose Lake chain: Skull Lake, requiring a 20-rod portage south from Newfound Lake, and Found Lake, 30 rods north of Newfound Lake.

26—Wood Lake (Map 6)

Canoeing Maps: Fisher—F-10
McKenzie—17

Motors are not allowed and congestion simply does not occur on peaceful Wood Lake. The fishing is excellent.

The trailhead is 13 miles east from the Ely Chamber of Commerce via Highway 169 and County Road 18. Look for a small parking lot on the north (left) side of the road. Nearby is the beginning of a signed 196-rod portage trail leading north to the south end of Wood Lake.

The portage is a challenge to inexperienced canoeists, but it is actually not difficult, sloping gently downhill on a good path. Day-trippers may enjoy exploring the small, shallow lakes north of Wood. Paddling and portaging all the way to Basswood Lake is not out of the question for energetic canoeists—a 12-mile round-trip journey through Hula, Good and Indiana lakes, involving nine portages. Along the way, you'll pass the site of a logging camp and dam that operated during the early part of this century.

27—Snowbank Lake (Map 7)

Canoeing Maps: Fisher—F-11
McKenzie—9

The southwest half of Snowbank Lake falls outside the BWCA Wilderness, and has no restrictions on motor size; several resorts and private cabins occupy the shoreline. The northeast corner of the lake is restricted to 25-horsepower motors. Anglers are drawn to the lake each spring because of its reputation for producing lake trout.

The trailhead is 22 miles east of Ely. From the Ely Chamber of Commerce, drive 18.8 miles east on Highway 169 and County Road 18. Turn left onto Township Road 95 and proceed another 4 miles to the road's end, where there is a fairly large parking lot next to the boat landing.

Day trips into Parent and Disappointment lakes involve two easy 0.25-mile portages. There you'll find that both scenery and fishing are definitely *not* disappointing. If the fish aren't biting and the kids are bored, you might want to explore the Snowbank and Old Pines trails that wind through the woodlands around Snowbank Lake (see "Snowbank Trail" in Chapter 4).

29—North Kawishiwi River (Maps 6, 7)

Canoeing Maps: Fisher—F-10, F-4
McKenzie—18

To access the North Kawishiwi River, paddlers must first cross Ojibway and Triangle lakes, portaging 10 rods between them, and then tackle a 190-rod carry from the south end of Triangle Lake to the river. All but the river fall outside the perimeter of the BWCAW. The north and west shores of Ojibway are populated with private cabins.

Because of the 190-rod portage, there are no easy outings beyond the south shore of Triangle Lake. For those who would rather shuttle cars than assault the portage twice in one day, you might consider a one-way day trip up the Kawishiwi River (eastbound) to the Lake One landing. The scenery is gorgeous, with several rapids along the route, and except for that 190-rod carry, portages along this 7-mile route (8, 40, 20 and 19 rods) are not difficult. Be sure to have a car waiting at Lake One—it's a long walk (5.5 miles!) back to Ojibway.

30—Lake One (Map 7)

Canoeing Maps: Fisher—F-10, F-4
McKenzie—18, 19

Lake One, the second most popular entry point in the BWCAW, offers canoeists entry into a chain of lakes (the "Numbered Lakes": One, Two, Three and Four) that is both easy and challenging at the same time—"easy" because only two short portages separate the northwest end of Lake One from the southeast end of Lake Four; "challenging" because the islands, bays and peninsulas that make this chain appealing to the eye also make it confusing to the inexperienced navigator. Be sure to bring your map and compass.

The trailhead is located at the end of Fernberg Road, which is 20 miles east of the Ely Chamber of Commerce via Highway 169 and County Road 18. There is a large parking lot near the boat landing at the north end of Lake One.

The Numbered Lakes are known for their good fish populations. If the fish aren't biting, a day trip through Hudson, Fire, Bridge and Rifle lakes might be in order. For those who would rather escape from the crowd, an excursion through Horseshoe, Brewis and Harbor lakes to North and South Wilder lakes might fill the bill. The easiest and closest refuge, however, is the north arm of Lake Two. Most folks paddle right past this quiet bay.

31—Farm Lake (Map 6)

Canoeing Maps: Fisher—F-3
McKenzie—18

Farm Lake is outside the Boundary Waters, so it has no restrictions on the use of motorboats. Private cabins and resorts dot the shoreline. Entry into the BWCA Wilderness is at the east side of the lake, where one channel leads to South Farm Lake (25-horsepower motors permitted) and another leads to the North Kawishiwi River (no motors).

To reach the trailhead, drive 1.5 miles east from the Ely Chamber of Commerce on Highway 169 to the junction with County Road 58-16. Turn right and follow St. Louis County Road 58, which becomes Lake County Road 16, 4.3 miles before the access road appears on the left. Turn onto the access road and head 0.25 mile north to a parking lot and boat ramp. All but the last mile of the road is blacktop.

A good destination for a daytime outing is Clear Lake, requiring just 5 miles of paddling from the Farm Lake landing up the North Kawishiwi River to a 0.5-mile portage over a low hill.

32—South Kawishiwi River (Maps 6, 15)

Canoeing Maps: Fisher—F-3
McKenzie—18

The South Kawishiwi, a wide, slow-moving river, gives one the impression of a series of small, narrow lakes joined by short stretches of white water.

The trailhead is located at the South Kawishiwi River campground, 11 miles south of the Ely Chamber of Commerce on Highway 1. Put in at the public landing on the left (east) side of the road, inside the campground entrance.

The landing is almost 4 miles from the edge of the BWCA Wilderness. During the first couple of miles, you'll see several private cabins along the shore and you may hear a few motorboats, but it's not congested. At the first of four scenic rapids is a cluster of buildings belonging to Voyageur Outward Bound School.

Visitors who prefer to enter the Boundary Waters more quickly may do so. Instead of stopping at the campground, continue driving south on Highway 1 an additional 0.25 mile to Spruce Road. Turn left and drive 4 miles on a good gravel road to a small parking area on the left side of the road. From there, a 140-rod portage leads northwest to the river. This part of the river is in the BWCAW. If you choose this access you'll bypass a few signs of civilization, but you will also eliminate a lovely part of the South Kawishiwi River. If you don't mind shuttling cars, in fact, this 4-mile stretch back to the campground makes a nice day trip. If the water level is suitable and your skills are appropriate to the task, you may be able to run some of the rapids. Always scout them first, however, and don't take any chances if you are not absolutely sure of yourself. Traveling in the other direction, when the water level is not too high, you may also be able to walk your canoe through the rapids, eliminating any need to portage. Use your best judgment and have fun.

33—Little Gabbro Lake (Maps 6, 15)

Canoeing Maps: Fisher—F-3
McKenzie—18

Depending on the condition of the portage, access to Little Gabbro Lake can be a challenge. In early spring and after periods of heavy rainfall, the long trail from the parking lot to the lake is quite muddy. But, overall, it's a good, wide, relatively smooth path that slopes downhill much of the way to the lake.

The trailhead is located east of Highway 1, 18 miles southeast of Ely. From the Ely Chamber of Commerce, drive 11.25 miles south on Highway 1 to Spruce Road. Turn left and drive 4 miles on this good gravel road to its junction with Forest Route 181. Continue straight ahead on F.R. 181 for 1.8 miles to the junc-

The Kawishiwi River swimming beach

tion with Forest Route 158. Turn left there and drive 0.6 mile on a rough, unimproved road to a large clearing at the road's end. (A vehicle with high clearance is recommended.) From there, a 265-rod portage trail leads north to the south end of Little Gabbro Lake. (*Note:* A new portage and parking area are planned at a location along F.R. 181 that will require less driving and won't be as muddy for portaging. The improved road should be suitable for all vehicles.)

Little Gabbro Lake offers a nice base for day trips into the Wilderness. From the north end, you can portage 122 rods northwest to the South Kawishiwi River and then loop around to the 140-rod portage from the river back to Spruce Road. The pretty 7-mile route ends 2.4 miles from the trailhead, so have a car waiting or be prepared to walk.

Anglers may be more interested in heading east from Little Gabbro Lake to Gabbro and Bald Eagle lakes. The region north of Gabbro and Bald Eagle is an excellent place to see moose and other forms of wildlife. Duck hunters frequent the area in autumn.

ISABELLA DISTRICT

Driving Directions. The trailheads for all the five canoeing entry points are accessible from graveled Tomahawk Road (Forest Route 173), which intersects Highway 1 midway between Ely and Isabella. Collectively, these are the entry points least known by people who don't live nearby. All offer good opportunities for quick seclusion, wildlife viewing and catching fish.

84—Snake Creek (Map 16)

Canoeing Maps: Fisher—F-4
McKenzie—18

Popular with local fishermen, Snake Creek provides quick access to Bald Eagle Lake, the only obstacles being three portages (160, 20 and 10 rods) and less than 1 mile of paddling. The marshy lower part of Snake Creek is home for many species of birds, and at least a dozen bald eagle and osprey nests exist in the region around Bald Eagle and Gabbro lakes.

The trailhead is located north of the Tomahawk Road, 28 miles from Isabella. From the Isabella Ranger Station, drive northwest on Highway 1 for 19 miles to Forest Route 173. Turn right and drive east on this good gravel road for 6 miles to Forest Route 381. Turn left and proceed north 1.5 miles to a Y intersection. Bear left there and continue for another 1.5 miles to the road's end. Because of the road's roughness during the final 3 miles, vehicles with high clearance are recommended, though not absolutely necessary. (There are plans to improve the road, but the project was awaiting funds from Washington when this book went to press.) From the barricade at the end of the road, a 0.5-mile portage trail leads northwest to the Snake River access.

Strong, seasoned paddlers might consider making a loop from the south end of Bald Eagle Lake up the Isabella River to the Little Isabella River, ending at Entry Point 75. The 13-mile route includes 10 portages (the longest is 190 rods) and ends 2.5 miles from the trailhead. Most canoeists prefer to spread this trip over two days.

75—North Kelly Road (Map 16)

Canoeing Maps: Fisher—F-4
McKenzie—18

There is no better place to find peace and seclusion than in the winding wilderness of the Little Isabella River, on the 5-mile journey to Quadga Lake.

The trailhead is located near Entry Point 84 (see directions above). At the Y on Forest Route 381, bear *right* and continue 1 more mile to the road's end. Because the road is very rough and often underwater in low places, a vehicle with high clearance is recommended, though not absolutely necessary (the road may be improved by the time you read this). From a small parking lot at the end of the road, a 20-rod portage leads downhill to the Little Isabella River.

There are three short portages along the slow, meandering Little Isabella, which is bordered by alder brush, black spruce and jack pine. It flows into the larger Isabella River about 1 mile west of the Quadga Lake portage. Ambitious paddlers could enjoy lunch on the lake, fish for a couple of hours and still make it back to the car well before dark.

67—Bog Lake (Map 16)

Canoeing Maps: Fisher—F-4
McKenzie—19

Bog Lake is a destination, not part of any route. There are no outlets leading to any other lakes. Surrounded by a low spruce-covered shoreline, it offers a typi-

Pine grosbeak

cally boreal scene. It's used mostly for day fishing trips, so there is little demand for the five campsites along its shoreline.

The trailhead is located 14 miles north of Isabella. From the Isabella Ranger Station, drive 1 mile east on Highway 1 to its junction with Forest Route 172 in "downtown" Isabella. Continue straight ahead on F.R. 172 for 0.8 mile to its junction with Forest Route 369. Turn left there and drive 5.8 miles north to the junction with Forest Route 173. Bear left at that Y intersection and continue northbound on F.R. 173 for 1.8 miles to its junction with Forest Route 373. Bear right at that Y intersection and drive another 3.5 miles to the junction with Forest Route 377. Turn right at the stop sign and proceed 0.8 mile to an unimproved road spur on the left. Turn left there and drive 0.75 mile to the road's end at the edge of the BWCA Wilderness. You'll be on good gravel roads all the way to the final turnoff from F.R. 377. The end of this rough access road, however, will probably be underwater (as much as a foot deep in spring) and high-clearance vehicles are imperative.

A hilly 230-rod portage leads from the small parking lot north to Bog Lake. There are plans to improve the access road, ending it just before the flooded area. The good news is, you won't need a high-clearance vehicle. The bad news: an already tough portage will be even tougher, because it will be 30 rods longer and there are no plans to construct boardwalks across the pond. Wear your knee-high waterproof boots!

34—Island River (Map 16)

Canoeing Maps: Fisher—F-4
　　　　　　　　McKenzie—19

The Island River is unique among entry points, because you can enter the Boundary Waters by paddling in either direction from the road.

The trailhead is located 4.5 miles east of Forest Route 373 on Forest Route 377, 18 miles north of Isabella (see Entry Point 67 for directions to the junction of Forest Routes 373 and 377). A boat access and small parking lot are on the northeast side of the river, just beyond the bridge.

Island River flows west to a confluence with the Isabella River about 1.5 miles from the landing. By paddling upstream (toward the southeast), however, you will find a small, obscure display of Indian pictographs near a Wilderness campsite less than 5 miles from the trailhead. Either option is suitable for day trips or for easy overnight outings.

The only short route that does not require backtracking is the 5-mile loop from the Island River bridge to Entry Point 35 at Isabella Lake. It involves four short portages and ends 1 mile north of the trailhead at the historic site of Forest Center (see Entry Point 35).

35—Isabella Lake (Map 16)

Canoeing Maps: Fisher—F-4
　　　　　　　　McKenzie—19

Anglers who want easy access to an area where motors are prohibited like Isabella Lake. Canoeists can use it as a base for day trips.

The trailhead is located at the Forest Center landing on Forest Route 377, 1 mile north of Entry Point 34 (see directions above) via Forest Route 377. A large parking lot there serves canoeists using this entry point and hikers using the Pow Wow Trail. A 35-rod portage leads north from the parking lot to the south shore of Isabella Lake.

Once in the lake, paddlers can head east to the Perent River by way of Boga Lake. Portages on the way are frequent, but short and easy. A lovely campsite rests along the Perent River near rapids less than 6 miles east of the Isabella Lake landing.

If you don't mind a long portage to acquire peace and quiet, Ferne Lake is a good destination. The hilly, 330-rod portage is reached by paddling up Pow Wow Creek from the Perent River, east of Isabella Lake. The Ferne Lake region has one of the highest concentrations of moose in Minnesota.

Paddlers may also steer west from Isabella Lake, travel down the Isabella River and then loop back toward the southeast on the Island River to Forest Route 377. This 5-mile loop involves four short portages and ends 1 mile from the trailhead. A pair of bald eagles nesting nearby can be seen from time to time flying overhead or perched on trees bordering Isabella Lake.

TOFTE DISTRICT

Driving Directions. The trailheads for all six canoeing entry points are accessible from the gravel Sawbill Trail (County Road 2), which begins at Highway 61 in Tofte and leads 23 miles north to Sawbill Lake.

36—Hog Creek (Map 17)

Canoeing Maps: Fisher—F-5
McKenzie—20

Narrow, winding Hog Creek is barely wide enough for one canoe, offering a delightful route through an area teeming with wildlife. More moose per square mile live in this region than in any other part of Minnesota.

The trailhead is located 30 miles northwest of Tofte. Drive 17 miles north of Tofte on Sawbill Trail (County Road 2) to the junction with County Road 3. Turn left and drive west on Cook County Road 3, which becomes Lake County Road 7, to Forest Route 354—a total distance of 10 miles from the Sawbill Trail. The turnoff to the Hog Creek parking lot is 2 miles northwest of County Road 7 on Forest Route 354. A 15-rod portage leads from the parking lot to the south bank of the creek.

Four miles from the trailhead, Hog Creek enters Perent Lake—a good destination for day-trippers as well as overnight visitors. Most are lured by the good fish population. Wildlife enthusiasts are enticed by the good possibility of seeing moose browse along the shoreline or bald eagles nesting nearby. If you're headed to Perent Lake just for the day, bear in mind that the return trip may take longer than the downstream journey. The current is not extremely swift, but it *is* noticeable.

If you decide to travel down the Perent River, leading west from the lake, be prepared for frequent (but short) portages. It's a lovely region, but progress is slow.

37—Kawishiwi Lake (Maps 8, 17)

Canoeing Maps: Fisher—F-5
McKenzie—20

Many Kawishiwi Lake visitors are anglers in pursuit of full stringers. Treks up to Kawasachong Lake are easy, following the Kawishiwi River from Kawishiwi Lake north to Square Lake. They require only two short portages between Square and Kawasachong lakes. Portages of 181 and 91 rods, however, separate Kawasachong from Polly Lake to the north. Though not particularly rough, these carries might be more than a canoeing novice would want to attempt in one day. Quiet paddlers should have little difficulty seeing moose during the twilight hours and, quite possibly, at any other time of day.

To find the trailhead, see directions for Entry Point 36. Drive 2.5 miles north of the Hog Creek entry point on Forest Route 354 to the parking lot and boat landing at the road's end, next to the Forest Service campground.

38—Sawbill Lake (Map 8)

Canoeing Maps: Fisher—F-5
McKenzie—20, 21

Sawbill Lake's portages are well maintained and receive frequent use. A 7-mile loop northwest to Kelso Lake makes a pleasant day trip from the Sawbill boat landing and provides a nice change of scenery, from big Alton Lake to tiny Kelso River. Only three short portages (30, 10 and 13 rods) are necessary. A railroad track at the portage between Alton and Kelso lakes was built by the CCC in order to provide speedy access for heavy boats in case of forest fires. Keep your eyes open for moose, eagles and ospreys, often seen in this area.

The trailhead is located at the end of the Sawbill Trail (County Road 2), 23 miles north of Tofte. A large parking lot is adjacent to the boat landing.

39—Baker Lake (Maps 8, 9)

Canoeing Maps: Fisher—F-6
McKenzie—21

Little Baker Lake and the northern lakes that drain into it compose the upper flowage of the Temperance River system, a scenic series of narrow lakes bordered by hills that tower up to 275 feet above the water. It's a delightful area to explore while camping at the Baker Lake Campground—ideal for canoeists not interested in roughing it.

For directions to County Road 2, see Tofte District driving directions in this chapter. From C.R. 2, 17 miles north of Tofte, follow Forest Route 165 northeast (right) 5 miles to F.R. 1272, which leads 1 mile north (left) to a small parking lot and boat landing next to the Baker Lake Campground.

Although no short round-trip loops are possible from the Baker Lake access, by shuttling cars to Sawbill Lake (Entry Point 38), paddlers can experience a moderately difficult 6-mile route through Burnt and Smoke lakes to the Sawbill Lake landing. Five portages are necessary; the longest is 230 rods. Watch for moose, bald eagles and ospreys.

40—Homer Lake (Map 9)

Canoeing Maps: Fisher—F-6
McKenzie—21

The eastern two thirds of Homer Lake, which lies outside the BWCA Wilderness, has no motor restrictions. Motorboats are not permitted in the western third, however.

The trailhead is located 23 miles north of Lutsen. From the Tofte Ranger Station, drive 10.8 miles northeast on Highway 61 to its junction with the Caribou Trail (County Road 4). Drive north on the Caribou Trail for 17.6 miles to its intersection with Forest Route 153. Turn left there and proceed west 1.7 miles to the junction of Forest Route 326, which leads 4 miles north to the east shore of Homer Lake.

Day trips southwest from the west end of Homer Lake through East Pipe Lake to the west end of Pipe Lake require only four short portages, the longest 20 rods. Along the way, you'll see the results of a violent windstorm that struck the

Bull moose seen from the portage connecting West Round and Round lakes

west end of Homer during the fall of 1986 and leveled many trees. The region west of Homer Lake and south of Brule Lake is one of the least visited parts of the entire BWCA Wilderness.

Ambitious paddlers could complete the 12-mile loop north to Brule Lake by steering west from Homer Lake through Whack, Verne and Juno lakes in one day. Five portages are crossed, the longest 70 rods. The route ends at the Brule Lake landing (see Entry Point 41), 2 miles north of the Homer Lake parking lot. Plan to shuttle cars or hike that final stretch on the road.

41—Brule Lake (Map 9)

Canoeing Maps: Fisher—F-6
McKenzie—21, 3

One could easily spend a whole day or longer exploring the extensive shoreline and numerous islands of Brule Lake. On a lake this large, it's best to stay close to shore. Strong winds can whip up large, treacherous waves. When out on the main part of the lake, always carry emergency provisions to enable a safe and comfortable layover should you find yourself windbound.

The trailhead is located 2 miles north of the Homer Lake access on Forest Route 326 (see directions for Entry Point 40). It is next to a public parking area at the end of the road.

One good destination is the palisades on Brule's west end. Canoeists who prefer smaller lakes might consider the loop down to Homer Lake (see Entry Point 40). Seasoned paddlers might also enjoy a day trip to Wanihigan Lake, a 12-mile loop that takes you north via the Cone Lakes chain to Cliff and Wanihigan lakes, then returns to Brule Lake by way of Grassy, Mulligan and Lily lakes. Nine portages are crossed, the longest a 200-rod trek between Grassy and Wanihigan lakes. This is not an easy one-day outing for most paddlers—better allow two full days if you're not accustomed to portages. Regardless, watch for bald eagles and ospreys soaring overhead.

GUNFLINT DISTRICT

Driving Directions. All but three of the 24 canoeing entry points are accessible from the Gunflint Trail (County Road 12), a good blacktop highway that begins in Grand Marais and leads 57 miles northwest to Gull Lake. The remaining three entry points are at the north end of the Arrowhead Trail (County Road 16), a good gravel road that begins in the tiny village of Hovland, 20 miles northeast of Grand Marais, via Highway 61, and leads 18 miles north to McFarland Lake.

43—Bower Trout Lake (Maps 9, 10)

Canoeing Maps: Fisher—F-13
McKenzie—3

Bower Trout Lake is the most isolated entry point along the Gunflint Trail, and the 4-mile trip west to Swan Lake is extremely scenic. The surrounding Misquah Hills reach to more than 500 feet above the headwaters of the South Brule River. Five short portages (the longest is 90 rods) are required, but none is difficult. A 292-rod portage might discourage day travel beyond Swan Lake, however.

An old railroad once skirted the north shores of Bower Trout and Swan lakes. A campsite at the north end of Swan Lake rests where a logging camp existed. Along the portage west of Swan Lake is evidence of a lumber camp that operated during the early 1920s.

The trailhead is located 23 miles north of Grand Marais. From the Ranger Station, drive 17 miles north on the Gunflint Trail to its junction with Forest Route 325 (1 mile past the Greenwood Lake Road). Turn left there and drive 6 miles west on this gravel road to its intersection with Forest Route 152. Turn left again and drive 0.25 mile southeast to a primitive road that spurs west (right). Bower Trout Lake is 0.5 mile west; there is a small boat landing and an even smaller space for parking. Vehicles with high clearance are recommended. (Note: If this unimproved road appears impassable, put in at the South Brule River bridge, 0.25 mile farther southeast on Forest Route 152. Starting there will necessitate a 72-rod portage from the river to the lake.)

44—Ram Lake (Maps 9, 10)

Canoeing Maps: Fisher—F-13
McKenzie—3

Ram Lake is nestled in the scenic Misquah Hills, which create an impressive background but are also responsible for some rather difficult portages between the small lakes northwest of Ram Lake.

The trailhead is located 0.75 mile northwest of the Bower Trout Lake access road, via Forest Route 152 (see directions for Entry Point 43). There is space for parking at the beginning of a 0.5-mile uphill portage to Ram Lake.

For most folks, the 2.5-mile journey into Little Trout Lake provides plenty of challenge for a day trip. Four portages connect Ram, Kroft, Rum and Little Trout lakes; the first and last involve some steep uphill climbing.

Energetic canoeists may want to continue north from Little Trout Lake through Misquah Lake to Vista Lake and then steer east through Jake and Morgan lakes back to Forest Route 152. It's a rugged loop with nine portages, the longest a 400-rod trail connecting the east end of Morgan Lake with Forest Route 152. The most difficult is the 190-rod trail connecting Little Trout and Misquah lakes. The loop is only 9 miles long, but it ends 4 miles north of your trailhead, so plan to either shuttle cars or end the trip with a long walk. Strong voyageurs could negotiate the loop in one long day. Most people, however, would be happier spreading the route over two days, with a night on Vista Lake.

45—Morgan Lake (Maps 9, 10)

Canoeing Maps: Fisher—F-13
McKenzie—3

Because of a long drive followed by a long portage, Morgan Lake is not very popular. The only bad part of the long portage, however, is the first few rods through a swampy area. It is relatively smooth and quite level much of the way, climbing over a low hill near Morgan Lake.

The trailhead is located 24 miles north of Grand Marais. From the Ranger Station, drive 20.8 miles north on the Gunflint Trail to its junction with Forest Route 152, the "Lima Mountain" road. Turn left and drive 2 miles to the junction with Forest Route 315. Bear right at the Y and proceed 2 more miles northwest to the beginning of the 400-rod portage that leads west (left) to Morgan Lake.

A 6-mile loop through four small lakes (Morgan, Carl, Lux and Jake) can be completed easily in just one day and requires only four short portages (in addition to the big one—twice). All of the lakes have recently been reclaimed for stream trout management.

Poplar Lake (Map 9)

Canoeing Maps: Fisher—F-13
McKenzie—3

The four BWCAW entry points described below are accessible from Poplar Lake. Three (Swamp, Lizz and Meeds lakes) lead south to the same general area and lend themselves well to short loop possibilities. Lizz Lake receives more use than the other three combined. The fourth entry point (Skipper Lake) leads to an isolated chain of lakes west of Poplar Lake.

Sitting entirely outside the BWCA Wilderness, Poplar Lake is dotted with resorts, outfitters and private cabins. Motorboats are permitted throughout the lake, but are not permitted to enter the Boundary Waters at any of the entry points.

The trailhead is located 33 miles northwest of Grand Marais. From the Ranger Station, drive 32 miles north on the Gunflint Trail to County Road 92. Turn left there and drive 0.5 mile west on this rough road to the junction with an unmarked, unimproved road that leads south (left) 0.5 mile to an 80-rod portage to the west end of Poplar Lake. This access should be used only by high-clearance vehicles with four-wheel-drive. If you're driving a "normal" car, you may park it and launch your canoe (for a small fee) at one of the resorts along the north shore of Poplar Lake, easily accessible from the Gunflint Trail.

46—Swamp Lake (Map 9)

Swamp Lake is the least popular entry point served by the Poplar Lake trailhead. It would receive even less use if it weren't for the fact that its neighbor to the west, Lizz Lake, is nearly always booked up. Swamp Lake offers the easiest alternative route to the same destination, Caribou Lake.

Unless you're an angler in search of northern pike, Swamp is not a particularly attractive destination. (It requires a 100-rod portage from the southeast end of Poplar Lake.) If your ultimate destination is Caribou Lake or beyond, you might want to consider a loop back to Poplar Lake through either Lizz Lake (9 miles and six portages) or through Meeds Lake (10 miles and seven portages).

47—Lizz Lake (Map 9)

Lizz Lake is the easiest and most popular of the entry points served by Poplar Lake. Two short loops are possible. One leads east from Caribou Lake to Swamp Lake and then back to Poplar Lake; it is 9 miles long and crosses six portages (round-trip from the public access), the longest at 155 rods. The other route loops west from Caribou Lake, enters the east end of Meeds Lake and returns to Poplar Lake via a challenging 220-rod portage. Seven portages (round-trip from the public access) are crossed on this 7.5-mile loop.

The easiest way to partake of the good fishing in this area is to use Lizz Lake for both the Wilderness entrance *and* the exit. Though the scenery is not spectacular, the fishing sometimes is, particularly for those who venture to Horseshoe and Vista lakes. Lizz Lake was reclaimed in the fall of 1985 and stocked with splake in 1986. Since the northern half of the lake is outside the BWCA Wilderness, motorboats are permitted there; but the southern half is exclusively for paddlers.

48—Meeds Lake (Map 9)

A challenging 220-rod portage from the southwest end of Poplar Lake leads to the east end of Meeds Lake. Day-trippers who don't mind tackling a long portage, however, might enjoy the 7.5-mile loop through Caribou to Lizz Lake (see Entry Point 47) or the 10-mile loop through Swamp Lake (see Entry Point 46). Each requires seven portages, with the routes starting and ending at the public access to Poplar Lake. The distances will be shorter if you start at one of the resorts on Poplar Lake.

49—Skipper Lake (Map 9)

A 320-rod portage near the west end of Poplar Lake leads to one of the least visited parts of the Gunflint District. The portage is not too difficult, but any carry of this length discourages all but the hardiest paddlers. That goes double for day-trippers, since they must cross the same portage twice in one day. The only short route that does not require backtracking leaves the Boundary Waters at the Portage Lake entry point and ends at the Iron Lake campground (see Entry Point 65).

If you have a strong inclination to escape from other people, the chain of lakes west of Skipper Lake (Little Rush, Rush and Banadad) affords the best opportunity in this part of the BWCA Wilderness. It is also one of the best areas in which to see moose.

65—Portage Lake (Map 9)

Canoeing Maps: Fisher—F-13
McKenzie—4

Portage Lake is entirely outside the Boundary Waters, but like Skipper Lake, it provides direct access to an isolated chain of lakes.

From the Grand Marais Ranger Station, drive 36.7 miles northwest on the Gunflint Trail to County Road 92. Turn left there and proceed 1 mile southeast to Forest Route 150, which leads south (right) 0.25 mile to the Iron Lake Campground and public access to Iron Lake. Portage Lake is southeast of Iron Lake, separated from it by a 40-rod portage.

The 240-rod portage from Portage Lake to One Island Lake is a rough entry into the BWCAW, climbing steeply for much of the first half. Because of the difficulty, few people venture to One Island, Rush and Banadad lakes. It's a great place to escape from the peak-season crowds. The only way to avoid backtracking is to shuttle a car to the Poplar Lake access (see "Poplar Lake," above) and exit the Boundary Waters at Entry Point 49, Skipper Lake. The 8-mile route crosses seven portages, the longest 320 rods. Add 4 more miles of paddling if you decide to search the shoreline of Rush Lake for browsing moose.

51—Ham Lake (Maps 8, 9)

Canoeing Maps: Fisher—F-12
McKenzie—7

Lying just north of the BWCAW border, Ham Lake is part of a chain of small lakes that compose the upper flowage of the Cross River. Though motors may be seen and heard on Ham Lake, the lakes to which it leads are exclusively for paddlers. It's a lovely and relatively easy way to enter a part of the Wilderness where moose abound.

The trailhead is located west of the Gunflint Trail, 47 miles northwest of Grand Marais. From the Ranger Station, drive north on County Road 12 for 46.2 miles to County Road 47. Turn left and drive 0.5 mile on this good gravel road to a boat landing and small parking area adjacent to the Cross River. Ham Lake is about 1 mile southeast of the road via the Cross River and two short portages (68 and 40 rods).

Canoeists who prefer the intimacy of narrow, winding lakes and streams will enjoy exploring the shores of Cross Bay and Snipe lakes. People with no aversion to portages might also want to complete one of two loops from Ham Lake to Round Lake. Both routes pass through Ham, Cross Bay and Snipe lakes. The shorter loop then crosses a 180-rod portage to Missing Link Lake and exits the BWCAW to Round Lake. Six portages are crossed on this 7-mile loop.

If time and ambition permit, the 10-mile loop through Copper, Hubbub and Tuscarora lakes to Round Lake is also a possibility. Nine portages are required for this all-day trek, including a tough 1.13-mile hike from Tuscarora Lake to Missing Link Lake (see Entry Point 52). Regardless of the route chosen, you'll end your journey at the Round Lake parking lot, more than a mile by road from your origin.

52—Missing Link Lake (Map 8)

Canoeing Maps: Fisher—F-12
McKenzie—7

Missing Link Lake is 142 rods southwest of Round Lake. Although the uphill portage is not too difficult, traveling anywhere beyond it is definitely a test of endurance. A 180-rod portage leads southeast to Snipe Lake, while a 366-rod path leads southwest to Tuscarora Lake. Unless you plan to loop east to the Ham Lake entry point (see Entry Point 51), you'll have to take your selected portage twice—a challenge, but not out of the question with a nearly empty canoe.

Tuscarora Lake is a big, attractive lake with nice fishing. A campsite on a big rock outcropping at the west end of the lake makes a great destination for anglers and picnickers alike. It sits 4.5 miles from the parking lot and requires four portages (round trip) totaling more than 3 miles in cumulative length, wearying even for seasoned canoeists.

The trailhead is located at Round Lake, 1 mile west of the Ham Lake entry point via County Road 47 and Forest Route 1495 (see Entry Point 51). Turn right onto F.R. 1495 and follow it 0.75 mile to the end. There is a fairly large parking lot near the landing.

53—Brant Lake (Map 8)

Canoeing Maps: Fisher—F-12
McKenzie—7

Brant Lake is 1.5 miles west of Round Lake, via three short portages and two small lakes. The scenery surrounding Round, West Round and Edith lakes and the south end of Brant Lake is considerably less than spectacular—low terrain covered with spruce and fir. Winding your way up Z-shaped Brant Lake from the southeast corner to the northwest end, however, the low, green shoreline squeezes the lake into a narrow channel bordered by rocky ledges. Campsites rest high above the water's edge on rock outcroppings. It's an appealing scene, resembling a narrow river more than a lake.

The 4-mile round trip to and from the north end of Brant Lake provides novice paddlers with a pleasant introduction to the Boundary Waters—small lakes, easy portages and a scenic picnic site at a campsite overlooking the narrow north channel of Brant Lake.

There are no short loops to consider. The best way to enjoy this entry point is to paddle a comfortable distance into the BWCAW, and then retrace your route to the trailhead.

The trailhead is at Round Lake (see Entry Point 52).

54—Sea Gull Lake (Map 8)

Canoeing Maps: Fisher—F-19
McKenzie—6

There are resorts and cabins at the northeast end of Sea Gull Lake, which lies outside the BWCAW. Ten-horsepower motors are permitted in the eastern half of the lake; the western half is reserved for paddlers.

The trailhead is located at Trail's End Campground, 57 miles northwest of Grand Marais via County Road 12. Drive northwest on this good blacktopped

Round Lake

road until you come to its end at a large parking lot adjacent to the campground entrance.

Blessed with more than 50 miles of shoreline, over a hundred islands and a plethora of bays and peninsulas—most of them within the BWCAW—there is plenty of pretty scenery for inexperienced canoeists to explore without ever crossing a portage.

Many visitors are attracted to the sheer granite cliffs along the north shore of the lake. Look closely and you'll see the rusty red prehistoric Indian pictographs near the base of the cliffs. Hikers may want to explore the 1.6-mile portage from the southeast shore of Sea Gull to Jap Lake—a wet, uphill climb, that takes a couple of hours. Or look for the 300-year-old Norway pine that reigns over Threemile Island. Swimmers will enjoy the nice sand beaches along the shore.

Seasoned paddlers might consider portaging from the west end of Sea Gull Lake to Alpine Lake and then looping northeast to Saganaga Lake. The 21-mile route starts and ends at Trail's End Campground, crosses five lakes and requires only three easy portages.

55—Saganaga Lake (Map 8)

Canoeing Maps: Fisher—F-19
                    McKenzie—6A

There is a good deal of daytime traffic, as well as campers, on this huge lake, due to several resorts, cabins and outfitters at the south end, which is outside the Boundary Waters. Twenty-five-horsepower motors are permitted on the U.S. side of the lake, east of American Point. There are no motor restrictions on the Canadian side, east of Cache Bay, or in the main "corridor" on the U.S. side from the public landing to the Canadian border.

The most convenient trailhead is located at Trail's End Campground, 57 miles northwest of the Grand Marais ranger station (see Entry Point 54).

Saganaga provides canoeists with a vast aquatic wilderness to explore without portaging. The Canadian border splits the lake from east to west, leaving the U.S. with the more interesting half, including more than 150 islands and 130 miles of shoreline with countless bays and tiny coves. Paddlers may venture into the waters of both nations, but the unprotected northern half is much more susceptible to the treachery of strong winds. You'll be safer in the island-studded U.S. waters.

80—Larch Creek (Maps 8, 9)

Canoeing Maps: Fisher—F-19
                    McKenzie—5

Narrow, shallow Larch Creek provides an appealing "back door" to the scenic Granite River system. The trailhead is located at the Sea Gull Guard Station, 49 miles northwest of the Gunflint Ranger Station in Grand Marais on County Road 12. Watch for the turn-off on the right side of the road.

Larch Creek meanders from the Gunflint Trail 1.5 miles northeast to Larch Lake, with maybe half a dozen beaver dams to pull over along the way. You may have difficulty paddling during dry seasons, but the stream is usually navigable.

One of the isolated campsites on either Larch Lake or Clove Lake, its neighbor to the east, makes a good destination for a leisurely half-day trip into the Wilderness. If you go farther than Larch Lake, however, you're more likely to encounter groups enjoying the Granite River flowage.

The only short loop that can be comfortably completed in one day requires car shuttling. It leads up the Pine River (south) from Clove Lake, leaves the BWCAW at Magnetic Lake and ends at the Gunflint Lake landing (see Entry Point 57). This interesting 7-mile trip requires five portages, the longest 110 rods, and passes scenic Little Rock Falls.

57—Magnetic Lake (Map 9)

Canoeing Maps: Fisher—F-12, 20
                    McKenzie—5

Magnetic Lake provides relatively easy access to one of the prettiest parts of the Boundary Waters: the Canadian border segment that includes the Pine and

Granite rivers. Both Gunflint and Magnetic lakes lie outside the BWCA Wilderness, so there are no motor restrictions, but beyond the north end of Magnetic Lake is a lovely wilderness world of winding streams, frothing white water, tranquil lakes and outstanding scenery collectively called the Granite River flowage.

The trailhead is located at Gunflint Lake, 44 miles northwest of Grand Marais. From the Ranger Station, drive 43.5 miles northwest on County Road 12 to County Road 50. Turn right onto this gravel road and proceed 0.5 mile east to the public boat landing and parking lot at Gunflint Lake. Magnetic Lake is accessed from Gunflint's northwest corner.

Many daytime visitors go no farther than the second portage, where the Pine River cascades 15 feet over Little Rock Falls. Although many of the rapids on the Pine and Granite rivers are tempting, only experienced whitewater canoeists should consider running them—and then only after careful scouting. Most daytime excursions into this region will necessitate backtracking to the trailhead. If you would rather not backtrack, you can end your journey at the Larch Creek entry point (see Entry Point 80).

58—South Lake (Map 9)

Canoeing Maps: Fisher—F-13
McKenzie—4, 2

Steep hills tower more than 400 feet above South Lake. Located on the Canadian border, the lake receives little overnight use and, because of its distance from the closest road, is barely accessible to day paddlers. The trailhead is at Gunflint Lake (see Entry Point 57). To get to South Lake, you must first paddle 12 miles east across Gunflint, Little Gunflint, Little North and North lakes. Two portages are required (20 and 80 rods), and the entire route is open to motorboats and highly susceptible to strong winds.

Along the way are several reminders of the rich history created by voyageurs, loggers and Native Americans. The 80-rod "Height of Land" portage that separates North and South lakes, in fact, was one of the most significant landmarks along the historic Voyageur's Highway. Now known as the Laurentian Divide, which separates the Atlantic Ocean and Arctic Ocean watersheds, it marked the point at which they would no longer be paddling upstream.

The best way for seasoned paddlers to experience this part of the Wilderness is to plan a route that ends at one of the entry points east of South Lake. The closest is Entry Point 60, which is accessible from a parking lot on the south shore of Bearskin Lake. The 22-mile route crosses nine lakes and six portages, the longest of which is 80 rods. Don't consider doing it in just one day unless there is a slight tail wind (from the west) or no wind at all. Even then, take emergency provisions in case you find yourself windbound or simply too tired to finish before dark. It's too much for a novice to attempt in just one day.

60—Duncan Lake (Maps 9, 10)

Canoeing Maps: Fisher—F-13
McKenzie—2

Duncan Lake, 0.25 mile west of Bearskin Lake, is popular with day-trippers because of its easy accessibility to the Canadian border and to Stairway Portage, an 80-rod trail at the northeast end of Duncan that leads north and drops steeply down to Rose Lake on a long wooden stairway originally constructed during the Depression by the Civilian Conservation Corps. The Border Route Trail bisects the portage and leads east to a spectacular overlook at the top of a dramatic bluff, affording a beautiful view across Rose Lake and well beyond the Canadian border. Getting there necessitates only 4.5 miles of paddling across Bearskin and Duncan lakes and portaging only 75 rods between the two lakes.

The trailhead is at Bearskin Lake (sometimes called West Bearskin Lake). From the Gunflint Ranger Station in Grand Marais, drive 27 miles northwest on County Road 12 to Clearwater Lake Road (County Road 66). Turn right and proceed another 3.2 miles on this gravel road to the public landing and parking lot at the east end of Bearskin Lake.

61—Daniels Lake (Map 10)

Canoeing Maps: Fisher—F-13
McKenzie—2

Peaceful Daniels Lake has several nice campsites near the east end, just 60 rods north of Bearskin Lake. A hiking trail skirts the southeast end of the lake on the bed of an abandoned railroad that served logging operations during the early part of this century, and meets the Border Route Trail at the Long Portage. Visitors who like to split their day between paddling and hiking will like Daniels Lake (see also "Daniels Lake Trail" in Chapter 4).

Like Duncan Lake, Daniels offers direct access to the Canadian border and beautiful Rose Lake, but novice paddlers and anyone who shuns long portages will probably be content to go no farther than the northeast end. From there, a 524-rod portage leads northwest to Rose Lake.

The trailhead is at Bearskin Lake (see Entry Point 60).

62—Clearwater Lake (Map 10)

Canoeing Maps: Fisher—F-14
McKenzie—2

Despite the fact that motorboats are permitted on the lake and the west end of the lake is home to a resort, an outfitter, a campground and many private cabins, if you enjoy fine scenery, you're bound to appreciate Clearwater Lake. Steep bluffs border this long, slender lake, and you can take a delightful day trip without ever portaging your canoe.

The trailhead is located 32 miles north of Grand Marais. From the Ranger Station, drive 27 miles north on County Road 12 to County Road 66. Turn right and follow this gravel road 5.1 miles to its end at the boat landing and small parking lot near the west end of Clearwater Lake.

An 11-mile round trip to the east end of the lake can be highlighted by stopping at the Mountain Lake portage, 4 miles from the boat landing. The Border Route Trail bisects the 90-rod portage, and from that intersection you can hike west on the Border Route Trail to palisades that afford panoramic views across the Canadian border and Clearwater Lake. It's an outstanding destination for photography buffs, especially in autumn.

A loop is possible by portaging 0.5 mile south from the east end of Clearwater Lake over a 150-foot hill to Caribou Lake, and then paddling to the west end of Caribou, where a 210-rod trail leads back to Clearwater Lake. Not recommended

Crossing West Round Lake

for a novice, this 10-mile loop will generate some sweat on the portages. Watch for bald eagles and ospreys soaring overhead.

64—East Bearskin Lake (Map 10)

Canoeing Maps: Fisher—F-13, 14
McKenzie—2

A resort, an outfitter and several private cabins are located along the north shore of East Bearskin Lake, which is mostly outside the BWCA Wilderness. Only the tips of the two eastern bays lie inside the Boundary Waters, and 25-horsepower motors are permitted there. Ten-horsepower motors are also allowed on Alder and Canoe lakes, east of East Bearskin, so you may have difficulty escaping the sights and sounds of other people on a day outing.

Nevertheless, the beautiful, hilly landscape is worth sharing with others. Virgin pines border Alder Lake and the east end of East Bearskin Lake, and the 7-mile journey from the boat landing to Canoe Lake is bordered by hills that rise more than 200 feet above the lakes. Only two easy portages (48 and 22 rods) are encountered.

If you have the strength, energy and time to spare, you might continue on to Pine Lake, where Johnson Falls awaits (see Entry Point 68). It's worth the effort even though the 0.75-mile portage from Canoe Lake to Pine Lake is one of the toughest in the BWCAW. Those who make it there usually continue in a counter-clockwise direction through Little Caribou, Caribou, Deer and Moon lakes back to the northeast end of East Bearskin Lake. The 15-mile route requires eight portages and will take even a seasoned canoeist a full day to complete.

To reach the trailhead at East Bearskin Lake Campground from the Grand Marais ranger station, drive 25.6 miles north on the Gunflint Trail to Forest Route 146. Turn right and proceed 1 mile east to the campground entrance. There is a large parking lot next to the boat landing.

66—Crocodile River (Map 10)

Canoeing Maps: Fisher—F-14
McKenzie—2

Because of its remoteness and, perhaps, because it leads to a route more easily served by the East Bearskin Lake entry point, the Crocodile River is the least used overnight canoeing entry point in the entire BWCA Wilderness. If you're looking for a quick way to escape from the midsummer crowds, the Crocodile River is your gateway to solitude.

To reach the trailhead from the Gunflint Ranger Station in Grand Marais, drive 15.8 miles north on County Road 12 to the Greenwood Lake road (Forest Route 309). Turn right and follow this good gravel road 4 miles to Forest Route 1386. Turn left onto this narrower, rougher gravel road and proceed 2.8 miles to Forest Route 313, which continues straight north another 2 miles to an unmarked trail on the left side of the road. The Crocodile River is three portages and two lakes north of the road.

To access the river, you must first portage three times (80, 75 and 100 rods) across two of the "vegetable lakes" (South Bean and Parsnip). The river then leads west to a 20-rod portage before merging with the slender east end of Crocodile Lake. Access to the lake is much easier and quicker by portaging south from East Bearskin Lake (see Entry Point 64). There are four campsites on the lake where you can fry up some bass.

68—Pine Lake (Map 10)

Canoeing Maps: Fisher—F-14
McKenzie—1

Pine Lake is surrounded by scenic hills towering as high as 500 feet above the surface. Seven and a half miles long and averaging about half a mile in width, it is a wide open expanse that can be treacherous on a windy day. Carry provisions for an emergency overnight stay.

To reach the trailhead from the Gunflint Ranger Station in Grand Marais, drive 20 miles northeast on Highway 61 to the small village of Hovland. Turn left there onto the Arrowhead Trail (County Road 16) and drive 18 miles north on this gravel road to the small parking lot and public landing at McFarland Lake. Pine Lake is accessed by a short portage at the west end of McFarland Lake.

Johnson Falls is the most scenic cascade in this part of the Wilderness. It can be seen by hiking 0.25 mile from the west end of Pine Lake along the south shore of a tiny creek. The 10-mile paddle there requires only a 2-rod portage between McFarland and Pine lakes around a small, gentle rapids that can usually be run on the return trip.

Portaging across Howl "Lake"

69—John Lake (Map 10)

Canoeing Maps: Fisher—F-14
                      McKenzie—1

John Lake is 10 rods north of Little John Lake, separated by a short, gentle rapids and a 10-rod portage that is usually not necessary—depending on the water level, you can normally line, walk or run your canoe through the channel. East Pike Lake lies west of John, requiring a 180-rod portage over a 100-foot hill. It's a quick route to solitude, the fishing is good and you just might see some interesting wildlife—osprey, moose and otters. The steep ridge along the south shore of East Pike looms more than 300 feet above the lake—an impressive scene that virtually glows in autumn.

The trailhead is located at Little John Lake, just past the McFarland Lake landing (see Entry Point 68).

70—North Fowl Lake (Map 11)

Canoeing Maps: Fisher—F-14
                      McKenzie—1

North Fowl Lake is part of the historic Canadian border route used by voyageurs of the 18th and 19th centuries. The lake is also rich in Native American history, and part of it is now listed on the National Register of Historical Sites.

109

The area entertains few campers, but there is frequent day use by fishermen, who are allowed to use 10-horsepower motorboats. A small, rustic resort sits on the U.S. side. Canadians can drive to the lake; there are some developments and no motor restrictions north and east of the border.

The trailhead is located at Little John Lake (see Entry Point 69). North Fowl Lake is 3 miles east of the landing by way of Little John and John lakes, the Royal River and Royal Lake. Three portages of 10, 78 and 160 rods are required to get there.

The 12-mile round trip to the north end of North Fowl Lake will provide plenty of challenge for most daytime visitors. The three portages are not tough, but the 0.5-mile carry will generate a good sweat. There are no short loops that can be completed in just one day.

PADDLING OUTSIDE THE BOUNDARY WATERS

Many people think Superior National Forest is synonymous with the Boundary Waters Canoe Area Wilderness. The BWCAW is just over 1 million acres in size, however, and that's only about a third of the total area within the Forest boundaries. Many canoeing experiences are possible outside the BWCA Wilderness, including large lakes, small lakes, winding streams and rushing rivers. As in the Wilderness, some lakes in each district are heavily used and some receive very light use. A few afford greater solitude than most places inside the Wilderness boundaries. Nearly all offer excellent potential for fishing, camping and wildlife observation.

There are 825 lakes in Superior National Forest outside the BWCA Wilderness. The Forest Service maintains over 30 watercraft launch sites in addition to those providing access to the Boundary Waters. The Minnesota Department of Natural Resources maintains additional boat landings. The launch sites range from paved lots and ramps to places where canoes must be carried down to the water ("carry-downs"). The remaining part of this chapter describes 14 canoe routes and 162 public boat accesses in Superior National Forest outside the BWCA Wilderness.

To many folks the most attractive feature of paddling outside the BWCAW is the lack of regulations. Cans and bottles are not prohibited. Group size is not limited to 10 people (although more than that is not recommended because of possible environmental damage at campsites). Permits are not required and there are no quotas. And even though motorized canoes and motorboats are allowed on all of the lakes outside the BWCAW, many of the lakes there are just as peaceful as any in the Wilderness.

In the following trip descriptions the map numbers following trip names refer to the maps in Chapter 2 on which their locations are shown. These maps, however, are not meant to be used for route finding. For that purpose detailed topographic maps are required.

LAURENTIAN DISTRICT

The southwestern part of Superior National Forest offers two canoe routes and 31 additional lakes and streams with public boat landings. Most of the lake and stream accesses in this district are served by good gravel roads that can accommodate passenger cars, but occasionally high-clearance vehicles are needed or recommended.

Stony River (Map 15)

Length:	8 miles (one way)
Difficulty:	Moderate, with some white water
Use level:	Light
Highlights:	A good rafting river
USGS Maps:	Slate Lake West, Babbitt NE

The trailhead is located where the river passes under Highway 1, 22.8 miles southeast of the Ely Chamber of Commerce. You'll need to shuttle a car to the take-out point at the junction of Forest Routes 424 and 178. The most direct route there is via F.R. 424, which intersects Highway 1, 21.1 miles southeast of Ely (1.7 miles north of the put-in). Drive 5.8 miles west on F.R. 424 to its junction with F.R. 178 adjacent to the Stony River bridge. There are no signs and no designated parking lot at the take-out.

This segment of the Stony River is mostly slow-moving pools with some rapids interspersed. The route can easily be completed in half a day or less. It penetrates some rough and scenic country, but receives very little use except for an occasional group of Outward Bound students. It is most suitable for canoeing in the spring and early summer or after heavy rainfalls—during other times of the year, it may be difficult to navigate because of low water and protruding rocks. There are no developed campsites and no developed portages, although there are some user-developed campsites along the river.

The Stony flows from east to west, and, for the most part, the current is noticeable only at the rapids. It eventually flows into the southeast end of Birch Lake, but is unsuitable for open canoes below the recommended take-out point, turning into a raging river of white water (the "Roaring Stony") that is best reserved for the rafters.

St. Louis River (Maps 14, 15)

Length:	12 miles (one way)
Difficulty:	Moderately easy
Use level:	Light to moderate
Highlights:	Wildlife habitat
USGS Maps:	Babbitt SW, Babbitt SE, Brimson NW, Toimi

You can put in and take out at Skibo Mill, 17 miles east of Aurora. From the corner of County Roads 100 and 110 in Aurora, drive 4.4 miles east on 110 to downtown Hoyt Lakes. Where County Road 110 turns left at the stop sign, continue straight for 1.5 miles on County Road 565. At the junction with County Road 569, turn right and follow this gravel road 7 miles southeast to a railroad crossing called Skibo. Just before reaching the tracks, you'll see a "dead end" gravel road called Pine Street that spurs off to the right (south). Turn onto Pine Street and follow this rough road 4 miles to its end at Skibo Mill. High-clearance vehicles are recommended on this final stretch.

The St. Louis River is, for the most part, a slow-moving stream that starts at the north shore of Seven Beaver Lake and meanders through the flat central lowlands of the Laurentian District. There are occasional fast-moving rocky sections,

Beaver lodge

some of which require portaging. Forest vegetation includes bog brush, muskeg swamp, aspen and birch, with some spruce, pine and cedar stands visible from the river. Wild rice grows in the shallow bays, moose and deer frequently feed along the banks, and there are many birds present.

There are six developed campsites along the route: two on Round Lake, one each on Seven Beaver and Long lakes, and two located along the river, one at Skibo Landing and one about midway between Seven Beaver Lake and Long Lake. A 60-rod portage south from the river is necessary to access Long Lake, one of the most isolated lakes in the Laurentian District. With no road access and no development except for the campsite on its north shore, Long Lake is usually a very quiet destination for people who wish to escape from crowds. Three more portages (100, 40 and 80 rods) may be necessary on the river between Skibo Mill and Seven Beaver Lake, depending on the water level and the direction you travel. The river flows from east to west.

There are no motor restrictions on any of these lakes, and seaplanes occasionally bring guests from nearby resorts. For the most part, the lakes are shallow and have swampy shorelines. Because of the boggy surroundings, biting insects are nuisances during late spring and early summer months—try early spring and autumn, when bugs are nothing more than a bad memory.

A three-wheeler trail leads south from Round Lake to Forest Route 418. The locals use it often, but it does cross private lands. Check with the district ranger for details if you'd like to explore this access for either a put-in or a take-out point. Otherwise, you'll need to return to the St. Louis River trailhead the way you came.

Table 4 — Other Lakes and Streams with Boat Accesses: Laurentian District

Lake/Stream	Depth	Size	Access	Development	Comments	Map
Arrowhead Lake	26	100	PC	2, 3	Boat landing used by swimmers	13
Bassett Lake	21	436	PC	4	Large landing maintained by the township	19
Big Rice Lake	4.5	2072	PC	2, 3	Rustic campground near boat landing	13
Bird Lake	14	9	PC	2	Picnic grounds next to lake; 5-rod portage	14
Breda Lake	4	137	PC	1	Access from Petrel Creek	19
Cadotte Lake	18	318	PC	4	Landing at USFS campground	19
Camp Four Lake	30	20	F	1	0.25-mile portage from C.R. 25	12
Chow Lake	11	43	F	1	10-rod portage to this peaceful little lake	15
Clear Lake	20	149	PC	3	Steep carry-down from C.R. 461	12
Cloquet River	N/A	N/A	PC	3	Easy access from F.R. 122, 8 mi. W. of Hwy. 2	19
Colby Lake	34	514	PC	4	Hoyt Lakes municipal access	14
Dark Lake	38	244	PC	2, 3	Blacktop roads most of the way	12
Dark River	N/A	N/A	F	2, 3	Walk-in access from N. and S. Dark R. Trails	12
Deepwater Lake	37	25	F	2	0.5-mi. portage; 1.5-mi. trail to campsite	12
Harris Lake	38	87	HC	1	Footpath connects Otto and Harris lakes	19
Hay Lake	N/A	114	PC	1	Access via the Pike River from C.R.64	13
Jammer Lake	33	19	PC	2	Adjacent to Hwy. 53	13
Knuckey Lake	9	71	PC	1	Wild rice attracts waterfowl	12
Otto Lake	27	168	F	1	0.5-mile portage from F.R. 416	19
Partridge River	N/A	N/A	PC	3	Easy access 6.5 miles east of Aurora	14
Pfeiffer Lake	26	57	PC	2	Campground, swimming beach, foot trail	13
Pine Lake	14	442	F	3	0.75-mile portage from F.R. 418	15
Rice Lake	3	41	PC	1	Access via the Pike River from C.R. 64	13
St. Louis River	N/A	N/A	PC	2, 3	Easy access at Norway Point Picnic Grounds	14

Lake/Stream	Depth	Size	Access	Develop-ment	Comments	Map
Salo Lake	20	149	PC	2, 3	Picnic grounds at boat landing	19
Sand Lake	12	506	PC	2, 3	4-rod carry-down from parking area	15
Shoe Pack Lake	30	50	PC	1	Isolated lake	12
Stone Lake	4	230	F	1	0.5-mile portage to good wild rice lake	15
Sullivan Lake	8	41	PC	2	State campground next to boat landing	20
Whiteface Reservoir	35	4980	PC	4	A busy lake with a popular campground	19
Whitewater Lake	73	1210	PC	4	Hoyt Lakes municipal park and campground	14

DEPTH: Maximum depth in feet
SIZE: Acres as listed in Division of Waters Bulletin No. 25
ACCESS: PC = passenger car, HC = high-clearance vehicles, F = foot trail
DEVELOPMENT: 1 = none, 2 = limited public, 3 = limited private, 4 = extensive development
MAP: Numbers refer to maps in this guidebook.

LA CROIX DISTRICT

The northwestern corner of Superior National Forest contains two excellent canoe routes and 17 lakes and streams with public boat landings. All of the lake and stream accesses in this district are served by good gravel roads that can be used by any passenger automobiles. Though some roads are rough, none requires high-clearance vehicles.

Vermilion River (Maps 4, 1)

Length:	36 miles (one way)
Difficulty:	Moderate
Use level:	Light (some parts moderate)
Highlights:	Outstanding scenery; extensive white water
Canoeing maps:	Fisher—F-8, F-15

The Vermilion River was extensively used during the fur trade era from 1768 to 1848. The first major voyageurs' highway, in fact, followed the St. Louis, Embarrass and Pike rivers to the Vermilion River. The route preceded the better-known "highways" that later paralleled the present U.S.-Canadian border.

The best place to put in is at Twomile Creek, 21 miles northeast of Cook. From Highway 53 in Cook, drive 21 miles north and east on County Road 24 to its intersection (the second one) with County Road 422. Turn right and proceed 0.3 mile south to the public landing at the creek. Take out at Crane Lake public landing (see directions for Entry Point 12 in the "Paddling the Boundary Waters" section of this chapter).

There is no public access at the dam that marks the beginning of the full 40-mile river route. Starting at Twomile Creek adds 1 mile of narrow, winding stream, but eliminates about 5 miles of the upper Vermilion River. To include all of the river and extend the route by several miles, you can put in at any one of several public landings on Lake Vermilion and then access the river by portaging 50 rods around Vermilion Dam.

The Vermilion's many rapids range in difficulty from class I (easy enough for anybody) to class VI (not runnable). Experienced whitewater canoeists will find the challenges delightful when the water level is sufficiently high. If the water level is low or if you don't wish to run the rapids, 11 portages, ranging in length from 8 rods to 330 rods, will take you around all the rapids. The other nine portages average 80 rods in length.

Allow at least three full days to enjoy the exceptional scenery along the Vermilion River, using campsites near Table Rock Falls (7 miles below the trailhead) and Snowshoe Narrows (13 miles farther downstream). That leaves 16 miles of paddling, but only three portages, for the final day.

Highlights include Table Rock Falls, a 20-foot cascade with several vertical ledges; Snowshoe Narrows, where pine-covered hills and cliffs tower nearly 100 feet above the river; Vermilion Falls, a 25-foot-high, narrow, twisting flume; and the Gorge, where the river makes a sharp bend and then tumbles over two steep ledges en route to a slender canyon with sheer 50-foot walls. Wildlife enthusiasts will find plenty of whitetailed deer, ruffed grouse and an assortment of ducks along the river, along with occasional wolves and moose.

Day-trippers can enjoy the river by putting in and/or taking out at locations other than Twomile Creek and Crane Lake. County Road 24 crosses the river at the townsite of Buyck, 25 miles upstream from the Crane Lake landing. Forest Route 491 crosses the river below Vermilion Falls, 4 miles west of Crane Lake. Ambitious day outings might include the 12-mile stretch from Twomile Creek to County Road 24 or the 20-mile stretch from C.R. 24 to Forest Route 491. An easy afternoon outing that includes Vermilion Gorge can be enjoyed by putting in at Forest Route 491 and paddling 4 miles downstream to Crane Lake. Two portages (40 and 240 rods) are required. Several other day routes are also possible.

For more information, write the Minnesota Department of Natural Resources, Trails and Waterways Unit, Rivers Section—B52, Centennial Building, St. Paul, MN 55155. Or call (612) 296-6699.

Astrid and Picket Creeks (Map 4)

Length:	22 miles
Difficulty:	Difficult
Use level:	Very light
Highlights:	Wilderness solitude; good wildlife potential
Canoeing maps:	Fisher—F-8, F-15
Warning:	**Route not suitable in low-water seasons**

This route passes through a cluster of five small lakes and two tiny creeks that see few visitors (except at the campgrounds). Canoeists are more likely to find complete solitude here than in most parts of the BWCA Wilderness. And since there are no quotas, it's a good destination when the BWCAW is booked up.

Use the trailhead at Lake Jeanette campground for putting in, and take out at Echo Lake campground. Both are accessed from the Echo Trail. (For directions

Large boulders border the Astrid Lake trail.

to the Echo Trail, see La Croix District driving directions in "Paddling the Boundary Waters".) Lake Jeanette is 12 miles east of County Road 24, and Echo Lake is 1.8 miles east of C.R. 24.

There are eight developed portages along the route, and you may also have to cross an occasional beaver dam on Picket Creek. The longest carry is nearly 1.5 miles, while two others are more than 0.5 mile each. This is not a good route, therefore, for inexperienced (or weak) canoeists.

In addition to the campgrounds at both ends of this route, there is one campsite each on Pauline and Nigh lakes, Astrid Lake has two developed sites and Picket Lake has three. Some sites sit next to sandy beaches, while others rest on rock outcroppings that afford excellent lake views. Those on Nigh, Pauline and Astrid lakes are accessible to backpackers using the Astrid Lake Trails (see Chapter 4). There are also six dispersed campsites on Lake Jeanette and three on Echo Lake. There are no developed sites along the 13-mile stretch of Picket Creek.

From the Lake Jeanette campground, you paddle only a short distance before portaging 0.5 mile southwest, across the Echo Trail, to Nigh Lake. A 60-rod portage connects Nigh and Pauline lakes. From the west end of Pauline Lake, follow Astrid Creek south to Astrid Lake and portage 200 rods on a good path that leads uphill to cross Forest Route 200 and then descends gradually to the east end of Maude Lake.

A 450-rod portage connects the west end of Maude Lake with a small beaver pond, which connects via another short portage to the east shore of Picket Lake. If you're planning to complete this route in two days, one of the three campsites at the west end of Picket Lake (about 8 miles from the trailhead) will be the most suitable for your only night on the trail.

From the west end of Maude Lake, you enter the winding wilderness of Picket Creek, which will lead you northwest to Echo Lake. Four portages (10, 25, 20 and 100 rods) will be encountered along the way. This is one of the best regions in Superior National Forest to see moose.

Picket Creek may be too shallow for a loaded canoe when the water level is down. If conditions are questionable, consult the district office before attempting this route.

| Table 5 | Other Lakes and Streams with Boat Accesses: La Croix District |

Lake/Stream	Depth	Size	Access	Develop- ment	Comments	Map
Ash Lake	25	678	PC	3	Easy access off Hwy. 53 north of Virginia	3
Astrid Lake	30	114	F	1	80-rod portage from F.R. 200; foot trail	4
Black Duck Lake	30	1264	PC	4	Among "Top 100 Walleye Lakes" in MN	3
Crane Lake	80	3396	PC	4	Access to Voyageur National Park & Canada	2
Echo Lake	10	1222	PC	2, 3	USFS campground; 3 dispersed campsites	4
Elbow Lake	60	1528	PC	3	Access at both north and south ends	4
Elephant Lake	30	782	PC	4	Among "Top 100 Walleye Lakes" in MN	3
Franklin Lake	18	145	F	1	225-rod portage from F.R. 203	1
Jeanette, Lake	15	638	PC	2	USFS campground; 6 dispersed campsites	5
Johnson Lake	88	1685	F	3	100-rod portage from F.R. 203; 6 campsites	1
Kjostad Lake	50	438	PC	2, 3	Picnic site adjacent to DNR boat landing	4
Maude Lake	26	88	F	1	120-rod portage from F.R. 200; 2 campsites	4
Meander Lake	15	101	F	2, 3	Short portage through picnic grounds to lake	5
Myrtle Lake	20	860	PC	3	Beautiful sand beach accessible by boat	4
Nigh Lake	12	40	F	1	160-rod portage from C.R. 116; 1 campsite	4
Pauline Lake	25	60	F	1	20-rod portage from C.R. 116; 1 campsite	4
Vermilion Lake	76	49,110	PC	4	Resorts, cabins, campgrounds, 8 campsites	4, 5

DEPTH: Maximum depth in feet
SIZE: Acres as listed in Division of Waters Bulletin No. 25
ACCESS: PC = passenger car, HC = high-clearance vehicles, 4WD = 4-wheel-drive
DEVELOPMENT: 1 = none, 2 = limited public, 3 = limited private, 4 = extensive
MAP: Numbers refer to maps in this guidebook.

KAWISHIWI DISTRICT

North-central Superior National Forest offers three canoe routes and 22 lakes and rivers with public boat accesses. Most of the boat landings in this district are served by roads that are good enough for passenger cars. Harris Lake is the only definite exception, although some roads may be rough or muddy in early spring or following periods of heavy rain.

Birch Lake (Map 15)

Length:	20 miles (one way)
Difficulty:	Easy
Use level:	Moderate to heavy
Highlights:	No portages
Canoeing map:	Fisher—F-3

Birch Lake is a long, relatively slender reservoir that extends from Highway 1 at the northeast end to Highway 21 at its southwest end, snaking like a river through the rolling woodlands, with some nice rock outcroppings along the shore. Because the shoreline is populated with private cabins, resorts and two National Forest campgrounds, Birch does not provide canoeists with wilderness tranquility, but it does offer an alternative that's easy enough for the whole family to enjoy. There are 16 dispersed campsites scattered around the lake, in addition to the South Kawishiwi River and Birch Lake campgrounds.

You can put in at either the northeast or the southwest ends of the lake. The South Kawishiwi River Campground lies at the extreme northeast end and is easily accessible by driving 11 miles south on Highway 1 from the Ely Chamber of Commerce. The public access at the south end of the lake is just east of Babbitt. From the Ely Chamber of Commerce, drive 1 mile west (through downtown) on Highway 1/169 to Highway 21. Turn left and follow Highway 21 16 miles south to County Road 70. Turn left again at the T-intersection and proceed 4 miles east to the turn-off (left) to the public landing and beach.

Since there are no portages along the route, and because other people are always around, Birch Lake is a good route for beginning canoe campers—a place to give it a try without being isolated from the rest of the world. One way to enjoy the lake is to put in at the South Kawishiwi River campground and paddle close to one shoreline as far southwest as you wish, then turn around and paddle along the opposite shoreline back to your car. Paddled as straight as possible, this route is nearly 20 miles long from end to end, but you'll add many more miles by paralleling the crooked shoreline. There are plenty of bays and creek inlets to explore along the way.

Bass and Fenske Lakes Loop (Map 6)

Length:	20 miles (round trip)
Difficulty:	Moderate
Use level:	Light
Highlights:	BWCA-type experience
Canoeing map:	Fisher—F-9

This route is an excellent substitute for the Wilderness, passing through a lovely region that is blessed with the same combination of rock hills, swamps, rivers, lakes and variety of vegetation as that found in the Boundary Waters. Ten portages are crossed, but none is too difficult. Only three are longer than 100 rods; most are less than 50.

You can start your trip at the Bass Lake Trail parking lot, which lies along the Echo Trail, 2.6 miles north of County Road 88 (for directions, see Kawishiwi District driving directions in "Paddling the Boundary Waters"). A 160-rod portage leads downhill to the west end of Bass Lake.

From Bass Lake, you paddle northeast to Low Lake and then veer north to enter the Range River. About 0.5 mile down this slow-moving, shallow stream, you intersect the mouth of the Grassy River and follow that tiny creek west to Grassy Lake. After crossing Tee, Sletten and Little Sletten lakes, enter the southeast end of Fenske Lake. The Fenske Lake campground is located at the northwest end of the lake, where you can take out to end a pleasant 10-mile trip 8 miles up the Echo Trail from County Road 88. This part of the loop is lightly traveled.

If you wish to complete the entire 20-mile loop, portage from Fenske Lake southwest to Everett Lake and the Twin Lakes, where there are half a dozen developed campsites along with a few remote cabins.

The Dead River will then lead you south to Burntside Lake. From the east arm of that gigantic lake, you'll portage south to Little Long Lake and return to the Echo Trail at the east end of that scenic lake. The portage from Little Long Lake to the Echo Trail crosses the property of Shig-Wak Resort. There has been no problem with the owners in the past, but it would be a nice gesture to ask for permission to walk on their property. The Bass Lake Trail parking lot is just a short trek down the road (left) from Shig-Wak Resort.

High Lake Route (Map 6)

Length:	3 miles (one way)
Difficulty:	Moderate
Use level:	Moderately light
Highlights:	Trout fishing
Canoeing map:	Fisher—F-9

High Lake has many rocky islands and points. Only 3 miles from the trailhead, at the Bass Lake Trail parking lot (see Bass and Fenske Lakes Loop above), it is an easy destination for day outings, with four campsites for those who wish to spend the night. Three portages are required to get there, but the first 0.5-mile carry may discourage those with little portaging ambition, even though it slopes downhill on a good path to Bass Lake. The 30-rod portage connecting Bass and Dry lakes bypasses a lovely little waterfall. An 80-rod portage separates Dry and High lakes.

Burntside Lake and Dead River Loop (Map 5)

Length:	9 miles (round trip)
Difficulty:	Moderately easy
Use level:	Moderate
Highlights:	Beautiful scenery
Canoeing map:	Fisher—F-9 or McKenzie—16

This loop lets you experience the North Woods without ever getting too far from civilization. Burntside is a deep, very clear lake, dotted with more than a hundred scenic islands. High rocky hills here are covered by an appealing blend of red and white pine, aspen and birch.

The trailhead is located 9.5 miles northwest of Ely. From County Road 88, drive 4.6 miles north on the Echo Trail to its junction with County Road 803. Turn left and drive 2 miles west to the public landing on the right side of the road. The small parking area near the landing will accommodate three or four vehicles.

Although the south and east shores of Burntside Lake are crowded with private cabins and several resorts, and the sound of motorboats is not uncommon anywhere on the lake, you can avoid most of the congestion by clinging to the north shore of the lake and entering the Dead River and West Twin Lake. Only one portage is necessary—a challenging 250-rod carry from West Twin Lake to the North Arm of Burntside Lake.

The loop can be extended several more miles by exploring East Twin Lake and as much of Burntside Lake as you wish. There are five campsites on the Twin Lakes and three along the shore of Burntside's North Arm narrows. You might be surprised just how nice and quiet it is in this lovely region.

Enjoying a quiet moment in the North Woods

Table 6	Other Lakes and Streams with Boat Accesses: Kawishiwi District

Lake/Stream	Depth	Size	Access	Develop-ment	Comments	Map
Agassa Lake	9	90	F	1	240-rod portage from C.R. 116; 1 campsite	5
August Lake	19	221	PC	1	Nice island campsite near the landing	15
Bass Lake	35	161	F	1	160-rod portage from C.R. 116; 2 campsites	6
Bear Island Lake	62	2667	PC	4	3 resorts, many cabins, 2 campsites S. end	14
Big Lake	18	2049	PC	2	2 resorts, good fishing, nice island campsite	5
Burntside Lake	126	10,236	PC	4	Many resorts & cabins, 5 campsites	5, 6
Everett Lake	15	123	F	3	30-rod portage from C.R. 116, 1 campsite	6
Fenske Lake	43	130	PC	2, 3	Campground & resort at W. end	6
Garden Lake	55	6427	PC	4	Resorts & many cabins, access to BWCAW	6
Harris Lake	13	121	HC	1	Isolated lake with 2 dispersed campsites	15
Johnson Lake	18	473	PC	3	1 dispersed campsite near center of lake	15
Low Lake	40	353	PC	3	2 dispersed campsites, access to BWCAW	6
Nels Lake	30	200	HC	1	1 dispersed campsite, access to BWCAW	6
Ojibway Lake	117	383	PC	3	Many cabins, long portage south to BWCAW	7
One Pine Lake	13	369	PC	3	Quiet little lake with several cabins around it	15
Perch Lake	13	91	F	1	35-rod portage from F.R; 1 campsite	15
Picket Lake	9	78	PC	3	Access to BWCAW	6
Shagawa Lake	48	2639	PC	4	Many cabins, resorts, city of Ely adjacent	6
Tofte Lake	70	134	PC	1	Pretty lake stocked with trout; 3 campsites	6
Whisper Lake	25	48	F	1	Lovely woods, 40-rod portage, 1 campsite	15
White Iron Lake	47	3429	PC	4	Many cabins, resorts, year-round homes	6

DEPTH: Maximum depth in feet
SIZE: Acres as listed in Division of Waters Bulletin No. 25
ACCESS: PC = passenger car, HC = high-clearance vehicles, 4WD = 4-wheel-drive
DEVELOPMENT: 1 = none, 2 = limited public, 3 = limited private, 4 = extensive development
MAP: Numbers refer to maps in this guidebook.

ISABELLA DISTRICT

South-central Superior National Forest contains two canoe routes and 33 lakes and streams with public boat landings. The roads in this district vary from excellent gravel routes to rough, rocky paths and muddy ruts that are barely passable for vehicles with high clearance.

Silver Island, Tee, and Windy Lakes (Map 17)

Length:	5 miles (one way)
Difficulty:	Moderate
Use level:	Light
Highlights:	Fishing in a BWCAW-type setting
Canoeing map:	Fisher—F-5

This trio of lakes offers paddlers a near-wilderness experience that is a good alternative to the Boundary Waters. Windy, Tee and Silver Island are dark-water lakes where there is usually good to excellent fishing. Windy is the deepest of the three. Tee and Silver Island lakes are quite rocky. The total length of this chain of lakes is about 5 miles, from the eastern tip of Windy Lake to the southwest end of Silver Island Lake. It can be enjoyed in one day, or, by paddling the shorelines, you could easily stretch the outing over a full weekend. There are 10 developed campsites throughout the chain, as well as one user-developed site next to County Road 7 along the portage between Windy and Tee lakes.

You may use the trailhead at Windy Lake and take out at Silver Island Lake (or vice versa). To get to either trailhead from Isabella, drive 0.8 mile east from Highway 1 on Forest Route 172. Turn left onto Forest Route 369 and drive 5.8 miles north to a Y intersection. Bear right on Forest Route 173 and continue 4 miles northeast to a large intersection of several forest roads at Sawbill Landing. Follow Forest Route 175 5 miles farther east to a new spur road that leads 1.5 miles north (left) to the southwest corner of Silver Island Lake, where there is a new concrete boat landing and where there are plans for a small campground. To access Windy Lake, continue driving past the spur road for 2.4 miles to County Road 7. Turn left and proceed 3.8 miles north to the Windy Lake access on the right.

After exploring Windy Lake, portage 165 rods west (across County Road 7) to Tee Lake and another 60 rods to Silver Island Lake. The first 45 rods of the 165-rod portage may be overgrown and somewhat difficult to negotiate, because it receives very little use (most folks who visit Windy Lake *drive* to it). After crossing County Road 7, however, the path is wide and relatively level. Nevertheless, there are many rocks and boulders that could easily cause a sprained ankle, so be careful.

Island River (Map 16)

Length:	7 miles (one way)
Difficulty:	Moderate
Use level:	Light
Highlights:	River travel; Indian rock paintings; moose
Canoeing map:	Fisher—F-4

The Island River skirts the south edge of the BWCAW. Though you're paddling upstream, there is little current with which to contend. Six short portages, ranging from 20 to 60 rods, are required—though not difficult, they might discourage a novice paddler.

The trailhead is off Forest Route 377, 18 miles north of Isabella (see Entry Point 34 in the "Paddling the Boundary Waters" section of this chapter). Take out at Comfort Lake, which is 3.7 miles northeast of Sawbill Landing (see directions on preceding page). From the junction of Forest Routes 173, 174 and 175, follow F.R. 174 0.3 mile north (left) to F.R. 356. Bear right and continue 1.5 miles on F.R. 356 to F.R. 913, which leads 1.9 miles north (left) to Comfort Lake.

The entire route can be completed in a day, but there are four developed campsites along the way for those who would rather spread the journey over several days. Anglers will want to cast in the pools below each of the rapids. Wildlife enthusiasts should concentrate on the shorelines; this is moose country. And historians will surely want to explore the north shore of the river about 5 miles downstream from the trailhead, where a prehistoric pictograph is located, although it appears to be little more than a reddish blob.

The route receives very little use, except during the fishing and duck hunting seasons. Wild rice grows in the shallow bays along the river, particularly near the west end. Rice attracts waterfowl, and fowl attract hunters; so wear your red hat when paddling in the fall.

Table 7 — Other Lakes and Streams with Boat Accesses: Isabella District

Lake/Stream	Depth	Size	Access	Development	Comments	Map
Beetle Lake	26	35	PC	1	Short carry-down to creek; unofficial campsite	16
Cloquet Lake	7	186	PC	1	2 dispersed campsites on this weedy lake	16, 20
Comfort Lake	7	38	F	1	10-rod portage to lake; no campsites	16
Dam Five Lake	38	92	PC	1	Short carry-down to south end of lake	17
Divide Lake	22	69	PC	2	Campground & 1 dispersed campsite	16
Dragon Lake	14	85	PC	1	2 campsites at boat landing; clear lake	16
Dumbbell Lake	40	476	PC	2, 3	Nice picnic grounds next to boat landing	16
Dunnigan Lake	18	84	PC	1	Pretty, little, clear lake	15
East Chub Lake	8	98	PC	3	User-developed campsite at landing	15
Eighteen Lake	12	113	PC	2	Small campground & trail near boat landing	16
Eikela Lake	30	13	HC	1	Remote state-managed brook trout lake	15
Elixir Lake	8	17	PC	1	At a pull-off from F.R. 172; unofficial campsite	17
Flathorn Lake	10	63	PC	2	Short carry-down from picnic grounds	16

Table 7 cont'd	Other Lakes and Streams with Boat Accesses: Isabella District				

Lake/Stream	Depth	Size	Access	Develop-ment	Comments	Map
Gegoka Lake	7	174	PC	2, 3	Resort & private cabins	16
Greenwood Lake	7	1469	PC	2, 3	State Forest campground across the lake	15
Harriet Lake	37	281	PC	1	Large meadow with 2 dispersed campsites	17
Hogback Lake	35	44	PC	2	Picnic grounds next to state trout lake	17
Homestead Lake	8	50	PC	1	Short carry-down through unofficial campsite	16, 17
Inga Lake	5	78	HC	1	80-rod portage from F.R. 177	16
North McDougal Lake	10	323	PC	2	Boat launch at National Forest campground	15, 16
Pike Lake	6	78	F	1	80-rod portage; high-clearance vehicles to trail	15, 16
Redskin Lake	5	10	HC	1	30-rod portage down a steep hill to the lake	16
Section 29 Lake	20	122	PC	3	2 nice unofficial camp-sites next to landing	16
Shamrock Lake	13	58	F	1	30-rod portage through nice stand of red pines	15
Silver Island Lake	12	1294	PC	1	5 dispersed BWCAW type campsites	17
Slate Lake	10	354	PC	3	Park & camp at site of a large gravel pit	15
Surprise Lake	9	38	F	1	40-rod portage from F.R. 386	16
Swallow Lake	40	158	HC	1	Carry-down to lake from unofficial campsite	15
Sylvania Lake	5	86	PC	1	Put in at creek draining into weedy lake	16
Tee Lake	15	307	F	1	120-rod portage; 2 BWCAW-type campsites	17
Trappers Lake	12	19	F	1	60-rod portage to clear state trout lake	16
Two Deer Lake	7	52	F	1	12-rod portage from F.R. 1491	15
Wye Lake	10	57	F	1	25-rod portage from F.R. 175	17

DEPTH: Maximum depth in feet
SIZE: Acres as listed in Division of Waters Bulletin No. 25
ACCESS: PC = passenger car, HC = high-clearance vehicles, F = foot trail
DEVELOPMENT: 1 = none, 2 = limited public, 3 = limited private, 4 = extensive development
MAP: Numbers refer to maps in this guidebook.

TOFTE DISTRICT

There are three good canoe routes and 22 lakes with public boat landings in the southeastern part of Superior National Forest. Most of the roads in this district have been upgraded during the past few years, and you can now get to all of these canoeing waters with passenger cars. A few, however, are more easily reached by high-clearance vehicles.

Timber and Freer Lakes Loop (Map 17)

Length:	9 miles (round trip)
Difficulty:	Moderate
Use level:	Light to moderate
Highlights:	Good potential to view moose and bald eagles
Canoeing map:	Fisher—F-5

The trailhead is at Whitefish Lake, 23 miles northwest of Tofte. From the ranger station, drive 1.6 miles southwest on Highway 61 to Forest Route 343, which leads 5.5 miles northwest to Forest Route 166. Turn left, proceed 5.5 miles west to County Road 7, turn right and continue 2.8 miles northwest to Forest Route 170. Turn right again and go 1.6 miles northwest to Forest Route 357. From there, it's 5 miles north (left) to the Whitefish Lake public access. There is a 6-rod carry-down from the parking lot to the northwest corner of the lake. The roads have good gravel surfaces all the way from Highway 61.

This interesting loop gives paddlers a good chance of complete solitude and some excellent fishing. The 9-mile loop crosses five lakes. Seven portages range in length from 5 to 140 rods. The lakes are fairly narrow and deep, surrounded by hills that reach more than 200 feet above the lakes. Several rock outcrops and a few sand beaches are found throughout the area. The portages are fairly level, but there may be occasional windfalls.

Eight BWCAW-type campsites are accessible only by water, including two on Whitefish Lake, two on Elbow Lake, one on Timber Lake, two on Frear Lake and one on Finger Lake. In addition, there are three gravel pads for campers at the access to Whitefish Lake. Seldom, if ever, are these campsites all occupied.

Look for moose along the shorelines and bald eagles overhead. This is the most productive eagle area in the Tofte District.

Ninemile Lake and Crooked Lake Area (Map 17)

Length:	7 miles (one way)
Difficulty:	Moderate
Use level:	Light to moderate
Highlights:	Scenic small lakes
Canoeing map:	Available from District ranger

The Crooked Lake Area Portage Trail System was developed to connect nearby lakes for a variety of recreational uses, including canoeing, fishing, hiking and camping. Opportunities for solitude are good. This is a picturesque region with low hills, a high cliff, small lakes and a variety of forest habitats ranging from climax maples and stands of mature cedar and spruce to mixed second-growth forests of birch, aspen, spruce and balsam fir.

Use the trailhead at either the Ninemile Lake Campground or the Crooked Lake public access. From the Tofte ranger station, drive 2.5 miles southwest on

Highway 61 to the village of Schroeder. Turn right onto Cook County Road 1 (which becomes Lake County Road 8) and follow it 10 miles to County Road 7. Turn right and proceed 4 miles north to the campground entrance on the left. To access Crooked Lake, continue driving past Ninemile Lake Campground 4 more miles to Forest Route 358. The turnoff to the Crooked Lake landing is 0.5 mile west of C.R. 7 (left) and leads 0.3 mile south (left) from F.R. 358.

A 110-rod portage leads west from the south shore of Crooked Lake to Bonanza Lake, a shallow minnow lake. It offers a lovely hike in the fall through a climax maple stand.

If solitude appeals to you, go south from Crooked Lake or north from Ninemile Lake to Meme Lake and follow the 120-rod portage from Meme Lake west to Thunderbird Lake, where there are two developed campsites. At the west end of Thunderbird Lake a 100-rod portage leads to Shoepack Lake, where a developed campsite perches on an outcropping of ledgerock on the north shore of the lake. About midway between Shoepack and Thunderbird lakes is a canoe rest at the base of a high cliff. It can be climbed easily for a spectacular view of both lakes. Both of these portages are relatively level and easy to negotiate.

There are several private cabins on both Ninemile and Crooked lakes, as well as an active resort at the east end of Crooked Lake. Nevertheless, these are two of the best lakes in the district to see ospreys. You'll find the most solitude on the lakes to the west of Meme Lake.

Crescent and Rice Lakes (Map 18)

Length:	5 miles (one way)
Difficulty:	Moderate
Use level:	Light (except near campground)
Highlights:	Fishing for walleyes, viewing bald eagles
Canoeing map:	Fisher—F-6

You'll find the trailhead at the Crescent Lake Campground. From the Sawbill Trail 17 miles north of Tofte (see Tofte District driving directions in "Paddling the Boundary Waters" in this chapter), drive 7 miles northeast (right) on Forest Route 165 to the campground entrance on the right.

From the campground at Crescent Lake, this route leads 5 miles south through a chain of small lakes and creeks to Rice Lake. It's a peaceful area with old white pines and large aspens, and one of the best areas in the Tofte District to view bald eagles. There is an eagle nest on Crescent Lake, as well as an osprey nest on Rice Lake. Once you depart from the campground, you aren't likely to encounter many other people as you ply the shallow waters of Fleck, Slip, Dogtrot, Bulge and Silver lakes. There are seven short portages along the way.

The 10-mile round trip route to and from Rice Lake can easily be completed in just one day. If you decide to stay overnight, however, there are two dispersed BWCAW-type campsites on Crescent Lake and two on Rice. District officials rate Rice as the best lake in the Tofte District on which to avoid other people.

If you'd rather not backtrack, it is possible to end the trip at Rice Lake, where there is a primitive, unimproved road leading from the south end of the lake to Forest Route 340. To get there from the campground entrance, drive 4 miles east of F.R. 165 to F.R. 340. Turn right and continue 6 miles south to F.R. 339. Turn right again and proceed 1 mile west to the unmarked turnoff (right) to Rice Lake. This road is recommended only for vehicles with high clearance and four-wheel drive.

| | | | Table 8 | Other Lakes and Streams with Boat Accesses: Tofte District |

Lake/Stream	Depth	Size	Access	Develop- ment	Comments	Map
Barker Lake	15	166	F	2	55-rod portage; Adirondak-type shelter	18
Caribou Lake	27	714	PC	4	Among "Top 100 Walleye Lakes" in MN	18
Cascade Lake	17	534	PC	1	2 dispersed campsites accessible by boat	9
Christine Lake	6	192	HC	3	Also accessible by PC w/a 10-rod portage	18
Clara Lake	15	418	PC	2, 3	Camping area near boat landing	18
Cross River Lake	5	77	HC	1	Carry-down to river, which leads to lake	17
Echo Lake	61	46	PC	1	Carry-down from C.R. 7	17
Four Mile Lake	19	593	PC	2	Camping area near land- ing; 2 dispersed sites	17
Goldeneye Lake	19	10	F	1	80-rod portage from C.R. 7	17
Gust Lake	6	159	PC	3	Put in along F.R. 165; cabins on south shore	9
Hare Lake	18	48	PC	1	User-developed carry- down from C.R. 7	17
Holly Lake	6	78	PC	1	Portage southwest to Mistletoe Lake	18
Lichen Lake	17	306	PC	1	Carry-down from F.R. 165; campsite W. end	9
Little Cascade Lake	9	262	HC	1	Can also portage 40 rods from C.R. 4	9
Little Wilson Lake	21	57	PC	1	Camping area nearby at Wilson Lake	17
Marsh Lake	13	63	PC	1	Carry-down through grassy unofficial campsite	17, 18
Moore Lake	8	64	PC	1	Carry-down from F.R. 165; may freeze out	18
Star Lake	13	120	PC	1	Carry-down from wide spot in F.R. 326	9
Toohey Lake	11	369	PC	2	Camping area near the sandy boat landing	17
White Pine Lake	10	374	PC	2	Camping area near the access; osprey nest	18
Wilson Lake	53	666	PC	2, 3	Camping area; 1 dispersed campsite	17
Windy Lake	38	469	PC	2	3 BWCAW-type camp- sites on S. shore	17

DEPTH: Maximum depth in feet
SIZE: Acres as listed in Division of Waters Bulletin No. 25
ACCESS: PC = passenger car, HC = high-clearance vehicles, F = foot trail
DEVELOPMENT: 1 = none, 2 = limited public, 3 = limited private, 4 = extensive development
MAP: Numbers refer to maps in this guidebook.

GUNFLINT DISTRICT

The northeastern corner of Superior National Forest has only one designated canoe route outside the BWCAW, but it offers the greatest number of lakes outside the Wilderness with public boat landings—38. Some of the roads leading to them may be rough, but passenger cars should make it to most of them.

Twin Lakes Loop (Map 10)

Length:	4-mile loop
Difficulty:	Moderately easy
Use level:	Light
Highlights:	Good fishing; few people
Canoeing map:	Fisher—F-7

The Twin Lakes loop offers paddlers a remote canoe camping experience with relatively easy access and few restrictions. It's in a lovely region, with neighboring hills rising to nearly 300 feet above the lakes. At one time, there was a railroad across Pine Lake (sometimes still referred to as Trestle Pine Lake). Now the only development in the area consists of a couple of cabins on West Twin Lake.

To reach the trailhead from the Grand Marais ranger station, drive 16.9 miles north on the Gunflint Trail to its junction with Forest Route 325 (1 mile past the Greenwood Lake Road). Turn left and drive 6 miles west on this gravel road to its intersection with Forest Route 152. Turn left again and proceed 4 miles south to the boat landings for East Twin Lake (left) and West Twin Lake (right).

The loop consists of four small lakes (West Twin, Tahus, Kemo and Pine) joined by four reasonably short portages. Visitors can also portage across the road from West Twin Lake to East Twin Lake to add a couple more miles of paddling to the loop. To accommodate overnight visitors, there are five dispersed BWCAW-type campsites in the area: two at the east end of East Twin Lake and one each on West Twin, Kemo and Pine lakes.

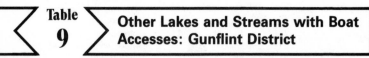

⟨ Table 9 ⟩ Other Lakes and Streams with Boat Accesses: Gunflint District

Lake/Stream	Depth	Size	Access	Development	Comments	Map
Ball Club Lake	25	231	PC	1	1 dispersed campsite; good moose area.	9
Bath Lake	24	36	HC	1	Short carry-down; 1 dispersed campsite.	9
Bearskin Lake	78	522	PC	3	3 dispersed campsites; access to BWCAW.	10
Binagami Lake	15	127	F	3	10-rod portage from F.R. 154; clear lake.	10
Birch Lake	76	266	F	3	80-rod portage from scenic overlook; 1 campsite.	9
Bogus Lake	25	22	PC	1	State-managed trout lake.	10
Boys Lake	13	23	F	1	80-rod portage to state-managed trout lake.	10

Lake/Stream	Depth	Size	Access	Development	Comments	Map
Carrot Lake	20	28	PC	1	Carry-down from F.R. 313; 1 campsite.	10
Chester Lake	35	50	HC	1	State-managed trout lake.	10
Deeryard Lake	20	358	HC	3	State's largest deeryard nearby; 1 campsite.	18
Devilfish Lake	40	417	HC	1	Short carry-down; 2 dispersed campsites.	10
Devil Track Lake	50	1873	PC	4	Campground, airport, many homes & cabins.	18
Elbow Lake	9	415	PC	1	2 campsites; good area to see moose.	10
Esther Lake	35	77	HC	2	State Forest campground adjacent to landing.	10
Flour Lake	80	352	PC	4	Campground, resort & cabins.	10
Greenwood Lake	112	2078	PC	2	2 dispersed campsites; Bald eagle area.	10
Gunflint Lake	200	4047	PC	4	Resorts, homes & cabins; access to BWCAW	9
Hand Lake	22	95	F	1	80-rod portage from F.R. 323.	9
Hungry Jack Lake	70	486	PC	4	Resorts, homes & cabins.	9
Iron Lake	19	138	PC	2	Carry-down thru SNF campground.	9
Junco Lake	5	45	F	1	0.5 mile portage to Junco Creek; moose area.	10
Kimball Lake	16	80	PC	2	SNF campground; stocked with trout.	10
Little Iron Lake	18	121	PC	1	2 dispersed campsites; moose area.	9
Little John Lake	8	39	PC	1	Access to E. end of BWCAW.	10,11
Loon Lake	202	1197	PC	3	A resort & cabins at E. end; 1 campsite.	9
Mayhew Lake	80	247	PC	3	1 dispersed campsite.	9
McDonald Lake	9	98	F	1	10-rod portage from F.R. 153.	9
Mink Lake	15	60	PC	3	Carry-down to state-managed trout lake.	10
Moss Lake	86	236	F	1	127-rod portage; BWCAW access; 1 campsite.	10
Northern Light Lake	7	443	PC	1	Good moose habitat; 1 dispersed campsite.	10
Pit Lake	17	29	PC	1	Carry-down from old gravel pit.	9,10
Round Lake	45	168	PC	3	Carry-down; resort; BWCAW access.	8

| | | | Table 9 cont'd | | Other Lakes and Streams with Boat Accesses: Gunflint District | |

Lake/Stream	Depth	Size	Access	Develop-ment	Comments	Map
Sunfish Lake	25	86	HC	1	10-rod portage; 1 campsite at access.	10
Thrasher Lake	27	29	HC	1	State-managed trout lake.	9
Trout Lake	77	277	PC	3	Resort & some cabins; 1 dispersed campsite	10
Two Island Lake	20	858	PC	2,3	Access at SNF campground.	9
Wampus Lake	18	33	F	1	Short carry-down from C.R. 66.	10
Ward Lake	13	44	PC	1	Carry-down; in state's largest deeryard.	18

DEEP: Maximum depth in feet
SIZE: Acres as listed in Division of Waters Bulletin No. 25
ACCESS: PC = passenger car, HC = high-clearance vehicles, F = foot trail
DEVELOPMENTS: 1 = none, 2 = limited public, 3 = limited private, 4 = extensive development
MAP: Location on district map, by coordinates

FOR MORE INFORMATION

Bell, Patricia, *Roughing It Elegantly.* Eden Prairie, MN: Cat's Paw Press, 1987. Excellent guide for novice canoe campers headed for the Quetico-Superior wilderness.

Beymer, Robert, *The Boundary Waters Canoe Area.* Berkeley, CA: Wilderness Press. Volume I (Western Region), 4th ed. 1988. Volume II (Eastern Region), 2nd ed. 1986. Comprehensive guides for Wilderness canoeists on the U.S. side of the border.

———, *Paddler's Guide to Quetico Provincial Park.* Virginia, MN: W.A. Fisher Company, 1985. Comprehensive guide for canoeists on the Canadian side of the border.

Cary, Bob, *The Big Wilderness Canoe Manual.* New York: Arco Publishing, Inc., 1983. Sound advice for folks en route to the BWCAW.

Drabik, Harry, *The Spirit of Canoe Camping.* Minneapolis: Nodin Press, 1981. More good advice for Quetico-Superior canoe campers, as well as thoughtful prose.

Jacobson, Cliff, *The Basic Essentials of Canoeing.* Merrillville, IN: ICS Books, Inc., 1988. Fundamentals for people in need of instruction.

———, *The New Wilderness Canoeing and Camping.* Merrillville, IN: ICS Books, Inc., 1986. General information about canoe camping by an author familiar with the Boundary Waters.

Schmidt, Ernest F., *Canoeing.* North Brunswick, NJ: Boy Scouts of America, 1981. Basic fundamentals for those who need canoeing instruction.

HIKING

Unlike most of the activities discussed in this guide, hiking may be enjoyed at *any* time of year in Superior National Forest. Though most people do their treks between Memorial Day and Labor Day, spring and fall are better suited to the sport. Even in winter, with the aid of snowshoes, hikers can enjoy the Forest footpaths.

Superior National Forest offers 60 designated trails across more than 400 miles of North Woods landscape, including long, challenging routes for seasoned backpackers, intermediate-length trail systems for ambitious day-hikers and a multitude of short, easy paths that are well suited to afternoon outings for the whole family, young and old alike. Most trails are signed and well maintained by the U.S. Forest Service or volunteer trail organizatons. Some trails penetrate the BWCA Wilderness; many do not. A few trails are ruggedly steep or frustratingly boggy, but most are neither. Many trails lead to breathtaking overlooks. Some follow the high crests of oak-covered ridges, others meander peacefully through dense stands of pine, birch and aspen or along the bird-infested edges of boreal spruce bogs.

Superior National Forest contains 15 trails long enough to accommodate backpackers and another 45 trails suitable for short hikes. All are described in this chapter. The map number (or numbers) following the name of each trail refers to the map in this book on which its location is shown (multiple maps are listed "in order of appearance" along the trail). These maps, however, are not meant to be used for route-finding during a trip. For that purpose a USGS topographic map is recommended. The appropriate maps are listed for each trail. For more information about any of these trails, contact the appropriate district office (see individual district listings in Chapter 2 for addresses and phone numbers).

OVERNIGHT TRAILS FOR BACKPACKERS

The trails suitable for backpackers vary in length from eight to 55 miles and take from one to seven days to explore. Eleven penetrate the BWCAW, and four lie completely outside the Wilderness. None is heavily used, and most are *very* lightly traveled except, perhaps, on the peak weekends of early autumn.

Because no comprehensive single source for detailed information about hiking trails in Superior National Forest existed prior to the publication of this guide, this chapter will do much more than simply identify the foot trails. It will also supply you with enough information about each trail to make a judgment about the trail's suitability to your needs and desires, and it will "take you by the hand" and lead you through each route, mile by mile.

MAPS

The USFS District offices issue maps covering most of the trails in this section. These maps are normally included as part of a Recreational Opportunity Guide (ROG)—a one-page handout that briefly describes the trail. For the most part, these maps are not detailed and do not include contour lines. As long as you stay on the trail, you should be fine, but don't even *think* about straying!

When hiking in a wilderness, always try to carry an accurate, detailed topographic map of the area. The USGS maps provide excellent detail, but sometimes they don't show the actual trails. F-series maps from the W.A. Fisher Company and McKenzie maps also provide good topographic detail, but they, too, don't always accurately depict the trails. The best way to have the most accurate "picture" of a trail described in this book is to carry both the appropriate USGS map and the USFS sketch. Combined, they should keep you on the right path.

LAURENTIAN DISTRICT

Only two trails in the Laurentian District are long enough to accommodate the yearnings of most backpackers. Both were constructed in the mid-1980s. They are fine trails that penetrate lovely parts of the Forest, yet few people outside the immediate localities are even aware that they exist. If you try these trails, be sure to stop by the district office to share your opinions. Feedback from the public is an essential part of future trail development in Superior National Forest.

Otto-Harris Lakes Trail (Map 19)

Length:	11.2 miles (round trip)
Hiking time:	1 to 2 days
Difficulty:	Easy
Elevation differential:	90 feet
Use level:	Light
Highlights:	Birch-maple forest
USGS Maps:	Fairbanks, Harris Lake

The Otto-Harris Lakes Trail consists of loops around Otto Lake (3.3 miles) and Harris Lake (1.9 miles) that are joined by a 2.5-mile path. Passing through a lovely forest of birch and maples, this trail is especially scenic in autumn, when the turning leaves bring the forest ablaze with color.

The few changes in elevation mostly follow an elevated ridge between and around the two lakes. Planks cross the few wet lowland areas. Currently, there are two campsites on Otto Lake, accessible by spur trails off the main loop, and one site on Harris Lake. Another Harris Lake site is planned.

To reach the trailhead from the corner of County Roads 100 and 110 in Aurora, drive 11 miles south on County Roads 100 and 99 to the junction with County Road 16. Turn left and drive 13.5 miles east to tiny Fairbanks. The small Otto Lake parking lot is 4 miles southwest of Fairbanks via Forest Route 416, a good gravel road.

From the parking area, hike northwest on the portage trail to Otto Lake. The trail dips through a marshy valley, then ascends gradually back to the low ridge that skirts the south shore of Otto Lake. Near the northeast end of Otto Lake, the trail intersects a loop around the lake. (One campsite is about 0.25 mile southwest of the junction, to the left. The other site rests on the north shore of the lake, about 0.75 mile from the portage, to the right.) The loop around Otto Lake is 3.3 miles long. Most of it is on dry ground, but there are wet bogs at both the southwest end and the north side of the lake.

Turn left at the junction, and find the connecting trail to Harris Lake at the southwest end of Otto Lake. Bear left there. The trail crosses over a low hill and then continues in a southwest direction on a maple-covered ridge. About 1 mile northeast of Harris Lake, the trail joins an old logging road for a short distance.

The Harris Lake loop is intersected near the northeast corner of the lake, 4.3 miles from the trailhead. The Harris Lake campsite is at the southwest end of the lake, near the midpoint of the route, making it a good overnight destination for a two-day trek. The campsite is accessible to vehicles with four-wheel-drive by way of an old logging road from Forest Route 121. Except during the grouse hunting season, however, you aren't likely to be bothered at this remote location.

After looping around Harris Lake, backtrack to the Otto Lake loop and then complete that route back to the portage trail and the parking lot.

Sturgeon River Trail (Map 12)

Length:	22.2 miles (round trip)
Hiking time:	2 to 3 days
Difficulty:	Easy to moderate
Elevation differential:	80 feet
Use level:	Very light
Highlights:	River ecology
USGS Map:	Dewey Lake NW

This trail was designed for both summer and winter use. The Sturgeon is a relatively large river, and offers varied vegetation and topographic relief, with steep slopes descending to the banks of the river and large, old growth silver maples lining the flood plain. Scenic overlooks are common. The trail also penetrates mature stands of pine, groves of young aspens, grassy openings and clearcut areas resulting from recent logging activity. Ruffed grouse, woodcocks, beavers, whitetailed deer and coyotes inhabit the area.

Parts of the trail may be wet at times. Even though small bridges span some of those areas, expect wet feet. The trail is fairly flat, except for the small, hilly loop around Jean Lake.

To reach the trailhead from the intersection of Highways 169 and 53 in Virginia, drive 17.5 miles west on Highway 169 to downtown Chisholm. Turn right onto Highway 73 and follow it 10.5 miles north to its junction with Forest Route 279. Turn left and you'll see the parking lot and trailhead on the left (south) side of F.R. 279.

Beaver handiwork

The trailhead is at the south end of the Sturgeon River Trail. Walk southwest to intersect the east end of a short loop around Jean Lake, about 0.5 mile from the trailhead. This 1-mile loop provides access to a three-sided log shelter on the east side of Jean Lake. Beyond the west end of the loop, the main trail swings toward the north and crosses Forest Route 279.

The trail splits into the first of two major loops 0.5 mile north of Forest Route 279. Turn right and cross a bridge over the East Branch of the Sturgeon River to parallel the river's east side. The first of two semideveloped sites lies 2.8 miles from the trailhead, where a fire ring was placed along the river for campers.

At the northern end of the first loop, bear right and you'll cross County Road 65 near the midpoint of the trail system, 5.7 miles from the trailhead. (This is an alternate trailhead for backpackers who prefer to hike only the north loop.) After crossing the road, veer west 0.25 mile to the junction with the north loop.

Take the right fork at this intersection. An Adirondack-type shelter makes a good destination for the night, 7.7 miles from the trailhead. Beyond it, the trail angles toward the northeast.

The trail parallels the west side of Highway 73 for 0.75 mile (a third access to the trail is located adjacent to the Highway) and then loops back toward the southwest to begin its southbound return along the west side of the Sturgeon River. The northern part of this loop is through an area that was clear-cut, and it may be difficult to follow. Watch carefully for signs of the trail.

Another fire ring sits—at a poor location for camping—on the west bank of the river, 16.1 miles from the trailhead. A half mile beyond, after completing the northern loop, the trail meets County Road 65. At the junction with the south loop, bear right this time to cross the East Branch of the Sturgeon River.

At the south end of the loop, you'll rejoin the final segment of the trail and backtrack to the parking lot.

LA CROIX DISTRICT

Four backpacking trails are administered by the La Croix District. The trailheads for three (the Sioux-Hustler, Astrid Lake and Stuart Lake trails) are located along the Echo Trail (St. Louis County Road 116). The fourth trail (Herriman Lake) is accessible from County Road 24, 5 miles north of the Echo Trail junction. All of these trails receive very light use throughout the year.

Astrid Lake Trail (Maps 4, 5)

Length:	7 miles (including 2 optional loops)
Hiking time:	4 to 6 hours
Difficulty:	Easy to moderate
Elevation differential:	170 feet
Use level:	Light
Highlights:	Pretty lakes, scenic overlooks and some virgin pines
USGS Maps:	Astrid Lake, Lake Jeanette; Fisher—F-8, F-15

This is the La Croix District's only trail for backpackers that lies completely outside the BWCA Wilderness. It connects Jeanette, Nigh, Astrid, Maude and Picket lakes, and consists of 1.3 miles of excellent canoe portage trails and 5.7 miles of less improved hiking trails. The oldest, most traveled and best-marked trail—the Jeanette–Maude Lakes Trail—is the main corridor between Lake Jeanette at the northeast end and Maude Lake at the southwest end of the system. In the middle are two loops that branch off toward the west and north from the main corridor: the Astrid Lake Loop and the Nigh–Pauline Lakes Loop.

The forest is characterized by dense, rolling stands of jack pine, oak-covered ridges, spruce-infested lowlands, groves of birch and maple, a blend of aspen and balsam fir, and a smattering of enormous red and white pines. Two large beaver ponds add "texture."

The trailhead is located at the Lake Jeanette Campground, 12 miles east of County Road 24 along the Echo Trail (see La Croix District driving directions in "Paddling the Boundary Waters" in Chapter 3). Turn left onto Forest Route 360 and proceed 0.1 mile north to a small parking lot (right) across from the trailhead (left). Trail intersections are not signed, except at the canoe portages. Blue ribbons attached to trees and shrubs help to mark the way on parts of the trail.

The *Jeanette–Maude Lakes Trail* (4.3 miles one way) leads west from the Lake Jeanette campground, paralleling the north side of County Road 116. After crossing the road, it joins the Nigh Lake portage and continues southwest on an excellent path that climbs over a small hill and then descends to the northeast shore of Nigh Lake. Nearby is a nice campsite on a high rocky point.

After skirting the western edge of a large swamp, you'll ascend to a high ridge through a scattered assortment of large white pines, estimated to be as old as 200 years. At the summit of the ridge is the junction with the Astrid Lake Loop. Bear left there and enter an area where many small oak trees are mixed with birch and aspen. The trail drops down from the ridge to cross a small creek on a half-log bridge and a beaver dam. It then skirts the south side of a large beaver pond en route to a rolling landscape covered with a blend of mature jack pines, paper birch and aspen. Charred stumps are evidence of a fire that burned over this region around 1900.

Near the east shore of Astrid Lake is a junction with the south end of the Astrid Lake Loop, 2.9 miles from the trailhead. Bear left. The trail descends into the valley of Crellin Creek, which feeds the south end of Astrid Lake. A beaver dam bridges most of the creek, with a short boardwalk attached to the west end of the dam.

Just west of Crellin Creek, a spur trail leads 50 yards north to an elevated rock outcropping on the south shore of Astrid Lake. Campers there are treated to a lovely view of the lake, but there are few (if any) good tent sites available.

Beyond the campsite spur, the trail hugs close to the south shore of the lake, crosses a small creek on a boardwalk, and then skirts the west shore of Astrid Lake. A sign marks the beginning of an 80-rod portage from Astrid Lake to Forest Route 200. This excellent path climbs more than 70 feet from the lakeshore to the gravel road. It then crossses the road, joins the Maude Lake portage and descends more gradually to the east shore of Maude Lake, 4.3 miles from the trailhead. This alternate starting (or ending) point is 2.5 miles south of the Echo Trail and 6.25 miles by road from the trailhead at Lake Jeanette.

The *Astrid Lake Loop* (1.6 miles one way) offers another route to the east shore of Astrid Lake. From the main corridor trail, hike west along the crest of the oak- and maple-covered ridge to an overlook that affords a panoramic view across Superior National Forest. Lake Jeanette is clearly visible to the northeast. Another scenic vista may be enjoyed at the end of a short spur trail that leads north from the main trail. Beyond that point, the trail begins a long, gradual descent through a dense forest of mature jack pines.

At a junction with the Nigh–Pauline Lakes Loop, bear left and surmount a small hill en route to a second junction with the loop, 0.25 mile beyond the first. You'll pass several huge red and white pines before arriving at the northeast shore of Astrid Lake. The trail follows the shore closely for a short distance and then veers inland. A fine campsite on the sandy shore of Astrid Lake has good sites for two or three tents amidst the large red and jack pines that shade the slope.

The Astrid Lake Loop rejoins the main corridor trail inland, about 60 feet above the shore of Astrid Lake. At that point, you may loop back toward the northeast and return to the trailhead via the Jeanette–Maude Lakes Trail for a

A beaver pond starts to ice up along the Astrid Lake trail.

trek totaling 6.3 miles, or continue westbound on the trail to Maude Lake for a one-way hike totaling 4.8 miles.

The *Nigh–Pauline Lakes Loop* (1.1 miles one way) provides an extension for the Astrid Lake Loop. From its junction with the Astrid Lake Loop, 2.7 miles southwest of the Lake Jeanette trailhead, hike north on a down-sloping path to cross a small creek connecting Nigh and Pauline lakes. At the portage trail that connects the lakes, turn left and proceed west to the shore of Pauline Lake. A nice little campsite sits adjacent to the portage, at the edge of a sandy beach.

Continue south along the shore of the lake, cross the creek draining Nigh Lake, and then angle southwest over a couple small hills en route to the second junction with the Astrid Lake Loop. Along the way, the trail passes between several enormous boulders ("erratics") that were left stranded when the glaciers receded some 10,000 years ago.

Herriman Lake Trail (Maps 2, 4)

Length:	14.7 miles (several short loops possible)
Hiking time:	1 to 2 days
Difficulty:	Easy, moderate and difficult loops
Elevation differential:	300 feet
Use level:	Very light
Highlights:	Scenic vistas, Echo River, several small lakes
BWCAW Entry Point:	13
BWCAW quota:	None
USGS Maps:	Crane Lake; Fisher—F-15

This scenic network of varied trails winds throughout a 10-square-mile region between the Echo River on the west and the Canadian border on the east. In between are rolling hills covered primarily with a mixed forest of jack pine, aspen, birch and balsam fir. Rocky ridges afford hikers outstanding views across the area. Five lakes and several beaver ponds add to the scenic appeal. More than half of the trail system lies within the BWCA Wilderness. No trail signs are used in the Wilderness, and only a minimum number of signs are used elsewhere.

Several loops and trail segments are short enough to be completed easily in one day or less, but to enjoy the entire system, plan to spend at least two days. One way to do this is to pack in to Knute Lake and use the centrally located campsite there as a base for side trips.

To find the trailhead, drive to the junction of County Road 24 and the Echo Trail (see La Croix driving directions in "Paddling the Boundary Waters" in this chapter). From this junction, continue driving 4.9 miles north on C.R. 24 to C.R. 424 (the Nelson's Resort Road). Turn right and proceed 1.5 miles northeast to the trailhead on the right side of the road. A small parking lot is on the opposite (west) side of the road. From County Road 424, hike east to the Echo River, where a good bridge allows hikers to safely cross the rapids. Just beyond is an intersection of two trails. The Little Vermilion Lake Trail continues eastbound, while the Echo River Trail leads south.

The *Little Vermilion Lake Trail* (3.2 miles one way) is the main corridor through this area, a good, wide path that is level to gently rolling much of the way to Little Vermilion Lake. The Dovre Lake Loop intersects the trail twice during the first 1.5 miles. Beyond the second intersection, a spur trail leads south to the northeast shore of Knute Lake and accesses the shoreline campsite there. Continue hiking east through the middle of an alder swamp, where you may have difficulty maintaining dry feet—especially during spring or after prolonged or heavy rains.

Soon after the trail climbs out of the swamp, it intersects the east end of the Knute Lake Loop. The north end of the Herriman Lake Loop is intersected 0.5 mile farther. Throughout this area, the gently rolling landscape is covered with a dense forest of mature aspen, balsam fir, jack pines and an occasional birch tree.

Bridge at the Echo River

The only notable change in elevation occurs when the trail descends more than 120 feet to cross a creek at the end of a long grassy beaver pond. From there, it's an easy trek to the west shore of Little Vermilion Lake and a long sand beach, 3.2 miles from the trailhead. Two small campsites sit close together near the east end of the beach. From either site, campers can enjoy an unimpeded view of the Canadian shoreline.

The *Echo River Trail* (3.7 miles one way) leads southeast to a bald ridge top south of Baylis Lake. During the first mile, the trail closely parallels the Echo River across level to gently rolling landscape. Large red and white pines occasionally add variety to the dominant forest of jack pine, aspen, birch and fir.

The Herriman Lake Trail intersects the Echo River Trail from the northeast. Continuing in a southeast direction, you'll start to gradually climb up from the river valley along a rocky ridge that eventually peaks at more than 230 feet above the river. As the summit of the ridge is approached, the trail divides to form a 0.9-mile loop around the bald knob, which is sparsely covered with oaks and maples—a lovely sight in autumn.

The *Knute Lake Loop* (0.3 mile) intersects the Little Vermilion Trail at two points, looping south to provide access to a campsite on Knute Lake. The campsite sits on a large rock outcropping—the only outcropping on the entire lake—surrounded by a dense stand of jack pines. Near the east end of the loop, it intersects a trail that leads 0.8 mile south across an oak-covered ridge to the Herriman Lake Trail. Rock cairns are used frequently to mark the path across the top of this rocky ridge.

The *Herriman Lake Trail* (2.8 miles one way) connects the Echo River Trail with the Little Vermilion Lake Trail. After crossing two creeks near the east end of the trail, it then uses switchbacks to climb the steep slope from the base of the valley to the top of an oak-covered ridge overlooking Herriman Lake. West of the lake, you'll use more switchbacks to descend from the ridge to a valley containing a large grassy pond and marsh.

After crossing a small creek, you'll intersect the junction of a spur trail leading north to Knute Lake near the base of a long uphill slope. Continue hiking northeast to the Little Vermilion Lake Trail.

The *Dovre Lake Loop* (4 miles) intersects the Little Vermilion Lake Trail at two points west of the Knute Lake Loop. It crosses a number of ledgerock ridges that afford outstanding views of beaver ponds, Dovre Lake and vast stands of dense forest. At the north end (and midpoint) of the loop, a short spur trail leads down to a campsite on the south shore of Dovre Lake.

Sioux-Hustler Trail (Maps 5, 2)

Length:	2 loops of 20 or 29 miles each
Hiking time:	2 to 4 days
Difficulty:	Moderate to difficult
Elevation differential:	300 feet
Use level:	Very light
Highlights:	Devil's Cascade, Pageant Lake, many beaver ponds and bogs, good moose habitat
BWCAW Entry Point:	15
BWCAW quota:	None
USGS Maps:	Shell Lake & Takucmich Lake (Fisher F-16)

The Sioux–Hustler Trail penetrates one of the most isolated parts of the BWCA Wilderness—a region of seldom-seen lakes, beaver ponds, bogs, tiny creeks, rocky ridges and rolling hills.

The trail was originally a 27-mile horseshoe-shaped USFS administrative route, built to permit quick access to the forest by fire crews. (A fire tower once stood near Devil's Cascade, and old telephone wire may still be seen along parts of the loop paralleling the Little Indian Sioux River.) In 1985, an extension from Elm Creek rapids to Meander Lake resulted in a 29-mile loop that starts and ends at the picnic grounds. To make the trail system more appealing to hikers with less time or ambition, the Forest Service split the loop in half by cutting a new trail just north of Shell Lake, and created a 20-mile loop too.

The trail is well signed in the part of the loop outside the BWCA Wilderness. Within the Boundary Waters, however, intersections may not be marked and some trail sections are difficult to follow, particularly in the grassy meadows that surround beaver ponds and bogs. Rock cairns are used only sparingly along bald ridges and at some major intersections. Tree blazes are helpful at times. This trail is not for the novice, but it's a fine trail for seasoned hikers who like to test their navigational skills in a wilderness setting.

Late summer and early autumn are, by far, the best times of the year to enjoy the Sioux–Hustler Trail—the water levels should be at their lowest, the bogs should be their driest and the creeks should be more fordable. (Some creeks could be nearly impassable in early spring or following periods of heavy rain.)

The trailhead is located at the Meander Lake Picnic Grounds (see La Croix driving directions in "Paddling the Boundary Waters" in Chapter 3). From County Road 24, drive 21 miles east on the Echo Trail to Forest Route 467. Turn left and go 1.7 miles north to the road's end at a small parking lot. The forest in this vicinity was virtually destroyed by a storm in 1988, ruining what had been a very lovely picnic site.

The Pageant Lake Loop. From the picnic grounds, hike 0.5 mile west along a low, rocky ridge to the west end of Meander Lake, where a signed intersection marks the beginning of the loop. Turn right and enter a vast region where nearly 15,000 acres of forest were destroyed by the Little Indian Sioux Fire in 1971. In the following 5 miles, the forest habitat alternates between large stands of young aspen, jack pine and spruce, and smaller patches of mature spruce and jack pine that were somehow spared by the inferno.

At the first of several beaver ponds, do not cross the large dam. The trail passes below the dam through an open, grassy area, crosses a boulder-strewn creek and then veers off to the right.

After skirting the west side of another grassy bog and then crossing another small creek, you enter the BWCA Wilderness amidst a mature stand of jack pine at the crest of a low ridge. Two more beaver ponds are passed before you leave the region that was burned and climb to higher ground. Occasional rock cairns mark the way across an oak-covered granite ridge.

More cairns mark the intersection of the Shell Lake Loop (left), 7 miles from the trailhead. Continue northbound on the main trail, which descends more than 100 feet to cross Shohola Creek. Beyond the creek, the trail gains 120 feet in elevation as it climbs to a rocky ridge above the eastern shore of Emerald Lake.

About 0.75 mile farther, a spur trail leads west from the main loop and drops 120 feet to the shore of Emerald Lake and a developed campsite, a good destination for the first night of a four-day trek.

Beyond the junction, the main loop trail continues northbound, descends to the northeast bay of Emerald Lake, and then climbs steeply over another high, rocky ridge. Near the east end of Hustler Lake, you'll intersect a canoe portage trail that connects Hustler and Oyster lakes. The well-worn portage leads west to an easy source of drinking water.

After crossing Weeny Creek on a good, old beaver dam, the trail angles toward the northwest and follows a rocky ridge that is sparsely forested with pine. The scene later changes to a dense forest of spruce.

Soon after Hustler Lake comes into view through the trees, watch for an unmarked access trail that leads southwest to a campsite on Hustler Lake. Located only 100 yards downhill from the main trail, this campsite is a good destination for backpackers planning to negotiate this loop in just three days.

Less than 0.5 mile beyond the campsite spur, the main trail drops down to the edge of Hustler Lake and crosses the Hustler River, followed by a swampy area where slippery logs and soft muskeg are treacherous.

Between Hustler and Range Line lakes, the hiking is rather uneventful, with few obstructions to slow your pace. Along the way, you'll see several huge white pines that somehow survived logging operations and fires during the past three centuries. In the lowland region bordering the northeast shore of Range Line Lake, a spur trail leads west to the third campsite along this route. Inaccessible to canoeists, this is a good place to feel truly isolated in a pristine wilderness setting, 13.1 miles from the trailhead.

Pageant Lake is a beautiful, isolated destination for backpackers at the northern tip of the Sioux-Hustler loop.

Near the north end of Range Line Lake, the trail crosses Range Line Creek at a scenic setting near a small falls. It then loops straight north to cross Pageant Creek on an old beaver dam, before veering west.

A lovely campsite near the west end of Pageant Lake is accessible by a short spur trail leading north from the loop. It marks the midpoint of this loop, 14.8 miles from the trailhead, and makes a great destination for the second night of a four-day outing. Pageant is a very scenic and peaceful lake that provides an intimate setting for the ultimate wilderness experience.

From that point, the loop begins its southbound return to the trailhead, first leading southwest to Heritage Creek. Use caution as you step on boulders to ford the creek, which flows rapidly most of the year. At an elevation of only 1180 feet, Heritage Creek marks the lowest point on this loop, 300 feet lower than the first ridge you crossed, just north of Meander Lake.

South of Heritage Creek is some of the wettest terrain since the early stage of this loop—three major bogs. The trail sometimes seems to disappear in the grassy mire, but beaver dams bridge the wettest parts of the route.

After crossing the bogs, the trail bends south and follows a ridge 200 feet above the Little Indian Sioux River. Devil's Cascade is a beautiful series of rapids and falls where the river plunges 75 feet through a narrow granite canyon, 20.1 miles from the trailhead. The campsite here rests on a flat, grassy plateau at the very brink of the gorge, near the midpoint of a 0.5-mile portage trail that receives considerable canoe traffic throughout the summer. It is the last developed campsite along the loop, a fine place to spend the final night of your three- or four-day trek.

From Devil's Cascade, the trail leads straight east on an excellent path that was once part of the USFS administrative route. About 1 mile from the cascade, you'll intersect the west end of the Shell Lake Loop. About 0.25 mile beyond this junction, the Sioux–Hustler Trail crosses the portage connecting Shell and Lower Pauness lakes. .

Continuing southbound, an excellent path crosses a gently rolling landscape, through a small, grassy bog and then along the northeast shore of the Little Indian Sioux River. The path may be muddy along the river at times.

At Elm Creek rapids, 24.1 miles from the trailhead, the trail skirts the edge of a lovely little waterfall, then climbs abruptly to the ridge above the river's east bank and parallels the river for over 1 mile. This part of the trail network combines old forest roads with newly cut paths, and may be a bit confusing at times. Watch carefully for signs and trail markers that direct hikers on and off the old road. Less than 1.5 miles southeast of Elm Creek rapids, the hiking trail angles off toward the southeast, away from the road, exits the BWCA Wilderness and then re-enters the region that was devasted by the Little Indian Sioux fire. Two small creeks are crossed on good board bridges, and the grassy meadow-marsh of a former lake is flanked on its south end.

Turn right at a good gravel road that leads south to the site of an old gravel pit located 0.13 mile east of the Echo Trail. From the gravel pit, hike east on a dirt road that affords good views of the burned area.

After crossing a small creek and then climbing more than 100 feet above the valley bottom, the trail veers north, away from the road, and crosses a barren ridge to end the loop near the west end of Meander Lake. From there, you'll have to backtrack the final 0.5 mile to the parking lot at the Meander Lake picnic grounds.

Shell Lake Loop. The cut-across trail that constitutes the northern part of this loop extends 5.2 miles from just south of Shohola Creek to just north of the Shell Lake–Lower Pauness Lake portage. Experienced hikers may complete the route in just two days, with an overnight stay in the vicinity of the Shell–Little Shell portage. There are no developed campsites there, but camping is permitted at any location (see "Regulations" in Chapter 6). For most folks, however, the loop is more enjoyable if spread over three days, to include camping at the developed sites at Emerald Lake and Devil's Cascade.

This loop shares the first 7 miles and final 7.8 miles of the Pageant Lake Loop. From the first intersection of the two loops at the crest of the ridge above Shohola Creek, hike west to the south shore of Little Shell Lake.

The trail intersects the Shell Lake–Little Shell Lake portage, then angles northwest along the side of a ridge overlooking Shell Lake. This is the most rugged part of the loop, but it is also the most scenic.

When the trail joins the Shell Lake-Heritage Lake portage, bear right and follow the portage about 50 feet to where it exits toward the west and crosses the creek connecting Heritage and Shell lakes. From that point on, you'll follow a ridgeline southwest to intersect the Pageant Lake Loop about 1 mile southeast of Devil's Cascade. A side trip to the falls is well worth the small amount of effort and time required.

Stuart Lake Trail (Map 5)

Length:	8 miles (one way)
Hiking time:	2 days (round trip)
Difficulty:	Easy to moderate
Elevation differential:	210 feet
Use level:	Very light
Highlights:	Stuart Lake, Stuart River rapids, nice stands of pine
BWCAW Entry Point:	18
BWCAW quota:	None
USGS Maps:	Lapond Lake, Lake Agnes, Iron Lake; Fisher—F-16

Perhaps the best thing about the Stuart Lake Trail is Stuart Lake. There are no panoramic overlooks along the trail itself; in fact, the trail avoids ridges altogether. Formerly known as the La Croix Trail, it was originally an administrative trail to a Forest Service cabin on Lac La Croix, used in the 1920s and 1930s. (Telephone wire and insulators can still be seen at many locations.) The trail was no longer needed after the 1940s and was not maintained until the Youth Conservation Corps reopened it in 1978 for recreational visits to Stuart Lake.

The trail was originally designed to avoid the steep slopes of ridges in favor of the low, flat valleys. What exists now is a relatively smooth, wide path over gently rolling terrain. In spring, after heavy rains or during unusually wet years, the trail is wet and muddy at several locations. Even during dry seasons, hikers may encounter a few wet spots where the trail dips into marshy valleys adjacent to swamps.

All but the first 0.25 mile of the trail lies in the BWCA Wilderness. The only reliable sources of drinking water are Stuart Lake and the Stuart River. Short side trips are possible on the two portage trails that intersect this trail. Ambitious hikers may also continue beyond Stuart Lake on the old La Croix Trail, but the trail is not maintained.

The trailhead lies 62 miles northeast of Cook. To find it, see the La Croix driving directions in "Paddling the Boundary Waters" in Chapter 3. Then drive 25.5 miles east from County Road 24 on the Echo Trail to a small parking space on the right (south) side of the road. The trail begins on the north (opposite) side of the road, at the site of the Portage River CCC Camp, Co. 711.

The Stuart Lake Trail begins at the site of an old gravel pit, now a grassy wildlife opening adjacent to County Road 116. Most of the portage trails, old plantations and roads in this area were built by the CCC, which had a camp here.

For the first 0.25 mile, the trail follows a forest road that loops around the old gravel pit and through the wildlife opening to the edge of the BWCA Wilderness. At that point, you enter a mixed forest of jack pine, balsam fir and occasional birch and aspen. In the first 0.75 mile, the trail crosses two small creeks and passes close to the west side of a large grassy swamp, where the path may be soft and muddy.

After skirting the bases of two high ridges, the trail descends steeply through a lovely forest of mature red pine, jack pine and aspen and then crosses a small creek draining into Mule Lake, visible 150 yards to the east. A nice stand of mature red pines occupies the hillside just west of Mule Lake. Beyond it, the trail again dips into a swampy area.

While crossing over the next low ridge, you'll see an enormous Norway pine that appears to be the matriarch of the smaller red pines that dominate the hillside. After looping through an open area of new growth, the trail returns to another ridge of lovely pines. Old telephone wire can be seen here.

A major muddy spot is encountered at the west edge of a swamp bordering Mule Creek. Signs of moose are plentiful in this region. After 1 mile of hiking on higher and drier ground, you descend rather abruptly to skirt another swamp, then climb over another low ridge.

As you approach a large beaver pond, watch for the foot trail to veer off to the left (west), while the old administrative route continues straight toward the pond. When the water is frozen, the old route is the most direct. During the ice-

A beaver enjoys warm sunshine at the only "hole" in his lake.

free season, however, you'll have to detour 0.25 mile around the west end of the pond, using a much rougher and narrower trail that is likely to be wet and muddy at the point where it crosses the western tip of the swamp. After the detour, the trail rejoins the old administrative route and continues northeastward over nearly level, drier terrain to the southern tip of Stuart Lake.

You must first ford the Stuart River above a scenic rapids that drains into the lake, 6.4 miles from the trailhead. It can normally be crossed easily by carefully stepping on rocks in the river. During high water, however, be very cautious. (You may find a balancing staff to be useful.)

Just beyond the river crossing, you intersect the portage trail canoeists use to bypass the rapids. There are picturesque scenes at both ends of the portage: one end offers a view of the tranquil Stuart River valley, while the other end is at the base of a small waterfall where the river pours into Stuart Lake.

As the trail climbs over a rocky ridge less than 0.25 mile north of the river, watch for a rock cairn next to the trail near the highest point on the ridge. From that point, you can leave the trail and hike due north through a sparsely forested area to a high, bald rock outcropping, 100 feet above the southeast shore of Stuart Lake. There you'll enjoy a marvelous view of Stuart Lake and the forested hills that surround it. The overlook is about 100 yards from the trail.

A quarter mile north of the overlook spur, the trail intersects a 0.5-mile portage connecting Stuart and Nibin lakes. The Stuart Lake Trail continues northbound, inland from the east shore of Stuart Lake. A half mile north of the Nibin-Stuart portage, the trail enters a grassy swamp and then skirts its western edge.

After the trail loops around the easternmost bay of Stuart Lake, watch carefully for the unmarked spur trail leading west to the campsite. The large campsite has a western exposure with a gently sloping rock outcrop that is ideal for swimmers.

KAWISHIWI DISTRICT

Four trails are administered by the Kawishiwi District for backpackers. The Angleworm and Cummings Lake trails are accessible from the Echo Trail north of Ely; the Snowbank and Kekekabic trails are accessed from the Fernberg Road (Highway 169 to County Road 18) east of town. All of them penetrate the Boundary Waters Canoe Area Wilderness.

Angleworm Trail (Map 6)

Length:	13.7 miles (loop)
Hiking time:	1 to 2 days
Difficulty:	Moderate to difficult
Elevation differential:	230 feet
Use level:	Light
Highlights:	Scenic overlooks, nice campsites
BWCAW Entry Point:	85
BWCAW quota:	2
USGS Maps:	Angleworm Lake, Fourtown Lake; Fisher—F-9

The Angleworm Trail offers high rock ridges with scenic overlooks and impressive stands of giant red and white pines, frequent access to lakes and ponds, and an occasional dip through lowland bogs and creek valleys. About a third of the trail utilizes an old logging road. The rest of the trail, for the most part, follows a rugged path along rocky ridges and creekside bluffs. The route is usually easy to follow, and blaze marks and rock cairns guide the way in the most confusing parts of the trail.

You may camp only at the nine developed campsites. For enhanced solitude, most of the sites are located at the end of short spur trails marked with a tepee symbol on a wooden post.

The 2.25-mile part of the trail joining the Echo Trail with Angleworm Lake is the most frequently used section, often by day-hikers, occasionally by canoeists and frequently by grouse hunters in autumn. Only eight times in 1987 was its quota filled, and only 38 BWCAW travel permits were issued throughout the entire five-month quota period.

The trailhead is located 16 miles northwest of Ely. From County Road 88 (see Kawishiwi District driving directions in "Paddling the Boundary Waters" in Chapter 3), drive 13 miles north to the trailhead and a small parking lot on the right side of the Echo Trail.

From the parking lot, hike northeast across rolling terrain covered with jack pine and a mixture of balsam fir, birch and aspen. As the trail begins its descent into Spring Creek valley, you pass a sign that marks your entry into the BWCA Wilderness. After dropping more than 150 feet, the trail intersects Spring Creek, where a log bridge spans the tiny stream, then climbs abruptly, ascending 100 feet to a high rocky ridge that affords a nice view across the valley. Another log bridge crosses a shallow, rocky flowage where one large swamp drains into another, a rather scenic location for a rest stop.

Near the south end of Angleworm Lake, 2 miles from the trailhead, is the junction of three trails and the beginning of the loop around Angleworm Lake. The portage trail to Trease Lake leads south, the route to the east side of the Angleworm loop veers east, and the trail to the south end of Angleworm Lake continues toward the northeast.

Bear left there. After 0.25 mile, the trail skirts the southwest shore of the lake and passes spur trails to three campsites. The first two sit relatively close to the lake, while the third lies on the west side of the trail, away from the lake. A quarter mile beyond the third campsite, you'll begin to climb steeply to a ridge 150 feet above the lake.

Atop the ridge is a nice stand of red and white pines and a lovely view across the slender lake. During the first half of this century, there was a lookout tower and a ranger cabin at the highest point on the ridge. Nothing is left of the cabin and the tower was buried, but you may still see some debris around the site.

Soon the trail veers away from the lake and passes through a logged-over region. Scattered amidst the new growth are a few enormous white pines dating back more than 200 years. The trail then curves back toward the northeast and gradually descends through a stand of younger red and white pines to the edge of the lake.

The fourth campsite sits away from the lake, on the west side of the trail, served by a short spur trail. This point marks the last contact you'll have with Angleworm Lake for 5 miles, until the trail loops around to the campsite on the opposite shore, barely a stone's throw away.

From the campsite, climb to a high ridge overlooking the deep valley of an intermittent creek lying west of the ridge. Beautiful in autumn, the crest of the ridge

Water is accessible at several points along the Angleworm Trail.

is forested with oaks and maples, yielding to a more typical northern forest of jack pines and aspens.

Just north of the highest point on the ridge, the trail bends sharply toward the east, dips through a steep gully, and begins its gradual 100-foot descent to Home Lake. A stand of mature red pines populates the hillside above the northwest shore of the lake, but many have been toppled by a storm.

There is no bridge across the creek draining the north end of Home Lake, so use caution. About 0.25 mile east of the creek is a short spur trail that leads to a campsite lying several hundred feet north of the lake in a pine forest. A short distance beyond the campsite, you intersect the portage trail that connects Home and Gull lakes. This marks the northernmost point on the Angleworm Trail loop, 6.7 miles from the trailhead.

On the west side of Home Lake is a spur trail that leads 0.1 mile to a fine campsite on the shore of the lake, a perfect destination for hikers who plan to walk the trail in two days.

From the campsite spur, the main trail angles toward the southeast, away from Home Lake, and gradually ascends to a high ridge. A beaver pond occupies the valley below the ridge, and Gull Lake is barely visible to the northeast.

After passing through another stand of large pines in the region northeast of Whiskey Jack Lake, the trail skirts the east edge of another high ridge that offers another vista across a large beaver pond. At that point, the trail veers back toward the west and descends to an isolated little campsite on the southeast shore of Whiskey Jack Lake—the most secluded of all the campsites along the Angleworm Trail, accessible only to hikers.

From the short spur trail to the campsite, the main trail continues westbound, passing to the south of Whiskey Jack Lake and then leading to the east shore of Angleworm Lake. Another short spur trail leads down a steep slope to a campsite on the shore of Angleworm Lake. The main trail leads south, angling away from the lake, through a mixed forest of jack pine, balsam fir, birch and aspen. You climb to another high ridge studded with red pines, only to drop back down again to the large east bay of Angleworm Lake.

A spur trail leads about 100 yards down to a beautiful campsite on the rocky shore of the bay. A large pile of lumber north of the campsite is all that remains of a logging camp. From the campsite spur, you hike away from Angleworm Lake and cross two more ridges en route to a panoramic view from atop a high ridge that overlooks a creek that feeds the south end of Angleworm Lake.

At the base of the ridge, the trail crosses the creek on a beaver dam and then follows a ridge along the south shore of the creek to the southwest end of Angleworm Lake. After skirting the southeast shore of Angleworm Lake, the trail turns west and enters a swampy area with boardwalks.

The junction of the Angleworm Trail portage and the Trease Lake portage marks the end of the loop around Angleworm Lake. From that point, backtrack 2 miles to the trailhead.

Cummings Lake Trail (Map 5)

Length:	5.8 miles (one way)
Hiking time:	1 to 2 days
Difficulty:	Easy to moderate
Elevation differential:	250 feet
Use level:	Light
Highlights:	Lovely pine forest
BWCAW Entry Point:	5
BWCAW quota:	6 (with Entry Point 4—Crab Lake)
USGS Maps:	Crab Lake, Shagawa Lake; Fisher—F-9

The Cummings Lake Trail is the longest of the North Arm Trails (see Chapter 5), a fine network of trails that wind across beautiful pine-covered hills and barren ridges in the region just north of Burntside Lake. It can be combined easily with one or more of the other trails for a more challenging trek. The final 3 miles of the trail fall within the BWCA Wilderness. Outside the Wilderness, you may see evidence of recent logging operations, as well as some vehicular traffic on this old logging road. Only five BWCAW travel permits were issued in 1987 to campers using the Cummings Lake Trail, all issued to paddlers.

Follow the Echo Trail (see Kawishiwi District driving directions in "Paddling the Boundary Waters" in Chapter 3) 8.8 miles north from County Road 88 to its junction with the North Arm Road (County Road 644). Turn left and proceed 3.5 miles to a parking lot across from Camp Northland. A sign there marks the "Coxey / Slim Trail."

Trails lead in three directions from the trailhead. Begin by following the left-hand route (the "North Star Run"), which leads abruptly uphill to the crest of a 100-foot ridge that parallels the North Arm of Burntside Lake. The trail then descends into a shallow valley containing "the Sentinels." These giant white pine trees are believed to be nearly 300 years old.

Just past the Sentinels is a junction with a trail leading west (Trolls Bridge Run); the North Star Run continues in a northwest direction. Bear left and ascend another 100 feet as you meander west to the old Coxey Pond Road.

Turn right at the road, the site of recent logging activity. This wide, smooth path leads northwest across a rolling, pine-covered landscape. Less than 0.25 mile farther, the trail enters the BWCA Wilderness. Though no longer accessible to vehicular traffic, the trail continues on a good, smooth, wide path. Along the route, you'll see signed and numbered intersections that mark spur trails for cross-country skiers.

In an open, grassy area adjacent to a small gravel pit, you'll bisect a short portage trail that connects Silica Lake and Coxey Pond. Fifty yards north is an appealing rest stop on the scenic southwest shore of Coxey Pond. The only developed campsite on the lake is located east of the portage, at the narrow neck of Coxey Pond.

The trail crosses a log bridge that spans a small creek and then continues to follow the old road west from the Coxey-Silica portage. Up to this point, the North Arm Trails are well maintained for the influx of skiing tourists who visit each winter. Windfalls blocking the trail are more common from here on.

Watch for pink ribbons marking the trail as it veers southwest, away from the old roadway, 3.4 miles from the trailhead. This is the old Cummings Lake Fire Trail, a much narrower and somewhat rougher trail than you've experienced thus far.

As the Cummings Lake Trail swings toward the west in a damp forest of black spruce, another trail continues to the southwest. Marked by yellow ribbons, the "Bog Trail" follows an old winter road across marshy terrain to the southeast corner of Cummings Lake (part of another loop used only by cross-country skiers).

The Cummings Lake Trail then ascends to higher ground, passes through a forest of 80-year-old jack pines and finally descends 100 feet to the northeast shore of Cummings Lake. A nice, large, developed campsite sits at the trail's end. During the summer, you may have to vie with canoeists for rights to the site.

Kekekabic Trail (Maps 7, 8)

Length:	38 miles (one way)
Hiking time:	4 to 5 days
Difficulty:	Difficult
Elevation differential:	460 feet
Use level:	Very light
Highlights:	Mueller Falls
BWCAW Entry Point:	28
BWCAW quota:	4 (with Snowbank and Old Pines trails)
USGS Maps:	Forest Center, Alice Lake, Kekekabic Lake, Ogishkemuncie Lake, Gillis Lake, Long Island Lake; Fisher—F-10, F-11, F-12

Formerly a fire access route for the Forest Service, the Kekekabic Trail was constructed during the 1930s to service the Kekekabic lookout tower, once located about midway along the trail. The trail extends from near the end of the Fernberg Road (Lake County Road 18) to the Gunflint Trail (Cook County Road 12), a journey of more than 175 miles via Highway 61 along Lake Superior's North Shore.

Because it was not built for recreational hiking, the Kekekabic Trail has few scenic vistas and no loop options. The landscape is level to gently rolling, with only a few steep grades. In spring and early summer, occasional swamps and water crossings may result in wet feet. *Lack* of water is a problem in late summer and in autumn—be sure to carry plenty of drinking water.

To find the trailhead, follow the directions for "Snowbank and Old Pines Trails," below.

The most scenic spot along the trail is at a log bridge that spans a creek between Mueller and Agamok lakes. The lovely cascade there entertains canoeists more often than hikers. Nearby is a developed campsite for backpackers, located about 12 miles from the trail's east end.

After construction of the Snowbank and Old Pines trails in the late 1970s, the central part of the Kekekabic Trail was abandoned by the Forest Service. In the mid-1980s, however, concerned citizens sought the reopening of this historic trail, and the Forest Service decided to once again include the "Kek" on its list of designated trails. But only as an *unmaintained* trail.

What does all this mean to you? First, unless maintenance is restored, most of the Kekekabic Trail, plagued with windfalls and receiving very little traffic, will be hard to follow. Only the west end (12 miles shared by the Snowbank and Old Pines trails) and a couple of miles at the east end are adequately maintained for pleasant hiking. Second, until the Kek Trail *is* maintained, a detailed description will not be included in this guide. You're on your own! If you like to bushwhack, this trail is the next best thing.

Snowbank and Old Pines Trails (Map 7)

Length:	40.5 miles (4 loops)
Hiking time:	2 to 5 days
Difficulty:	Moderate to difficult
Elevation differential:	360 feet
Use level:	Light
Highlights:	Scenic overlooks, virgin pines
BWCAW Entry Point:	74
BWCAW quota:	4
USGS Maps:	Snowbank Lake, Lake Insula, Ensign Lake SW, Ensign Lake SE; Fisher—F-10, F-11

The Snowbank and Old Pines trails provide backpackers with a wonderful network of footpaths to high rock ridges, through 300-year-old pines and to no less than a dozen pristine Wilderness lakes. The Snowbank Trail is a 22.25-mile loop around Snowbank Lake. The Old Pines Trail spurs off the Snowbank Trail to form loops around Disappointment Lake and several smaller lakes east of Disappointment, with optional treks ranging in length from 7 to 16 miles. To experience it all, plan to spend no less than four days hiking.

Sixty BWCAW travel permits were issued to trail users in 1987. Nevertheless, a reservation is seldom necessary—only once in 1987 was the quota filled. Since most of the trail is within the BWCA Wilderness, all federal regulations apply and you may camp only at developed campsites.

The trailhead is located off the Fernberg Road, 19.25 miles east of the Ely Chamber of Commerce via Highway 169 and County Road 18.

The *Snowbank Trail* begins at a small parking lot. Near the south end of Snowbank Lake is a junction with a short spur trail that leads north to the lake. Two miles farther, near the south end of Parent Lake is another junction with the trail that loops south to Becoosin and Benezie lakes—a 2-mile spur that also intersects the Old Pines Trail 0.75 mile east of the Snowbank Trail. There are two campsites on each of those lakes.

About 0.25 mile past the Becoosin loop junction, 4.9 miles from the trailhead, is the junction with the Old Pines Trail (described later). Bear left and follow the Snowbank Trail northeast as it parallels the east shore of Parent Lake. There are three campsites on Parent Lake, but only one is easily accessible to hikers.

At the northeast corner of Parent Lake, the trail joins the 0.25-mile portage connecting Parent and Disappointment lakes. It skirts the west shore of Disappointment and Birdseye lakes before heading overland to the northeast corner of Snowbank Lake. Along the way, you'll see campsites on Disappointment Lake and Snowbank Lake.

About 0.25 mile beyond the spur trail to the campsite on Snowbank Lake is the northern junction with the Old Pines Trail, 9 miles from the trailhead. Bear left. For the ensuing 10 miles, the trail follows the scenic north side of Snowbank Lake, where high rock ridges offer several excellent overlooks. Along the way, you'll have access to seven more campsites on Snowbank Lake and one on Grub Lake. (If peaceful solitude is your goal for the night, the Grub Lake campsite is the best choice.) Snowbank Lake is quite popular during the fishing season, and 25-horsepower motorboats are permitted inside the BWCAW there. Resorts and private cabins line the south shore of the lake, which lies outside the Boundary Waters.

Near the west end of Snowbank Lake is the intersection with the Flash Lake portage. Cross it and continue south to the Snowbank Road. From there it's a 2-mile hike on the road back to the trailhead. When you get to the Fernberg Road, turn left and proceed 0.75 mile to the parking lot.

The *Old Pines Trail* leaves the Snowbank Trail north of Becoosin Lake. At about 0.75 mile, pass the east junction of the loop from Becoosin and Benezie lakes and then proceed northeast to the south shore of Disappointment Lake. Near the southeast corner of Disappointment Lake, a shortcut leads north to parallel the east shore of the lake. It provides access to a lakeside campsite, and after 1.5 miles rejoins the Old Pines Trail.

Continuing on the Old Pines Trail, you come to a campsite on tiny Drumstick Lake. About 1.5 miles farther east is the highlight of this loop: a stand of large, virgin white pines. The trail then swings northeast to a cluster of small lakes at the east end of this trail system.

The old Kekekabic Trail starts near Moiyaka Lake, 7.4 miles from the beginning of the Old Pines Trail. Nearby are two campsites, one on Medas Lake and one on Moiyaka Lake. Medas and Moiyaka are two of the most isolated, accessible lakes in the Kawishiwi District. A campsite on Alworth Lake marks the northeast corner of this loop.

After crossing a small creek at the southwest end of Alworth Lake, the Old Pines Trail leads west to pass the south side of Disappointment Mountain and then intersects the shortcut trail that leads to the campsite on Disappointment Lake.

There are two campsites near the 25-rod portage connecting Disappointment and Ahsub lakes, one on each lake. Canoeists frequent these lakes, so you aren't likely to experience the same kind of wilderness solitude here that you might have enjoyed on Medas or Moiyaka lakes.

From the portage junction, the trail continues west and eventually intersects the Snowbank Trail near the northeast corner of Snowbank Lake.

ISABELLA DISTRICT

Two trails are administered for backpackers in the Isabella District. While the Hogback Lake Trail is short enough to be hiked in its entirety in just one day, the Powwow Trail is long enough to occupy several days of exploration. The Hogback Lake Trail is entirely outside the BWCA Wilderness, while the Powwow Trail is fully within.

Hogback Lake Trail (Map 17)

Length:	5 miles (several loop options)
Hiking time:	1 to 2 days
Difficulty:	Moderate
Elevation differential:	82 feet
Use level:	Light
Highlights:	Hogback ridges with scenic overlooks, trout lakes
USGS Maps:	Silver Island Lake, Wilson Lake

Enjoy day hikes or short backpacking treks into a rugged North Woods setting on two good loops of 3 or 4 miles each, or start at the picnic grounds and end at County Road 7 by any one of three possible routes ranging in length from 1.75 miles to 4 miles.

All of the routes traverse sharply crested ridges ("hogbacks") and skirt sparkling trout lakes. (Hogbacks are formed from steeply inclined layers of rock that are very resistant to erosion.) Winding through this area is the Laurentian Divide, a subtle geologic ridge that determines whether continental watersheds flow north to the Arctic Ocean or south and east to the Atlantic Ocean.

To find the trailhead, drive 12 miles east of Highway 1 at Isabella via Forest Route 172 to the Hogback Lake picnic grounds and parking lot on the right side of the road.

From the picnic area, the trail follows the birch-covered north shore of Hogback Lake. Near the lake's east end, the trail veers inland and begins a gradual ascent toward the east. As the trail loops toward the southeast, the climb becomes much more abrupt.

At the top of the steep ridge, the trail intersects the Scarp Lake loop. To enjoy a beautiful trek around Scarp Lake, bear left at the intersection and continue hiking southeast on the narrow crest of the hogback. You will soon be afforded panoramic views of Scarp Lake from the sparsely forested ridge. A spur trail drops 50 yards off the ridge to a scenic campsite in a birch grove on the lakeshore.

After the spur junction, the ridge slopes down to form a low barrier between Mound and Scarp lakes. A small creek, easily crossed by stepping on boulders, connects Scarp and Mound lakes. This man-made canal was once used by loggers to float logs out of remote areas. Beyond it, the ridge rises again and the trail climbs to an intersection at the crest of a hill, 1 mile from the trailhead.

The trail leading east from there traverses level to gently rolling landscape en route to Steer Lake (0.25 mile) and County Road 7 (0.75 mile). A campsite on

Steer Lake sits in a stand of scrubby balsam fir trees located about 100 feet from the main trail.

Back at the intersection, the Scarp Lake loop trail turns south and descends a steep hill into a wet lowland region where a short boardwalk crosses the wettest part of the swamp. Soon, the trail loops toward the west and passes the south shore of Scarp Lake, before ascending steeply to a high ridge overlooking the lake. You'll see a nice stand of cedar trees along this part of the route.

The junction with the Lupus Lake loop is in a small open area sparsely forested with birch, 1.5 miles from the trailhead. The intersection is not marked and it's easy to miss.

From that point, the Scarp Lake loop continues westbound high above the south shore of Scarp Lake. It again intersects the Lupus Lake loop near Canal Lake. At that point, 2 miles from the trailhead, a spur trail leads down to the southeast shore of Canal Lake.

One-tenth mile northeast of the second intersection with the Lupus Lake loop is the beginning of a spur trail leading 0.13 mile east to a campsite on Scarp Lake, a lovely, open site on the tip of a sparsely wooded peninsula. Although it doesn't have a fire grate or latrine, it appears to be the most popular of all the campsites along the Hogback Trail.

Just past the campsite spur, the hiking trail joins the east end of the level, sandy, 15-rod canoe portage connecting Scarp and Canal lakes.

You can still see the remains of an old railroad trestle that once bridged the narrows between Hogback and Canal lakes, as well as an old dam and sluiceway built during the early part of this century.

At the narrows, the trail turns sharply back toward the east and climbs up the gradually sloping ridge between Hogback and Scarp lakes to a nice view of Scarp Lake overlooking the campsite at its west end. At the end of the loop around Scarp Lake, backtrack down the steep hill that leads to the north shore of Hogback Lake and back to the picnic area, a total of 3 miles.

You can extend your hike 1.2 miles by adding the Lupus Lake loop to the south end of the Scarp Lake loop and eliminating the 0.5-mile stretch along the south side of Scarp Lake. The trail slopes gently downhill from the ridge above Scarp Lake, levels out and then passes a swamp where there is considerable evidence of moose. Beyond the swampy area, the trail skirts the base of a large hill covered by a lovely, pure stand of paper birch, then gradually descends into another wet lowland area. A short boardwalk spans the wettest part of the marsh.

Soon thereafter, Lupus Lake comes into view. As the trail undulates along the north shore of the lake's east arm, you're likely to see many signs of moose in the mixed forest of birch, spruce and pine. Trees felled by beavers are also in this area. Watch for an old square post with scribing on it: in the 1930s, the CCC used posts to mark work projects.

A campsite on Lupus Lake sits in a densely wooded area adjacent to the main trail. The shoreline is weedy, but there is a good view of the lake.

As the trail leaves the campsite, it loops north and follows close to the east shore of the lake's north arm, then turns inland and heads northeast across a level to gently rolling, low, damp landscape. Blaze marks on trees mark the way. Steep cliffs rise 60 to 70 feet above parts of the trail. As you approach the south shore of Canal Lake, you'll enter a nice stand of red pines before climbing up to a ridge above the lake's south shore. Canal is a pretty little lake bordered on all sides by

Moose are most abundant in the Perent River Region.

an appealing forest of spruce and birch. The Lupus Lake loop re-intersects the Scarp Lake loop at a point 0.5 mile west of the other junction.

Powwow Trail (Maps 16, 7)

Length:	26.5 miles (round trip)
Hiking time:	3 to 4 days
Difficulty:	Difficult
Elevation differential:	110 feet
Use level:	Very light
Highlights:	Solitude, scenic variety, moose habitat
BWCAW Entry Point:	86
BWCAW quota:	None
USGS Maps:	Isabella Lake, Quadga Lake, Snowbank Lake; Fisher—F-4

Although the loop begins as an easy trek across a gently rolling landscape, this route is by no means recommended for inexperienced hikers. Intersections are not signed, much of the trail is not marked and the Forest Service does not have the staffing capabilities to adequately maintain the trail. As a result, new beaver dams have flooded portions of the trail in lowland areas, dense brush has overgrown other parts, windfalls may obstruct much of the path in the western extremes. Although some of the old logging roads enable an easy, quick pace, other parts of the trail require the use of "all fours" to negotiate steep rock ledges. Strong hikers may average as much as 3 miles per hour at the east end of the loop, but may struggle to cover 1 mile per hour (or less) at the west end. Most back-packers should have no difficulty completing the route in three days, but anyone who likes to fish and/or relax along the way may want to stretch it over four or five days.

This is one of the best areas in the country to see moose, so walk softly as you approach bogs, beaver ponds and lakes. There are also good populations of grouse and beavers in this area. And on still August nights, you may hear the high-pitched howling of wolf pups emanating from unidentifiable points on the horizon.

The trail begins at the Isabella Lake parking lot, 19 miles northeast of Isabella (see Entry Point 35 in Chapter 3). From the parking lot south of Isabella Lake, the trail follows an old railroad bed west through a young stand of pine. Red ribbons mark the route. An old gravel road is intersected and the route veers northwest (right) along this wide, smooth path. Large boulders on the road mark the boundary of the BWCA Wilderness. The trail continues in a northwest direction on a level path that crosses a small creek twice.

One mile from the parking lot the Isabella River passes through large culverts under the old road bed. This scenic location affords views east toward Isabella Lake and west down the river. A small picnic site with a fire grate is located on the river's south shore. A good, well-worn portage trail intersects the Powwow Trail on the north side of the river.

From the river, the trail leads almost due north, continuing on an old roadbed. About 2 miles from the trailhead is your first clear view of the Rice Lake Fire zone, where 1100 acres of pine and aspen burned in 1976. Started by lightning, the fire burned so hot that it destroyed the top soil and seed source. Native grasses and tree species were then planted, but the new aspen and pine will take years to conceal the scattered charred trunks that loom over the young forest. The northern edge of the burned area is clearly evident from this vantage point. Farther on, a beaver dam has flooded parts of the old road. Wet feet may be unavoidable during the ensuing 0.25-mile stretch.

A couple of rock cairns mark the intersection of two old roads in the middle of the Rice Lake burn area, 2.6 miles from the trailhead. They mark the beginning of a large loop. Turn left and follow the westbound trail. A log straddles a small creek that feeds Pelt Lake (not visible to the south). Then the trail enters a brushy area where the path may be hard to see at times.

At the south end of Fallen Arch Lake (a name that is, hopefully, not descriptive of your physical condition), the trail crosses another small creek amidst an alder thicket, the first of many dense patches of shrubbery along this trail.

The landscape is somewhat hillier in the region southwest of Marathon Lake. Less than 1 mile beyond the lake, you cross a small creek and then climb abruptly, gaining about 50 feet in elevation. Descend gradually to Diana Creek, where there is a log across the creek draining Diana Lake, visible to the north. In the region west of the lake are many signs of moose and timber wolves—walk softly and watch carefully.

After the trail starts to bend toward the south, it crosses a small creek and enters an open, grassy area with a developed campsite, 8 miles from the trailhead. Campfire Lake, about 70 yards west of the site and not visible from the trail, is the last dependable source of water until you reach Superstition Lake.

A half mile southwest of the campsite, the trail veers toward the west and crosses another small creek, this one draining Myth Lake. The path then skirts the south end of a beaver pond and crosses a beaver dam.

Beyond the dam, the trail gets rougher and starts to narrow as it bends toward the north and approaches Superstition Lake. By the time you reach the

Wolf tracks

south end of the lake, the road will have completely yielded to a narrow, winding, undulating path through a dense forest of jack pine, spruce and balsam fir along the east shore of Superstition Lake. A spur trail leads downhill about 50 yards to a nice, developed lakeshore campsite, 9.8 miles from the trailhead, that provides adequate space for one or two small tents and is a good source of drinking water.

Following the shoreline, the trail continues to the northeast end of the lake, where a beaver dam must be crossed. The terrain from there to the south end of Mirror Lake is nearly level, but windfalls may slow your progress, depending on how long it has been since the last maintenance crew passed through this region. Watch carefully for a cold spring about midway between Superstition and Mirror lakes.

About halfway up the west shore of Mirror Lake is another small, developed campsite on the left side of the trail, sitting up a ways from the lakeshore. (This is not a very convenient place to renew your water supply.) Beyond the campsite, the trail rises and falls across rock outcroppings that afford some nice views of the lake. At one point, however, the trail passes precariously close to the water's edge.

North of Mirror Lake, the trail crosses a sturdy old beaver dam that should not endanger dry feet. From there, the path angles northeast along a creek until it reaches the southwest end of Path Lake, where there is a scenic overlook from a high rock ledge. Near the northwest corner of the lake, the trail drops down to the water's edge, where a nice campsite sits beneath a huge white pine, next to a gently sloping, smooth rock outcrop. The site has easy access to drinking water, as well as to a good "beach" for swimming.

North of the campsite, the trail veers away from the lake and enters a delight-ful forest of young maples interspersed with large white pines. The hike from Path Lake to Rock of Ages Lake—up and down steep, rocky ridges covered with moss and jack pine—is short but exhausting, and may require the use of "all fours" at times. It also may be difficult to see where the trail goes. Watch for blaze marks on trees and rock cairns on the ground.

A campsite lies at the scenic northern tip of Rock of Ages Lake, 12.7 miles from the trailhead. Atop a steep rock outcrop, it's a fine place for stargazing, bug-free lounging and diving.

The trail continues northbound from Rock of Ages Lake to the southeast corner of Lake Three. This section is much easier to follow, and, except for a couple of short uphill climbs, most of the route is level or slopes downhill, drop-ping a total of 150 feet through a forest of mature aspen, birch and balsam fir. Abundant flowers, ledges and mossy black spruce groves provide an excellent backdrop for photographs.

Soon after the trail touches the south shore of Lake Three, you come to a rock outcrop that serves as a good watering hole, as well as a beautiful place to rest.

The trail leads east to a creek that can be crossed either on a big fallen cedar tree or, during low water, by stepping from rock to rock. Use caution when the log is wet and slippery—it may be safer to walk through the creek. Uphill from the creek, the trail winds through an old logging camp, where the remains of old foundations and miscellaneous debris can still be seen along the trail all the way to the Horseshoe Lake portage, which intersects the Powwow Trail near the northwest corner of Horseshoe Lake.

At the northern tip of Horseshoe Lake, 14.4 miles from the parking lot, is a designated campsite on a high rocky bluff with a nice view across the lake. The tent pads and box latrine are located behind the bluff in a more protected area.

About halfway between Horseshoe and North Wilder lakes, the trail dips to cross a creek at a beaver pond. The path may be hard to see, but it extends straight across the creek. Beyond that point, the hilly mixed forest gradually yields to a woodland of mossy jack pines.

Another developed campsite is situated high above North Wilder Lake, across from a small island. One tenth mile beyond it is the intersection with the portage trail connecting North Wilder and Harbor lakes. South Wilder Lake is about 1 mile to the southeast, through a black spruce forest that eventually gives way to birch and aspen. The trail dips into a valley and crosses a small creek. It's a bit confusing, since the portage connecting North and South Wilder lakes also crosses the creek at that point, but the portage veers left and is a much more beaten path than the hiking trail. After crossing the creek, watch for the blazed tree that marks the continuation of the hiking trail.

Yet another developed campsite rests high above the west end of South Wilder Lake. Because of the steep drop to the lake, it is not a convenient place to get water. The view of the lake is not all that great, either, but the site does offer a good vantage point to watch for wildlife drinking in the narrow bay below.

After leaving the campsite, descend to the water's edge and closely follow the shoreline to the west end of the lake and then southeast, undulating over low hills and into boggy valleys and crossing several small creeks. The terrain is damp, cloaked by a mossy forest of black spruce.

There is a good vista across a large, open swamp on the north side of the trail, 20 miles into the route. The path then descends from a high ridge to a wet lowland region, crossing several small creeks en route to a major creek that drains a large beaver pond on the south side of the trail. After crossing the creek, climb a short distance up to a scenic vantage point overlooking another large swamp.

Just before the trail loops back toward the northeast, it joins the route of an old, unimproved logging road. This can be confusing, so watch carefully for the correct route—though not smooth, it is obviously wider and more level. The forest here is an appealing blend of young maples, paper birch, pine and spruce. Nevertheless, the route passes through a very wet, boggy region as the trail loops north and then east.

A blazed tree on the left side of the trail marks the beginning of a spur trail to Pose Lake. It leads northwest to a small and rustic campsite on the southeast shore of the lake.

The main trail intersects another old logging road in a large grassy opening. Turn right and follow this good, level path 1.3 miles southeast to another T intersection. Turn right again and hike southwest through an alder thicket on this good, old road. The trail passes along the edge of a swamp, and soon re-enters the region that was burned by the Rice Lake Fire.

Two rock cairns mark the completion of the loop at the first intersection you encountered, 2.6 miles from the trailhead. From that point, backtrack on the southbound trail to the parking lot.

TOFTE DISTRICT

Only one trail in the Tofte District is designed for backpackers, and it is not yet complete. When finished, it will surely be one of the longest and finest trails in the Midwest, paralleling Lake Superior's scenic North Shore from Duluth to Grand Portage and eventually to Thunder Bay, Ontario. Ultimately, this trail may be joined with the North Country Trail and a Canadian trail along the entire north shore of Lake Superior, resulting, some day, in a continuous, 2000-mile footpath around Lake Superior.

Superior Hiking Trail (Maps 17, 18)

Length:	50 miles (one way)
Hiking time:	5 to 6 days
Difficulty:	Moderate, with some difficult sections
Elevation differential:	1050 feet
Use level:	Moderate (heavy along some stretches)
Highlights:	Panoramic views, cascading streams, maple and birch forests, whitetailed deer, peregrine falcons
USGS Maps:	Schroeder, Tofte SE, Tofte NE, Lutsen, Deer Yard Lake, Mark Lake, Devil Track Lake, Grand Marais

The initial plan for this trail, a joint effort of the USFS, the DNR, local resort owners, residents and hikers, calls for a 186-mile trail from Duluth to Hovland, linking two state forests and seven state parks. Along the way, the trail will cross 3 dozen swift creeks and rivers, including several choice trout streams, and deliver hikers to some of the most incredible scenic overlooks in the Midwest. While trekking along the majestic crest of the Sawtooth Mountains, hikers will never be far from civilization. Frequent trailheads will enable short day outings as well as extended treks. Hikers who prefer not to camp will be able to walk from resort to resort via spur trails, or drop down to restaurants for meals.

Most of the completed trail lies in the Tofte District, but when finished, it will also extend across the Gunflint District. None of it is within the BWCA Wilderness. In the spring of 1988, the trail extended from Temperance River State Park to about 10 miles north of Cascade River State Park. The description below covers the continuous 50-mile segment between the village of Schroeder and County Road 12 that was scheduled for completion by the summer of 1989. To keep abreast of further developments, contact the Superior Hiking Trail Association, Box 2157, Tofte, MN 55615.

There are several good access points for this trail along the North Shore. To get to the southwest end, drive 2.7 miles southwest from the Tofte ranger station on Highway 61 to Schroeder. Parking space is next to the Cross River bridge.

If you hike the Superior Hiking Trail from southwest to northeast, you can start there and proceed 1.5 miles northwest to a falls in the Cross River and then northeast to the Temperance River valley. The trail crosses the Temperance River about 1 mile north of Highway 61; a spur trail joins it with a trailhead at Temperance River State Park. That trail begins at the parking lot adjacent to Highway 61, on the east side of the river, and extends for 1.25 miles along the brink of a steep, narrow gorge gouged out by the frothing white water below. It's a highly developed trail with railings at potentially dangerous overlooks and a path that is beaten by thousands of visiting day-hikers each summer season.

From the Temperance River, the trail climbs 875 feet en route to Carlton Peak, crosses four log bridges and several log walkways, climbs two sets of wooden steps, and leads to two developed scenic overlooks, including an overlook of the Temperance River valley. You pass through a lovely birch forest that eventually yields to a forest of mature maple trees. Spruce plantations line the trail near Britton Peak.

The spur trail to the summit of Carlton Peak is rather steep and sometimes slippery; part of it may be rerouted to eliminate those problems. Gnarled jack pines grow out of rock crevices at the summit, affording panoramic views in every direction.

The Britton Peak trailhead and parking lot lie on the east side of the Sawbill Trail (County Road 2), 2.8 miles north of Highway 61 in Tofte. Gently undulating across the maple-covered highlands, the main trail is easy to hike, with few steep slopes. There are three developed campsites along the route, evenly spaced about 2 miles apart. The entire segment can be hiked in four or five hours, including two steep side trips to scenic overlooks at Britton Peak and Leveaux Mountain.

The first spur trail is encountered within 100 yards of the Britton Peak trailhead. Watch for it on the right. It leads up a short, steep slope to the summit of Britton Peak, which has a nice view toward Lake Superior. Allow 10 to 15 minutes for this breathtaking side trip.

Beyond the spur, the main trail continues in a northeasterly direction, penetrating a lovely forest of mature maples and crossing a couple of old forest roads that are, in winter, part of the popular Sugarbush Ski Trail network. Eventually, you also cross three streams on log bridges. Several scenic views, rock outcrops and extensive talus slopes add variety to the route.

Just before Springdale Creek, you pass by a homestead site. The former occupant hung a piece of chain on a maple sapling and forgot to retrieve it. The chain is now imprisoned forever in the tree.

At Leveaux Creek, the trail is routed around an inactive beaver dam and you'll be treated to the pungent aroma of moist, decaying vegetation and the opportunity to view marsh marigolds in bloom during the month of June. A developed campsite is located next to the creek.

At the base of Leveaux Mountain, a spur trail leads south, up a steep slope to the summit of the peak (see "Leveaux Mountain Trail" in the "Day Hikes" section of this chapter). Allow at least an hour for this side trip, which is well worth the extra effort. The other end of the Leveaux Mountain Trail loop intersects the Superior Hiking Trail about 0.1 mile beyond the first junction.

Fifteen miles into this route, cross the Onion River on an old, sagging bridge. Beyond it is a flat, grassy area scattered with young balsam fir and spruce trees. This is a good place to see moose or deer, particularly in the early morning. A campsite sits near the river.

The Onion River trailhead and parking lot lie at the base of Oberg Mountain, 2.1 miles north of Highway 61 via Forest Route 336, about midway between Lutsen and Tofte. The trailhead is used most often by day-hikers en route to the summits of Leveaux and Oberg mountains.

After crossing the large parking lot at the Onion River trailhead, hike about 100 yards on the spur road to Forest Route 336. At the junction, the trail re-enters the woods and immediately intersects the spur loop that leads to the summit of Oberg Mountain. Allow a couple of hours for this 2.25-mile side trip. Along the good, well-beaten path, you'll enjoy several outstanding scenic views across Lake Superior, Oberg Lake and the rugged Sawtooth Mountain landscape. It's a very popular trail, especially in late September.

Back on the main trail, hike northeast from the base of Oberg Mountain across a rolling landscape that enables easy walking through a variety of forest

Picnicking on top of Oberg Mountain

habitats and over many small streams. A bridge spans Rollins Creek 1.25 miles from the Oberg Mountain loop; a developed campsite sits next to the creek. Beyond the site, the route climbs nearly 600 feet in less than 0.25 mile to a scenic overlook atop Moose Mountain. Continue along the lower ridge of the mountain and enjoy several more vistas from the highest elevations achieved thus far (950 feet above Lake Superior).

The trail descends along the north side of Moose Mountain to a cedar spruce swamp. After crossing Rollins Creek a second time, the trail winds toward the Lutsen Mountains Ski Area through a hilly landscape cloaked with a mixed hardwood forest. A bridge over the Poplar River is owned and maintained by the Lutsen Mountains Corporation, which operates the ski hill. Nearby is a developed campsite.

The trailhead serving this part of the trail is located at the ski chalet parking lot, 2 miles north of Highway 61 via County Road 36 (7.5 miles northeast of Tofte). This is the most developed part of the entire trail system. Besides the alpine ski facilities, a water slide and a condominium development account for a good deal of summer activity in the area.

The 6-mile section of trail connecting the Lutsen Ski Area with County Road 4 includes many overlooks. After crossing the Poplar River, the trail passes over several hills that afford panoramic overlooks, then steeply descends to skirt the scenic east shore of the river. Watch for the huge stump of an ancient white pine in this area—it measures about seven feet in diameter.

Soon the trail veers east, away from the river, and passes through a region that has been logged over—a good area to spot moose, deer and wolf. Next, climb to a couple of superb overlooks before descending to the west shore of Lake Agnes, where a bridge crosses Agnes Creek, a lovely stream with several small waterfalls. There is one campsite on the north shore of Lake Agnes, and two more sites are planned.

From Lake Agnes, the trail leads southeast to cross County Road 4 (the Caribou Trail) 3 miles north of Highway 61. Watch for spur trails leading north to the Caribou Lake public access and White Sky Rock. There is no designated parking space where the main trail intersects County Road 4; park at the Caribou Lake landing, 4 miles north of Highway 61.

After crossing the Caribou Trail, climb steeply to an overlook above Caribou Lake. From there, the trail continues through maple-covered hills to a series of old beaver ponds. An old beaver dam serves to bridge a low area. Soon you penetrate an area covered by young spruce plantations with a panoramic view of the rugged Lake Superior shoreline, then descend 300 feet to Spruce Creek.

A steep climb follows the creek crossing. Between Spruce Creek and Indian Camp Creek are north-facing palisades that allow breathtaking views across the maple highlands—gorgeous in autumn. From the highest point on the ridge (950 feet above Lake Superior), steeply descend about 600 feet to cross Indian Camp Creek, where there is a developed campsite.

A more gradual ascent from the creek to Lookout Mountain takes you through a forest of birch and cedar. From there, the trail gradually descends 550 feet to cross the Cascade River.

Parking space is available at Cascade River State Park, 36 miles northeast of your original trailhead, where a frothing river plunges toward the shore of Lake Superior. A campground here accommodates overnight visitors (see Table of Campgrounds in Chapter 6).

The 14-mile trail section between Cascade River State Park and County Road 12 was not complete when this book went to press in 1988. Plans call for the trail to follow close to the east bank of the Cascade River for a couple of miles and then angle northeast toward the Bally Creek Road (Forest Route 158). Along the way, the trail will cross several high peaks, including the highest point along this trail (1100 feet above Lake Superior). As the trail nears Grand Marais, it crosses a low, wet area that may require boardwalks.

The trail will cross the Gunflint Trail (County Road 12) 2 miles north of Grand Marais at the Sawtooth Mountain scenic overlook, also the trailhead for the Pincushion Mountain Ski Trails (see Chapter 5). A spur trail leads down to Grand Marais.

GUNFLINT DISTRICT

The Gunflint District administers only two trails long enough to entice backpackers, but both are noteworthy for different reasons. One of them—the Border Route Trail—is the "granddaddy" of all Forest trails. It is longer and entertains more overnight visitors than any other trail in Superior National Forest. The other—the Eagle Mountain Trail—leads to the highest peak in Minnesota.

Border Route Trail (Maps 9, 10, 11)

Length:	55 miles (one way) in Superior National Forest, 70 miles total (one way)
Hiking time:	5 to 7 days
Difficulty:	Difficult
Elevation differential:	700 feet
Use level:	Light to moderate
Highlights:	Towering cliffs, panoramic views, virgin forests
BWCAW Entry Points:	81 (west end), 82 (central) and 83 (east end)
BWCAW quota:	5 (three locations combined, BWCAW section only)
USGS Maps:	Gunflint Lake, South Lake, Hungry Jack Lake, Crocodile Lake, Pine Lake West, Pine Lake East, South Fowl Lake, Farquhar Peak; Fisher—F-13, F-14

The Border Route Trail affords panoramic vistas at many locations along its course, 40 miles of which lie inside the BWCA Wilderness. During the busiest season—late summer and early autumn—it's a good idea to reserve your visitor permit in advance. The entry point numbers and quotas for this part of the trail are: 81 (west end), one group per day; 82 (center), two groups per day; and 83 (east end), two groups per day.

The middle section of the trail usually entertains the most hikers. During the summer of 1987, 25 permits were issued to backpackers using Entry Point 81, 41 permits for Entry Point 82 (booked up 11 times) and 26 permits for Entry Point 83 (quota filled only three times).

Although the Border Route Trail is actually 70 miles long, only a 55-mile segment is described here. The east end of the trail penetrates Grand Portage State Forest, and continues all the way east to Lake Superior, crossing the Grand Portage Reservation and, finally, joining the historic Grand Portage trail. Since the Reservation is not public land and not part of Superior National Forest, that part of the Border Route Trail—the last 15 miles—is not included in this guide.

Most hikers will find plenty of satisfaction along the section of the trail that is included. Much of the route follows high, pine-covered ridges. Some parts can be hiked quickly and easily, while other sections are extremely rugged—not unlike mountain hiking out west, but without the oxygen starvation. Only the most seasoned, strong hikers should anticipate a pace averaging more than 1 mile per hour.

Although overnight use of the Border Route Trail is light, many of the developed campsites along the trail are also accessible to canoeists. In the peak periods—late July through early September—you'd be wise to make camp early if you prefer a developed lakeside site.

To access the west end of the Border Route Trail, drive 38 miles up the Gunflint Trail from Grand Marais to County Road 51 (a sign points right to Loon Lake Lodge). Turn right and proceed 0.9 mile (past the lodge) to a small parking lot at the road's end near the Loon Lake public landing.

The first 3 miles of this route are referred to as the Crab Lake Trail. From the parking lot, the trail first climbs north along a power line right-of-way. Soon it veers east, away from the power line, and follows a good, wide path that skirts the southeast shore of Crab Lake. At the east end of Crab Lake, the trail enters the BWCA Wilderness. Just beyond is a junction with a spur trail that leads north to Bridal Veil Falls (the first of two spur trails to the same attraction). Continue hiking in an east-northeasterly direction and soon you'll pass the west end of Whisker Lake and ascend gradually to the crest of a ridge.

For the next 52 miles, the trail roughly parallels the Canadian border, affording hikers many scenic views across the Canadian and Minnesota wilderness. Before hiking east, however, you might enjoy a side trip to Bridal Veil Falls, 1.8 miles straight west of this intersection.

To begin your eastbound journey, hike along a high ridge that parallels the south shore of South Lake, 250 to 300 feet above the water. The trail is relatively level to gently rolling, permitting a quick pace in the initial stages of this long route.

After crossing Topper Creek, you cross a portage trail near the shore of Topper Lake that leads north to South Lake. Soon the path intersects a signed spur trail leading south to a developed campsite on the north shore of Topper Lake, a lovely first night's destination for those who take the side trip to Bridal Veil Falls.

At 5.7 miles into this route, a spur trail leads south from the Border Route Trail to the Mucker Lake Trail. From this point, the Gunflint Trail is just 2 miles southwest, via Forest Route 317, an appropriate point of exit for hikers enjoying an easy overnight outing or a long day hike.

Less than 0.5 mile farther, a signed spur trail leads south to Sock Lake, while the main trail leads southeast to a scenic overlook. The vista southeast across Mucker and Dunn lakes offers a clue to the type of rugged topography that lies ahead. From that inspirational point, the trail descends more than 250 feet to fringe the north shore of Mucker Lake.

The Mucker Lake Trail intersects the Border Route Trail in a grassy opening that was once the site of a sawmill. A large pile of sawdust is still visible just north of the intersection. The trail sections in this area that are wide and relatively smooth were once used as logging roads, so thank the loggers for the relatively easy going so far.

Dropping down from a high ridge, you intersect the South Lake Trail at the base of a shallow valley. From that point, it is 3.5 miles south to the Gunflint Trail and about 0.5 mile north to the east end of South Lake, where a nice campsite is tucked away in a small bay. Beyond this junction, the route climbs back up to the crest of the high ridge.

An easy-to-miss spur trail leads south from the ridge to a lovely campsite at the northeast end of Partridge Lake, but few hikers bother to seek this isolated refuge. To get there, cross a beaver dam that spans a small creek draining into the lake.

About 0.75 mile past the spur trail, you arrive at the first of several spectacular cliffs that grace the international border. Towering more than 400 feet above the narrow west end of Rose Lake, the sheer bluff affords an incredible view across Rose, Rat, South and North lakes and miles of woodland wilderness. It's a grand place to catch your breath and prepare for the more difficult terrain ahead.

After climbing over the summit of a 2000-foot peak (your highest point thus far—nearly 500 feet above Rose Lake), descend abruptly into the valley of a creek that drains Duncan Lake into Rose Lake. There you cross Stairway Portage, a path used by hundreds of canoeists every summer. Before proceeding east, hike down the first set of wooden stairs to view a picturesque waterfall that has been photographed almost as often as the vista from above the falls.

After crossing the creek on a narrow wooden bridge, you begin a long and sometimes steep climb to the famed cliffs overlooking Rose Lake. About 0.25 mile east of the Stairway, watch for a spur trail that leads steeply upward to the top of the bluff, where you'll be rewarded with a breathtaking panorama.

You may also see a trail that spurs off to the south. Recently constructed to provide a more direct route to Stairway Portage and the palisades, the Split Pine Trail leads 3 miles south to County Road 65 at the northwest corner of Hungry Jack Lake.

East of the cliffs, is a long, steep downhill stretch that uses switchbacks to arrive at the shore of Rose Lake. There, three campsites near the lakeshore have been developed for backpackers (although two are also accessible to canoeists).

After skirting the south shore of Rose Lake for more than a mile, the Border Route Trail joins the northwest end of the Long Portage, 15.4 miles from the Loon Lake trailhead, and follows the course of a small creek leading east to Rove Lake. The first part of the portage trail is relatively smooth and wide, using the abandoned route of an old railroad that served logging operations in this area.

About 1.5 miles farther, watch for the signed junction of the trail to Rove Lake. The wider trail continues southbound to Daniels Lake, exits the BWCAW and eventually reaches County Road 66, 3.4 miles away, a good ending point for a two-day trek that spans more than 20 miles from Loon Lake. The trail leading east to Rove Lake is narrower, hillier and rougher than the old railroad grade to Daniels Lake.

Upon reaching the west end of Rove Lake, the Border Route Trail veers south from the portage trail and closely parallels the south shore of the lake for more than a mile on a rocky, rooty path. It then turns south and climbs steeply through a narrow hollow, past a field of talus boulders, to an intersection at the crest of the ridge separating Watap and Clearwater lakes.

A spur trail continues southbound, leading to a small, developed campsite on the north shore of Clearwater Lake, about 0.25 mile past the intersection. It commands a nice view of Clearwater Lake.

Turn left at the intersection and proceed along the highest ridge of the entire route, at one point reaching 2050 feet above sea level. During the next 4 miles, you'll enjoy several spectacular views in all directions from the ridge, the first atop west-facing cliffs that stand 350 feet above Watap Lake. The trail then crosses to the south side of the ridge, where there is a less spectacular view toward Clearwater Lake. Finally, a breathtaking vista toward the east encompasses both Clearwater and Mountain lakes, as well as a vast part of the wilderness on both sides of the Canadian border.

From the last overlook, the trail descends in a loop that passes beneath the cliff and then continues gradually down to intersect a portage trail connecting Mountain and Clearwater lakes, 23 miles into the route. Drinking water is easily available from both lakes, 0.13 mile downhill in either direction.

After crossing the portage, climb steeply to another panoramic vista at the brink of a sheer, west-facing cliff. The trail then leads northeast, first along the wooded edge of the bluff, then farther inland. It's a lovely ridge, covered with large, mature white, red and jack pines.

At the east end of Clearwater Lake, follow the path of a well-traveled canoe portage for just over 0.5 mile to a signed junction near the west end of West Pike Lake. At that point, the trail turns right, crosses a creek and angles southeast to the north shore of Gogebic Lake. Looping around the west end of the lake, the trail passes a couple of user-developed campsites before entering a USFS developed site on the northwest shore of the lake, 26.7 miles from the trailhead.

After skirting the west end of the lake, the trail climbs over a low hill and then crosses a beaver dam at a pond draining into Gogebic Lake. From there, climb nearly 500 feet to the crest of a ridge that provides some of the most rugged landscape encountered thus far. Don't expect a rapid pace, as you encounter several steep ascents and descents, but along the way, you'll be treated to several nice views across Gogebic and West Pike lakes.

A portage trail connecting West Pike and Pine lakes is intersected at the base of a steep hill, 32 miles into the route. South 0.75 mile is a campsite at the north shore of Pine Lake. If you need a resupply of water, the 0.25-mile hike north to West Pike Lake is the most convenient source.

The Border Route Trail continues across rolling terrain with no noteworthy vistas for several miles. The hills are not as steep, and there are longer stretches of nearly level landscape as you progress farther east.

At a junction with the portage trail connecting McFarland and East Pike lakes, bear left and follow the portage downhill to near the south shore of East Pike Lake. As the lake comes into view and the portage begins its steepest descent, the Border Route Trail branches off toward the east, where it follows a fairly level ridge about 100 feet above the lake. One mile east of the portage, the trail goes up a 120-foot hill, then loops toward the southeast and begins a long, gentle decline along a ridge that eventually parallels the southwest shore of John Lake.

After a long stretch without any exceptional viewpoints, a sparsely wooded hillside affords a fine overlook toward the south end of John Lake, your last panoramic view in the BWCA Wilderness. From that point, the trail bends south, drops off the ridge, exits the BWCAW and gradually descends through a moist forest of cedar trees. Upon intersecting a private gravel road, bear left for about 50 yards to its junction with another road. Turn left again and you'll soon come to the wooden bridge that spans the creek draining McFarland Lake into Little John Lake.

The small parking lot just east of the bridge marks the trailhead for BWCAW Entry Point 83, 40 miles from the Loon Lake trailhead, the end of a delightful four-to-five-day trek on that part of the Border Route Trail contained fully within the Wilderness.

Nearby, the trail re-enters forest on the north side of the road and begins its journey into Grand Portage State Forest. The trail first leads northeast, ascends a small hill and then loops toward the south. About 1 mile from the trailhead is a steep, 300-foot climb to a ridge that affords outstanding views across the Royal River valley and South Fowl Lake to the east. After a steep dip through a trough in the ridge, the trail climbs back to the summit of a hill that towers nearly 400 feet above the south shore of South Fowl Lake, then angles toward the southeast and descends into the Pigeon River valley.

Along the turbulent 1-mile stretch of the river just south of South Fowl Lake, are two developed campsites. Beyond the second site, the trail leads straight south, away from the river, crosses the Stump River and continues south through a low, wet, relatively level region. Two miles farther, a developed campsite sits at the point where the trail crosses Portage Brook, flanked on the south by a high ridge.

About 0.75 mile past the campsite is the junction with the Otter Lake Trail, which leads 1.6 miles southwest to the Swamp Lake Road. After crossing the brook, hike southwest and climb to another high ridge that yields several panoramic overlooks. This is the newest part of the Border Route Trail; it receives very little use and, in the past, infrequent maintenance.

This part of the trail ends at the Swamp Lake Road where it crosses the Swamp River, the easternmost trailhead for the 55-mile uninterrupted part of the Border Route Trail that lies in Superior National Forest. If you wish to continue hiking all the way to Lake Superior through Grand Portage Reservation, contact the Minnesota Rovers Outing Club, P.O. Box 14133, Dinkytown Station, Minneapolis, MN 55414.

Eagle Mountain Trail (Map 9)

Length:	9 miles (one way)
Hiking time:	1 to 2 days
Difficulty:	Moderate to difficult
Elevation differential:	560 feet
Use level:	Light to moderate
Highlights:	The highest point in Minnesota
BWCAW Entry Points:	78 (northwest end) and 79 (southeast end)
BWCAW quota:	2 (one at each end)
USGS Maps:	Mark Lake, Eagle Mountain, Brule Lake; Fisher —F-6

The highest peak in Minnesota (elevation 2301 feet), Eagle Mountain is a worthy destination for day-hikers as well as campers, with its outstanding view across Superior National Forest, including a chain of small lakes that compose the upper flowage of the Cascade River.

The most heavily used part of the trail is the 3-mile segment from Forest Route 153 to the summit of Eagle Mountain, a trek that takes a minimum of three to four hours. This part of the trail is well maintained and easy to follow. Thirty-seven BWCAW visitor permits were issued during the summer of 1987 to overnight users of the Eagle Mountain Trail; 78 percent of the visitors began at the south end. If you're planning a trip during the peak season of late summer and early autumn, a reservation is necessary to ensure a permit.

To reach Entry Point 79, from Highway 61 at Lutsen, drive 18 miles north on County Road 4 to its junction with Forest Route 153. Turn right and drive 3.8 miles east on F.R. 153 to the junction with Forest Route 158. The parking lot is on the north side of this intersection.

To reach Entry Point 78, follow directions above, but turn *left* at the junction of County Road 4 and Forest Route 153. Drive 1.5 miles west to the Brule Lake Road (Forest Route 326). Turn right and drive 4 miles north to the signed trailhead. A large parking lot is available 0.5 mile north of the trailhead at the Brule Lake landing.

From the parking lot adjacent to F.R. 153, the trail begins on a rough, rocky path that winds through a forest of spruce, birch and balsam fir. About 1 mile from the parking lot, the trail enters the BWCA Wilderness. You cross three creeks and boggy areas during the first 2 miles, but all of the wet areas are planked. After the third crossing, the forest habitat abruptly changes to birch, and the trail leads west to the south shore of Whale Lake.

The trail meets the lake at a small opening with a good view north across the lake toward a steep hill just east of Eagle Mountain. The trail continues to skirt the south shore of Whale Lake, passing through a large clearing at the southwest corner of the lake, the site of an old logging camp. The remains of an old cabin can still be seen near the right side of the trail. A developed campsite is located nearby.

At the northwest corner of the lake, 2.3 miles from the trailhead, the trail splits. The left branch leads northwest and steadily ascends to the summit of Eagle Mountain, nearly 500 feet above Whale Lake. The views from the bluffs are spectacular: Crow, Eagle, Shrike and Zoo lakes can be seen to the west; the Misquah Hills are to the north; and the Brule Lake lookout tower is to the northwest. On a clear day, you may even be able to see Lake Superior toward the south. Follow the rock cairns up from the southwest bluffs to the summit. A metal plaque imbedded in rock commemorates the "rooftop" of Minnesota. Camping is not permitted on the peak.

From the junction at the base of the mountain, the trail to Brule Lake veers north, leading away from Whale Lake. Just beyond the junction, a spur leads to another developed campsite on the northwest corner of the lake. Paper birch and aspen dominate the wooded landscape.

The trail from Whale Lake to Brule Lake passes through several boggy areas, and windfalls often clutter the route. This section is no longer maintained by the Forest Service, so approach it with caution. From the northwest corner of Whale Lake, the trail leads north through a deep valley east of Eagle Mountain. As it swings northwest, the trail borders the west side of a large swampy area before climbing to higher ground. After crossing Ball Club Creek, the trail angles northwest toward the south shore of Fishhook Lake, 4 miles from the parking lot. From that point on, the trail crosses a rolling landscape and skirts the south shores of three small lakes and ponds.

Near the west end of the trail, a spur trail leads south to the Brule Lake lookout tower, the only one in Superior National Forest. Beyond the spur, the main trail goes west a short distance to Forest Route 326. The Brule Lake parking lot is 0.5 mile to the north.

DAY HIKES

Forty-five signed and maintained trails totaling 88.5 miles are suitable for day hikes in the Forest. Only 12 of them penetrate the BWCA Wilderness. Countless miles of portage trails, old logging roads, ski trails and snowmobile routes also lend themselves to short hikes. For all practical purposes, the opportunities are unlimited.

Although the name of the appropriate USGS map is included with the introduction to each trail, please understand that very few of these trails are shown on the USGS maps. In most cases, the only maps that show these short routes are in the USFS Recreational Opportunity Guides (ROGs). The ROGs, however, do not reveal topographic details. For the clearest "picture" of what to expect, therefore, you may want to carry both.

LAURENTIAN DISTRICT

Nine short trails, from 0.25 to 4 miles, have been identified in the south-ernmost district of Superior National Forest. Most are short, not difficult, and suitable for the whole family. None enters the BWCA Wilderness. The only two "fitness trails" in the Forest are located here, one near Hoyt Lakes and one near Virginia. In addition to the trails described below, you may also want to explore parts of the Big Aspen Ski Trail, the Bird Lake Ski Trail north of County Road 569 (see Chapter 5) and the Taconite State Trail. Though designed for, and used mainly by, winter recreationalists, many parts of all three trails are suitable for hiking. Furthermore, the 4.3-mile loop around Otto Lake (see "Otto–Harris Lakes Trail" in this chapter) provides an ideal day trip for hikers.

Big Lake Trail (Map 15)

Length:	2 miles (one way)
Hiking time:	2 to 4 hours
Difficulty:	Easy to moderate
Highlights:	Stone and Big lakes
USGS maps:	Babbitt SE, Babbitt SW

Lightly used Big Lake Trail follows the north shore of Stone Lake, and then leads northeast to Big Lake. Big Lake is noted for its northern pike population, while Stone Lake is well known for its wild rice.

From the corner of County Roads 100 and 110 in Aurora, drive 4.4 miles east on C.R. 110 to the stop sign in downtown Hoyt Lakes. Continue straight ahead on County Road 565 for 1.5 miles to its junction with County Road 569. Turn right and drive 4.8 miles southeast on C.R. 569 to the junction of Forest Routes 120 and 128. Continue straight on F.R. 120 for 7.7 miles to a T intersection. Turn right and drive 0.3 mile to a small parking area at the road's end.

From the parking lot, a newer trail leads southwest to a junction with an older trail. To the right is a 0.25-mile portage to Stone Lake. The trail to Big Lake (left) parallels the northwest shore of Stone Lake on a low ridge above the lakeshore. Near the midpoint, however, the trail drops through a boggy area with boardwalks and corduroy. Just before Big Lake, cross a railroad track. Alongside it is a three-wheeler path that accesses Big Lake from the south. From the tracks to Big Lake, a distance of less than 0.25 mile, the trail is much wider and smoother, but heavily used by ATVs. Boats are anchored at the southwest end of Big Lake.

Beyond the boat access, the trail crosses a marshy area on a board bridge and then skirts the northwest shore of Bungalow Bay, where there are two dispersed campsites. An Adirondack shelter is at the closer site.

Although the trail is not too difficult, it is probably not suitable for families with small children. Quite a few ATVs visit the lake on the railroad right-of-way.

Longyear Physical Fitness Trail (Map 14)

Length:	0.25 mile (one way)
Hiking time:	10 to 20 minutes
Difficulty:	Easy
Highlights:	Longyear drill site, exercise stations
USGS map:	Allen

Eight exercise stations designed to accommodate 14 different exercises line the trail, which leads to the site of the first diamond drilling rig on the Mesaba

Big Lake Trail

Iron Range (see "Longyear Drill Site" Chapter 6). Each station is designed for both beginners and longtime exercise buffs, and signs clearly define the regimen to be followed.

From the corner of County Roads 100 and 110 in Aurora, drive 4.4 miles east on C.R. 110 to downtown Hoyt Lakes. Turn left at the stop sign and continue on C.R. 110 another 3.3 miles to the USFS Firefighters Fitness Trail on the right side of the road.

Visitors can jog or walk at their own pace, utilizing the stations as they wish.

Lookout Mountain Physical Fitness Trail (Map 13)

Length:	0.5 mile (one way)
Hiking time:	15 to 30 minutes
Difficulty:	Easy
Highlights:	Exercise stations
USGS map:	Virginia

Straddling the Laurentian Divide, this scenic trail consists of 14 exercise stations along a 0.5-mile jogging path. Signs at each station describe and illustrate each exercise (including chin-ups, sit-ups, parallel bars, etc.). The trail is ideal for individual or group training, and offers safe, healthful exercise, regardless of your age or condition. Progress at your own rate and do as many or as few repeats as you wish, or simply jog the trail and ignore the exercises altogether.

The Lookout Mountain Physical Fitness Trail begins at the Laurentian Divide Picnic Area, 3 miles north of Virginia along Highway 53.

The trail is a popular place for leisurely walks, especially in autumn, when the leaves change colors. It connects with several miles of scenic paths used by cross-country skiers in winter (see "Lookout Mountain Trails" in Chapter 5), as well as the Laurentian Snowmobile Trail.

North Dark River Hiking Trail (Map 12)

Length:	1.3 miles (one way)
Hiking time:	1 hour
Difficulty:	Easy
Highlights:	50-year-old jack pine forest
USGS map:	Dark Lake

This short trail is well suited for families with small children. There is evidence of beaver activity both along the trail and in the river. In late spring and early summer, moccasin flowers beautify the landscape.

From the junction of Business Route 169 and Highway 73 in downtown Chisholm (17.5 miles west of Virginia via Highway 169), drive 15.5 miles north on Highway 73 (right) to County Road 688. Turn right and 0.8 mile to the trailhead, just beyond the Dark River Bridge.

The trail parallels the Dark River, a state-managed trout stream, on an elevated ridge 50 feet above the water. Most of the terrain is level to gently sloping, with only one short dip through a small ravine. Hikers can see across the river valley at many points along the trail, but the river itself may be obscured by dense alder brush and other wetland shrubs.

The trail eventually joins a smooth, grassy forest road that returns in a straight path back to County Road 688. On the right side of the road is a plantation of young Norway and jack pines, while on the left is a narrow strip between the road and the river on which the tall jack pines were planted back in 1939.

Pfeiffer Lake Trail (Map 13)

Length:	3 miles of short loops
Hiking time:	1½ to 2½ hours
Difficulty:	Easy
Highlights:	BWCAW-type campsites
USGS maps:	Lost Lake, Biwabik NW

The trail is mostly level, and parts may be wet at times. It's easy enough for the whole family to enjoy, and afterwards, everyone can enjoy a refreshing swim at the campground's nice sand beach.

The trailhead is located at Pfeiffer Lake Campground. To get there from the junction of Highways 169 and 73 in Virginia, drive 22 miles north and east on Highway 169 to Highway 1. Turn left and follow Highway 1 5 miles west to Forest Route 256, which leads south (left) 1.8 miles to the campground entrance (right).

The trail begins at the boat landing in the campground and extends in several short loops along the east side of Pfeiffer Lake. One branch leads to two remote campsites, each with table, latrine and tent pads, located about 1.3 miles from the campground. Either site is a good destination for a picnic lunch.

The Taconite State Trail (see Chapter 7) can be accessed from one of the eastern loops, an extended hike for those want more, but the ground may be muddy in places. Bear left at each loop intersection, and you can't miss it.

An overlook across the Dark River valley

South Dark River Hiking Trail (Map 12)

Length:	0.8 mile (one way)
Hiking time:	1 hour
Difficulty:	Easy
Highlights:	Dark River overlooks
USGS map:	Dark Lake

The trail penetrates a mixed forest of tall jack pine, aspen, spruce and many Norway pines. The smooth path provides an easy walk for young and old alike; the landscape is generally flat to gently rolling, with only one major climb into a steep ravine near the trailhead. Part of the trail follows an old railroad grade, adjacent to a red pine plantation planted by the Civilian Conservation Corps.

From Chisholm (see directions for North Dark River Trail) drive north on Highway 73 for 13.4 miles to County Road 65. Turn right and drive 1.5 miles to Forest Route 271, a narrow one-lane dirt road that dead-ends after 1.5 miles at a DNR gate blocking the road just south of the Dark River. Turn-arounds there will accommodate several parked vehicles. A large sign marks the beginning of the trail.

After about 0.5 mile, hikers encounter the first of three small loops that swing north to overlook the Dark River valley from about 50 feet above the river's edge. Because of dense wetland shrubs along the shore, the view of the river may be somewhat obscured. Look for evidence of beaver and porcupine. Moccasin flowers are abundant here in late spring and early summer.

From that point on, the trail follows close to the shore of the river and offers several scenic vistas. At the end of the third loop, hikers must backtrack to the trailhead.

St. Louis River Hunter Walking Trail (Map 14)

Length:	4 miles (several loops)
Hiking time:	2 to 3 hours
Difficulty:	Easy
Highlights:	Ruffed grouse and whitetailed deer habitat
USGS map:	Markham NE

This trail system is an assortment of short loops and spur trails that meander through an area along the St. Louis River that is managed for ruffed grouse. The trail is wide and smooth, providing a good, easy path that leads to the river at two different locations. It is used mostly by hunters on autumn weekends.

From the corner of County Roads 100 and 110 in Aurora, drive 4.4 miles east on C.R. 110 to the stop sign in downtown Hoyt Lakes. Continue straight ahead on County Road 565 for 1.5 miles to its junction with County Road 569. Turn right and drive 1.2 miles southeast to Forest Route 130, which leads another 2 miles south (right) to Forest Route 790. Turn left and proceed 0.8 mile to the trailhead and small parking lot.

Maps are available in a box at the trailhead, and you-are-here signs mark the intersections.

Trailhead for the Dark River South Scenic Hiking Trail

Sturgeon River Grouse Management Area (Map 12)

Length:	3.5 miles of loops
Hiking time:	2 to 3 hours
Difficulty:	Easy
Highlights:	Ruffed grouse and whitetailed deer habitat
USGS map:	Dewey Lake NW

From Chisholm (see directions for North Dark River Trail) drive 13.4 miles north on Highway 73 to County Road 65. Turn left and proceed 1.9 miles west to a dirt road, turn right and drive 0.75 mile north to the parking area and trailhead.

This new trail network is composed of several loops that meander through a region managed for ruffed grouse along the west side of the Sturgeon River. The trails are virtually flat and easy enough for anyone to hike. They are mostly used by hunters during the fall grouse and deer seasons. If you're not a hunter, that's a good time to avoid the area.

Whiteface Trail (Map 19)

Length:	2.5 miles (loops)
Hiking time:	1 to 2 hours
Difficulty:	Easy
Highlights:	3 dispersed campsites, lake views
USGS map:	Markham SW

You'll find the trailhead at the Whiteface Reservoir Campground. To get there from Aurora, drive 11 miles south on Highways 100 and 99 to County Road 16. Turn left and drive 4.4 miles to Forest Route 417. Turn right and continue 2.7 miles to the road's end at the parking lot, where the trail begins. From there, the trail loops around a large peninsula at the north end of Whiteface Reservoir, southwest of the campground, picnic area and swimming beach. It passes through some big pine trees and leads to three dispersed campsites on the shore of Whiteface Reservoir. One site is at an opening in the forest where a homestead once stood, a fine destination for a picnic lunch. The longest single loop is less than 1.5 miles long and easy enough for the whole family to enjoy.

LA CROIX DISTRICT

Four trails in this district provide lovely destinations for day-hikers. They range in length from 2 to 3 miles each (one way), and all of them enter the BWCA Wilderness. Day-hikers should also consider using parts of the Herriman Lake and Astrid Lake trails (see "Overnight Trails for Backpackers" earlier in this chapter); they both offer several short loops. Several portage trails along County Road 116 are also suitable for short hikes, and easy enough for the whole family to enjoy (see BWCAW Entry Points 14, 16 and 19 in Chapter 3). Finally, there are cross-country skiing and snowmobile trails near Crane Lake and Lake Vermilion (see "La Croix District" in Chapter 5), some of which are suitable for hikers during the "off season."

Blandin Trail (Map 5)

Length:	2.7 miles (one way)
Hiking time:	3 to 5 hours
Difficulty:	Moderate
Highlights:	Wildlife habitat
USGS maps:	Shell Lake, Lake Agnes

The overgrown remnant of an old logging road, this trail is used far more often by moose than by humans. Even on a sunny summer afternoon, the trail is likely to be wet and muddy, and during June and July the bugs could carry you away. It is used mostly in winter by northern pike anglers.

From the Echo Trail, 21 miles east of County Road 24 (see La Croix District driving directions in "Paddling the Boundary Waters" in Chapter 3), drive 0.7 mile north (left) on Forest Route 467. Turn right onto an unmarked, unimproved forest road. If you don't have a high-clearance vehicle, park here. Walk or drive the remaining 0.8 mile north to a grassy clearing at the edge of the BWCA Wilderness.

The trail begins at Meander Creek, where a ditch prevents motor vehicles from entering the Wilderness, and follows grassy old Blandin Road northeast to near the south end of Lamb Lake. The path is relatively smooth and level, as it traverses a wet lowland area much of the way. About 2 miles from F.R. 467, you cross Meander Creek on a beaver dam. In another 0.5 mile, the trail bends toward the east and enters the wettest, most overgrown part of the route. Finally, it takes a sharp left and intersects the portage trail connecting Nina-Moose and Lamb lakes, 0.25 mile south of Lamb. From there, you must backtrack to the trailhead.

Big Moose Trail (Map 5)

Length:	2 miles (one way)
Hiking time:	2 to 3 hours
Difficulty:	Easy
Highlights:	Big Moose Lake, pine forest
USGS maps:	Bootleg Lake, Lapond Lake

The Big Moose Trail winds its way across a gently rolling landscape covered with jack pine, red pine and aspen. Though all but the final 0.25 mile of trail is outside the BWCAW, it ends at a Wilderness campsite on the scenic north shore of Big Moose Lake.

While the trail can be hiked in half a day, it is also an excellent overnight route for families with young children or backpacking neophytes who want to take it easy on their first outing.

The trailhead is located 62 miles northeast of Cook. From County Road 24 (see La Croix District driving directions in "Paddling the Boundary Waters" in Chapter 3), drive 24 miles east on the Echo Trail to Forest Route 464, turn right and proceed 1.5 miles south to the signed trailhead (left) and small parking area (right).

The trail first passes through a recently logged area and crosses a couple of logging roads. (It's somewhat confusing and the path may be difficult to see.) After crossing the second road, you'll enter lovely forests of jack pine and then birch. Watch for rock cairns marking the way. As you approach Big Moose Lake, the trail skirts the east side of a large grassy pond with dead snags—good nesting and roosting sites for wildlife. The path then follows the crest of a low, rocky ridge before bending sharply to the right.

The quiet campsite on Big Moose Lake sits in a beautiful stand of Norway pines on a rocky shoreline with a southwest exposure. The developed site has sufficient space for two or three tents.

Norway Trail (Map 5)

Length:	2.5 miles (one way)
Hiking time:	3 to 5 hours
Difficulty:	Moderate
Highlights:	Large Norway pines, Trout Lake
USGS maps:	Astrid Lake, Bootleg Lake

Originally part of an 8-mile Forest Service trail connecting County Road 116 with a fire watchtower, the Norway Trail now provides a lovely route to the

North Arm of Trout Lake. (Timber sale activity south of F.R. 471 may change the trailhead in the future, bringing it even closer to Trout Lake.) The final 0.5 mile is part of the BWCA Wilderness. There are no developed campsites anywhere along the trail, and the terrain is challenging enough to discourage small children or people who have difficulty walking.

The trailhead is located 55 miles northeast of Cook. From County Road 24 (see La Croix District driving directions in "Paddling the Boundary Waters" in Chapter 3), drive 12.3 miles east on the Echo Trail to Nigh Creek Road (Forest Route 471). Turn right and continue 6 miles south to the signed trailhead.

The trail begins on a ridge above the south side of Norway Creek and extends 1.5 miles southwest into a stand of magnificent old Norway (red) pines that once sheltered a ranger cabin. You can see where the old trail leads up the rocky ridge to the former site of the fire lookout tower, and you may see telephone wire and insulators in the area. After crossing a beaver drainage, the trail enters the BWCA Wilderness and finally ends at the northern tip of Trout Lake.

Pine Lake Trail (Map 5)

Length:	2.5 miles (one way)
Hiking time:	2 to 3 hours
Difficulty:	Easy
Highlights:	Bear Creek, Pine Lake
USGS map:	Chad Lake

When the water level is high—in spring or after heavy rains—Bear Creek may swell to a roaring rapids, and could be difficult, if not impossible, to cross, since there is no bridge. The creek is easy to cross during normal water.

From downtown Tower (see La Croix District driving directions in "Paddling the Boundary Waters" in Chapter 3), drive 10 miles east on Highway 1/169 to the junction with County Road 408. Turn left and follow the Mud Creek Road 9 miles northwest to its end at the entrance to Glenwood Lodge. The trailhead is alongside the resort's metal storage building, just west of the entrance.

The user-maintained trail leads north from Glenwood Lodge, enters the BWCA Wilderness, crosses Bear Creek and terminates at the south end of Pine Lake. Along the way, you'll enter a nice stand of red pines and see a few giant, old white pines, but most of the forest is a mixture of second-growth aspen and spruce. Several spur trails lead off from the main trail, and intersections are not signed. Backtrack from Pine Lake.

KAWISHIWI DISTRICT

Four trails are designated for day-hikers in the north-central part of Superior National Forest, ranging in length from 1 mile to 5.5 miles. Two enter the Boundary Waters; all offer a special look at some unique aspect of the Forest. Day-hikers may also want to consider all or parts of the Angleworm and Cummings Lake trails (see "Overnight Trails for Backpackers" earlier in this chapter). When it's snow-free, the North Arm Ski Trail (see Chapter 5) provides a splendid network of trails across lovely pine-covered, rocky ridges adjacent to the Slim Lake Trail. The Taconite Trail, a state multiple-use trail designed primarily for snowmobiling (see Laurentian District in Chapter 7), also offers a good, smooth path across a gently rolling landscape. Finally, don't overlook the portage trails in this district (see BWCAW Entry Points 6, 22, 26, 32, 33 and 77, as well as Agassa Lake, in Chapter 3).

Bass Lake Trail (Map 6)

Length:	5.5 miles (loop)
Hiking time:	3 to 5 hours
Difficulty:	Moderate
Highlights:	Dry Falls, ledge rock vistas, Bass and Low lakes
USGS maps:	Shagawa Lake, Ely

Prior to 1925, the surface of Bass Lake was 55 feet higher than it is today, separated from Low Lake by a high ridge of glacial gravel. In 1925 the ridge washed out, and in just 10 hours Bass Lake shrank to about half its original size, creating Dry and Little Dry lakes at the southwest end of the former Bass Lake.

Parts of this trail pass over what was once lake bottom, where more than 250 acres of land demonstrate primitive plant succession and forest invasion. Compare the vegetation in the valley that was once under water, with that in the highlands, which have always been dry: where the trail drops off, cedars grow out of what used to be the rocky lakeshore, birch and balsam fir are the dominant species in the valley, red and jack pines blanket the ridge. Along the path are many rare plants and at least one very poisonous mushroom—fly agaric—so stay on the marked trail and don't disturb them. None of this area lies in the BWCA Wilderness. Much of the the Bass Lake Trail is nearly level or gently rolling, but there are several steep hills. The only reliable sources of drinking water along the trail are at Dry Falls and the northeast end of Bass Lake.

From County Road 88 (see Kawishiwi District driving directions in "Paddling the Boundary Waters" in Chapter 3), drive 2.6 miles north on the Echo Trail (County Road 116) to the signed trailhead and parking lot on the right side of the road.

The route starts at the parking lot and makes a large circle around Bass Lake. It begins by following a canoe portage on a down-sloping path for 0.13 mile to an intersection. Go left, descending steeply to the old lake bottom. The trail crosses a creek, then climbs steeply to a rocky ridge nearly 100 feet above the creek. Look for blueberries and raspberries here from late July through early August.

One mile from the trailhead, the trail drops steeply to a bridge that crosses a creek connecting Dry and Bass lakes. Dry Falls, a small cascade below the bridge, provides a lovely place for a picnic or an afternoon swim.

Beyond the bridge, the trail crosses a canoe portage and ascends into an elegant stand of Norway pines. A post with a tepee on it marks a spur trail to two campsites on Bass Lake. After skirting the north shore of Dry Lake, you emerge from the old lake bottom and climb to a high bald ridge with a nice overlook across Bass Lake. Rock cairns mark the route.

A campsite located in a grassy meadow near the northeast end of Bass Lake marks the midpoint of this loop. Beyond it, the trail crosses the gravel washout area that separates Bass and Low lakes. On a hot day, this is a great place for a refreshing swim, but watch out for a patch of poison ivy at the west end of the portage. At the east end of the washout area, the trail loops back toward the south, crosses a bridge and follows a high ridge above the south shore of Bass Lake back to the portage.

Hegman Lakes Trail (Map 6)

Length:	1 mile (one way)
Hiking time:	1 to 2 hours
Difficulty:	Easy
Highlights:	Old pines and lovely lakes
USGS map:	Angleworm Lake

One of the most vivid displays of ancient Indian rock paintings (pictographs) in the Quetico-Superior region adorns the cliffs between North Hegman Lake and Trease Lake. Unfortunately, this attraction is not accessible to summertime hikers—the only way to see them is by canoe. Nevertheless, this popular trail leads to two of the loveliest lakes in the Boundary Waters.

From County Road 88 (see Kawishiwi District driving directions in "Paddling the Boundary Waters" in Chapter 3), drive 10.8 miles north to the parking lot and trailhead for the South Hegman Lake portage. From the parking lot, a wide, smooth, well-beaten portage leads 0.25 mile down a gradual slope to the southwest corner of South Hegman Lake and an impressive stand of pines. Just before the portage reaches a log stairway leading down to the lake, it intersects a more obscure trail that goes north to the south shore of North Hegman Lake. This 0.75-mile trail is not used nearly as often as the portage, and may be hard to see when the summer foliage forms a canopy over it. The path passes through a scenic pine forest on level to gently sloping terrain, and ends at a rock outcrop adjacent to the creek connecting North Hegman and South Hegman lakes. It's a fine location for a picnic.

Secret and Blackstone Lakes Trail (Map 7)

Length:	3 miles (including one loop)
Hiking time:	2 to 4 hours
Difficulty:	Easy, moderate and difficult
Highlights:	Technical rock-climbing site on Ennis Lake
USGS map:	Snowbank Lake

This small trail system offers three distinctly different trails that branch off in three directions: the Flash Lake portage, the Blackstone Lake loop and the Ennis Lake trail. Built in 1981 by a crew of deaf Youth Conservation Corps folks, it receives moderate traffic throughout the summer, mostly Moose Lake cabin owners, rock climbers and the Boy Scouts, who have a High Adventure base there.

From the Ely Chamber of Commerce, drive 16.5 miles east on Highway 169 and the Fernberg Road (County Road 18). Turn left onto the Moose Lake Road (Forest Route 438) and drive 2.5 miles north to the trailhead on the right side of the gravel road. A parking lot is located at the Moose Lake public landing, 0.25 mile north of the trailhead.

The Flash Lake portage junction is 0.1 mile east of the trailhead, and continues eastbound for a total of 0.8 mile to the west bay of Flash Lake. This trail is the easiest of the three and it receives the most traffic.

Leading south from the portage is the trail to Blackstone, Secret and Ennis lakes. Skirt the edge of a grassy beaver pond, cross two small creeks, then ascend to the junction with the Blackstone Lake loop. This 1-mile loop leads north, crosses Blackstone Creek and veers east to pass along the scenic north shore of

Climbers from Voyageur Outward Bound on the cliffs at Ennis Lake

Blackstone Lake. Hiking is easy, through a lovely stand of Norway pines. A beaver dam at the east end of the lake bridges another creek, then the trail swings back toward the west and skirts the north shore of Secret Lake before rejoining the trail to Ennis Lake.

A nice campsite sits in a stand of jack pines on the west shore of Blackstone Lake, accessible via a short spur trail about midway between the two junctions of the Blackstone loop. It's an easy overnight destination for families with small children or for neophytes.

The Ennis Lake trail continues for 0.9 mile beyond the second Blackstone Lake loop junction. The rugged, rocky path passes over two steep ridges and provides scenic overlooks across beaver ponds and small lakes, penetrates a forest of birch and aspen and ends at the top of a dramatic cliff overlooking Ennis Lake.

A box latrine sits at the top of the ridge, with several undeveloped sites for camping nearby. It's a long way down to the water, so carry drinking water to this spectacular picnic site. The cliff is also a playground for technical rock climbers—the best site in the Ely area.

Slim Lake Trail (Map 5)

Length:	1 mile (one way)
Hiking time:	1 to 2 hours
Difficulty:	Moderate
Highlights:	Old Baldy, Slim Lake
USGS map:	Shagawa Lake

This short hiking trail is part of a much larger network—the North Arm Trails, constructed for cross-country skiers (see Chapter 5).

From County Road 88 (see Kawishiwi District driving directions in "Paddling the Boundary Waters" in Chapter 3), drive 8.8 miles north to the junction of County Road 644. Turn left there and follow the North Arm Road 3.5 miles west to a parking lot on the right side of the road, across from the entrance to Camp Northland.

There are actually three routes to the south end of Slim Lake. The Indian Rock Ski Trail skirts the base of a ridge running northeast from the trailhead. As it approaches Slim Lake, it joins the Slim Lake Ski Trail for the final stretch down to the shore of Slim Lake.

The most interesting (and oldest) route to Slim Lake is the original Slim Lake Hiking Trail. It's the most rugged route, crossing a high ridge en route to the lake. Since several trails intersect it along the way, it may be a bit confusing to follow.

About 0.25 mile from the trailhead, a signed intersection marks a split in the trail. The right fork is the Slim Lake Ski Trail, while the left fork is the Slim Lake Hiking Trail. Old red blazes on trees mark the original hiking trail, while red ribbons mark a newer trail. Both lead to the same destination. Along the way, watch for a spur trail to Old Baldy, a high rock ledge that affords a panoramic view across the North Arm of Burntside Lake.

At the base of the ridge's north slope, the old trail continues northbound to a developed campsite at the southern tip of Slim Lake. Though much of the trail lies outside the BWCA Wilderness, the campsite is in the Boundary Waters. This is a lovely place for a picnic, as well as an easy destination for an overnight outing.

ISABELLA DISTRICT

There are eight designated hiking trails in the south-central part of Superior National Forest, ranging in length from 0.25 mile to 5 miles. Four are associated with campgrounds or picnic areas, two are managed primarily for hunters, one is a short interpretive trail and only one enters the BWCA Wilderness. Ambitious hikers may also cover the entire Hogback Lake Trail network in one day (see "Overnight Trails for Backpackers" section of this chapter). Many old logging roads here offer easy trails for hikers as well as bikers (see Chapter 7). Finally, consider the portage trails used by canoeists to enter the Wilderness (see BWCAW Entry Points 84 and 67 in Chapter 3).

Arrowhead Creek Trail (Map 16)

Length:	5 miles (loop)
Hiking time:	2 to 3 hours
Difficulty:	Easy
Highlights:	Wildlife habitat
USGS map:	Sawbill Landing

The trailhead lies 7.5 miles northeast of Isabella. From Highway 1 at Isabella, drive 0.8 mile east on Forest Route 172. Turn left onto Forest Route 369, continue 5.8 miles north to Forest Route 173 and bear right at the Y intersection. Proceed east for about 0.8 mile to just beyond Arrowhead Creek, and watch for a turnoff on the right side of the road. The trail is not marked, but the creek is.

The Arrowhead Trail is approximately 5 miles of maintained old logging roads that wind through a lowland area rich with wildlife. Firm, level and open, the trail passes through an older pine plantation, some mixed forest habitat and a moist, brushy lowland area. These habitats provide food and shelter for many kinds of wildlife, including ruffed grouse, whitetailed deer and moose. During fall migrations, woodcock can be found in the moist lowlands.

Although the trail is essentially managed for grouse hunters, it is also a pleasant, easy hike for wildlife photographers and sightseers. Narrow footbridges span the Arrowhead Creek crossings to prevent any vehicle access to the trail.

Divide Lake Trail (Map 16)

Length:	2 miles (loop)
Hiking time:	1 to 2 hours
Difficulty:	Easy
Highlights:	Lakeshore scenery, birch forest, trout fishing
USGS maps:	Isabella, Cabin Lake

Constructed by the Youth Conservation Corps in 1984, the Divide Lake Trail provides an easy route through the pretty birch forest that surrounds Divide Lake. Three log benches are located at intervals where scenic views exist.

Drive 4.8 miles east from Highway 1 at Isabella on Forest Route 172 to the Divide Lake Campground on the right side of the road, where there is a small parking area. The trail begins at the south end of the portage to the boat landing by the parking lot.

The trail leads around the lake from the boat access to Forest Route 172, 0.5 mile east of the campground. Along the way, look for large patches of blue flag iris, abundant beaver chews, views of Crosscut and Tanner lakes and a family of loons. Rocky barriers at the south end of the lake serve as bridges across streams, but their main purpose is to prevent fish from migrating upstream. Near the halfway point, a spur trail leads left to a dispersed campsite at Blueberry Point, a peninsula that juts into the lake. A log swing is at a rest stop above the east shore of the lake.

At the north end of the lake, you'll be walking along the Laurentian Divide, the ridge that separates the headwaters flowing north to Hudson Bay or south to the Gulf of Mexico.

Eighteen Lake Trail (Map 16)

Length:	2.5 miles (loop)
Hiking time:	1 to 2 hours
Difficulty:	Moderate
Highlights:	Large pines, scenic overlooks
USGS map:	Sawbill Landing

Log benches are located along the trail every 0.25 to 0.5 mile; split log bridges provide easy walking adjacent to the lakeshore. Constructed in 1985 by the Youth Conservation Corps, the trail provides a scenic, quiet and sometimes vigorous hike. Look for the loons that nest here every year.

To reach the trailhead from Highway 1 at Isabella, 1 mile east of the Ranger Station, drive 0.8 mile east on Forest Route 172. Turn left onto Forest Route 369 and proceed 1.75 miles north. Turn left on the signed gravel road that leads 0.75 mile west to Eighteen Lake. You pass a camping area just before reaching the large parking lot where the trail begins.

This rolling lakeside trail climbs some steep hills with panoramic views, winds through a stand of mature red pines and skirts a swamp of huge, mossy cedar trees. Thick stands of maple and birch trees on the hillsides turn the trail into a colored corridor during late summer and early autumn. Also of interest are fire-scarred, old-growth pines, a regenerating clear-cut area, rock outcrops and patches of blueberries.

Flathorn Lake Trail (Map 16)

Length:	2 miles (loop)
Hiking time:	1 to 1½ hours
Difficulty:	Easy
Highlights:	Lakeside views, Little Isabella River
USGS map:	Mitawan Lake

Drive to the trailhead at the Flathorn Lake Picnic Grounds. From the Isabella ranger station, follow Highway 1 5.2 miles west to Forest Route 177. Turn right and proceed 0.7 mile north to the picnic grounds.

Blueberry pickers

This easy, lakeside trail begins at the north end of the picnic ground, loops around Flathorn Lake, and ends at the road to the old Environmental Learning Center. Along the route, are pine stands, hardwood-covered hills and spruce lowlands. You will also witness signs of forest fires, scenic rapids in the Little Isabella River and a variety of birds and wildflowers. Ambitious hikers can extend the hike by branching out on parts of the Flathorn-Gegoka Ski Trail, which intersects this trail (see Chapter 5).

Kane Lake Trail (Map 20)

Length:	4 miles of loops
Hiking time:	2 to 3 hours
Difficulty:	Easy
Highlights:	Grouse management area
USGS maps:	Kane Lake, Legler Lake

In this area, managed for ruffed grouse, wildlife photographers and sightseers may also see whitetailed deer and other wildlife. Wear red or blaze orange during the hunting season!

From the Isabella ranger station, drive 13.1 miles west on Highway 1 to County Road 2. Turn left there and drive 26 miles south on good blacktop to Kane Lake Road (County Road 203). Turn left and proceed 2.5 miles east to the intersection with Forest Route 107. Turn right on an old logging road that leads 0.75 mile south to the trailhead.

The Kane Lake Trail winds across a rolling landscape of aspen woods and alder brush, and crosses a beaver dam at the east end of the network.

McDougal Lake Trail (Map 16)

Length:	1 mile (loop)
Hiking time:	½ to 1 hour
Difficulty:	Easy
Highlights:	Lakeshore overlook, birch forest
USGS map:	Slate Lake E

The trailhead is located at the McDougal Lake campground. From the Isabella ranger station, drive 9.2 miles west to Forest Route 106. Turn left and proceed 0.5 mile to the campground entrance (right). The trail—signed and clearly visible—begins and ends at the parking lot next to the boat landing.

This short nature trail provides an easy hike through a lovely birch forest and into a bog about halfway around the loop. Part of it follows the lakeshore, to a split log bench at a scenic overlook. There are many wildflowers and the remains of old-growth pines along the route.

87—Powwow Trail (Map 16)

Length:	3 miles (one way)
Hiking time:	2 to 4 hours
Difficulty:	Easy
Highlights:	Perent River, beaver ponds, wildlife
USGS maps:	Isabella Lake, Perent Lake

This is now the only day trail in the Isabella District that enters the BWCA Wilderness. Originally, a 55-mile network for backpackers was served by two

BWCAW entry points, but the eastern half of the system was abandoned in 1987. The western half—served by Entry Point 86—is described in the "Overnight Trails for Backpackers" section of this chapter.

The densest population of moose in Minnesota is found in the area around Ferne Lake, just north of the trail. A variety of forest habitats covers the rolling landscape, ranging from stands of mature pines to areas with very young seedlings, open bogs or beaver ponds.

Drive 1.5 miles east of the Isabella Lake parking lot (see Entry Point 35 in Chapter 3), where there is a turnoff large enough to accommodate only one vehicle at the end of the one-lane road. Parking is easier at Isabella Lake, but that will add 1.5 miles (each way) to your hike.

Entering the Wilderness at Entry Point 87, hike 3 miles to the picturesque Perent River, where there is a nice campsite for picnickers and overnight visitors. Wet in some places and brushy in others, the route follows an old logging road across gently rolling hills and through boggy lowlands. The wide, smooth path permits easy walking, and boardwalks and bridges have been constructed over the wettest parts of the trail.

White Pine Interpretive Trail (Map 20)

Length:	0.25 mile (loop)
Hiking time:	10 to 20 minutes
Difficulty:	Easy
Highlights:	200-year-old white pines
USGS map:	Whyte

From the Isabella ranger station, drive 13.1 miles west on Highway 1 to County Road 2. Turn left there and drive 18 miles south to the turnoff on the left (east) side of the road.

Pamphlets for this self-guided nature trail are available at the trailhead; they are coordinated with marked stations along the trail to provide natural history information. Near the parking area, a cut old-growth pine and its stump have been left for viewing. The entire hike should take no more than 15 minutes, and there is a picnic area adjacent to the trail.

TOFTE DISTRICT

There are seven designated trails for day-hikers in the Sawtooth Mountain region of Superior National Forest, ranging from 0.25 mile to 3.5 miles. Most require varying degrees of climbing, only one is truly easy. Most, however, do have good paths that receive considerable traffic well into autumn. You may also hike parts of the Superior Hiking Trail (see the "Overnight Trails for Backpackers" section of this chapter) or the North Shore State Trail (see Tofte District in Chapter 7). Although both trails are designed for extended travel, they are segmented by road crossings that provide frequent points of access. Sections of the North Shore Mountains Ski Trail are also suitable for hiking (see Tofte District in Chapter 5).

Britton Peak Trail (Map 17)

Length:	0.25 mile (one way)
Hiking time:	15 to 30 minutes
Difficulty:	Difficult

Highlights: Panoramic overlook
USGS map: Tofte

From the Tofte ranger station, drive 1.1 miles northeast on Highway 61 to the Sawbill Trail (County Road 2). Turn left there and go 2.6 miles north to the parking lot and trailhead on the right side of the road.

This short, steep trail up the side of Britton Peak begins at the north end of the parking lot and leads northeast through a maple and birch forest to a junction with the Superior Hiking Trail. The right fork leads uphill to Britton Peak. Use the resting bench about halfway up the slope—the last half of the trail is extremely steep and rocky.

At the summit, the only development is a memorial to W. L. Britton. There you'll enjoy scenic views of Lake Superior, Carlton Peak, the Temperance River valley and parts of the Sawtooth Mountain range.

Leveaux Mountain Trail (Map 18)

Length: 3.5 miles (loop)
Hiking time: 2 to 3 hours
Difficulty: Moderate
Highlights: Panoramic overlooks
USGS maps: Tofte SE, Tofte NE

This trail is especially scenic in autumn, when the surrounding maple-covered hillsides are ablaze in red-orange colors. One of only two National Recreation Trails in the Arrowhead, it was built by the Youth Conservation Corps in 1976–1978. The trail is well maintained and easy to follow, but it does have some steep slopes, so plan accordingly.

From the Tofte ranger station, drive 5.8 miles northeast on Highway 61 to Forest Route 336 (marked by a sign designating "Superior Hiking Trail"). Turn left and follow the Onion River Road 2 miles north to the parking lot on the left side of this gravel road. This is the trailhead for the Oberg Mountain Trail and the Superior Hiking Trail, as well as the trail to Leveaux Mountain.

The first part of the trail, shared with the Superior Hiking Trail, begins at the west end of the parking lot and soon crosses a flat, grassy area with scattered spruce and fir trees—a good area to watch for moose and deer, especially during the early morning hours. A half mile from the trailhead, cross the Onion River on an old bridge and begin your ascent.

The Leveaux Mountain Trail spurs off the Superior Hiking Trail at two points along the northwestern base of the mountain. Bear left on either of these paths to begin the steep climb to the summit. There are rest benches along the route. Two loops wind across the top of Leveaux Mountain, affording excellent vistas across the Sawtooth Mountains and a panoramic view of Lake Superior.

Ninemile Lake Trail (Map 17)

Length: 2.5 miles (loop)
Hiking time: 1 to 2 hours
Difficulty: Easy
Highlights: Wildlife potential
USGS map: Cramer

The trailhead is located at the Ninemile Lake campground. From the Tofte ranger station, drive 2.5 miles southwest on Highway 61 to County Road 1. Turn right and proceed 10 miles west on C.R. 1 (which turns into C.R. 8) to County Road 7, which leads 4 miles north (right) to the campground entrance. Parking space is available next to the boat landing, and the trailhead is east of (across from) the campground entrance.

This recently constructed trail, a recreational diversion for campers at the popular Ninemile Lake campground, is largely sheltered by a forest canopy and passes through a swampy area—good for bird watching.

Oberg Mountain Trail (Map 18)

Length:	2.25 miles (loop)
Hiking time:	1 to 2 hours
Difficulty:	Moderate
Highlights:	Spectacular vistas
USGS map:	Tofte NE

The summit of Oberg Mountain towers almost 1000 feet above Lake Superior and provides nine superb overlooks. One of only two National Recreation Trails in the Arrowhead, the trail there was built by the Youth Conservation Corps in 1974–75. It is well maintained and easy to follow. The gradual slope is not too difficult, but there are numerous rock cliffs and ledges at the top, so youngsters should be carefully supervised. To reach the trailhead, see directions for Leveaux Mountain Trail, above.

The trail begins at the east end of the parking lot, across the Onion River Road. You quickly ascend via a series of switchbacks. Benches are located along the route for those who need rest breaks. Near the summit, the trail forks and forms a large loop that leads to the scenic overlooks.

Fall is the best time of year to visit Oberg Mountain. The brilliant reds and oranges of the inland maple ridges are laced with the yellows and golds of aspens and birch and accented by dark green conifers. Nature's prism is made complete by the vivid blues of Lake Superior and the clear autumn sky.

Onion River Trail (Map 18)

Length:	0.5 mile (one way)
Hiking time:	½ to 1 hour
Difficulty:	Moderate
Highlights:	Scenic Onion River, trout fishing
USGS map:	Tofte

This user-developed trail parallels the scenic east bank of the Onion River. Unknown to most hikers, it is used primarily by anglers in search of the trout that inhabit the stream. The river cascades through a lovely forest of birch and spruce, highlighted by an occasional ancient white pine.

To get to the trailhead, drive 4.8 miles northeast from the Tofte ranger station on Highway 61 at the Ray Berglund State Scenic Memorial Wayside (left side of the road).

The trailhead is not easily sighted from the parking area. After climbing a steep bank on the west side of the parking lot, you'll see a small sign marking the trail. From that point on, there are no further markers or constructed pathways.

The view across Oberg Lake from atop Oberg Mountain

The trail is steep in places, leading to cliffs that afford nice views of the boiling rapids below. There are no guard rails, so keep children under close supervision.

Temperance River Trail (Map 17)

Length:	1 mile (one way)
Hiking time:	1 to 2 hours
Difficulty:	Moderate
Highlights:	The cascading Temperance River
USGS maps:	Schroeder, Tofte

This popular trail closely follows the scenic, rocky edge of the Temperance River, which cascades more than 250 feet through the Sawtooth Mountains to Lake Superior.

Drive 1.4 miles southwest of the Tofte ranger station on Highway 61 to Temperance River State Park. A parking lot is along Highway 61 next to the bridge. The trail begins on the northeast side of the highway bridge.

The first half of the trail requires a gradual uphill hike. Waterfalls and rapids squeeze through slender canyons that can be viewed from stone overlooks built by the Civilian Conservation Corps during the 1930s. The last half of the trail, part of a cross-country ski trail, levels out at the seventh overlook and continues inland to the eighth pool in the river. At a fork near the trail's end, bear left (the ski trail goes right) and you'll arrive at a small gravel beach that provides a good place to swim or to enjoy a picnic lunch.

A second, short trail on the lower side of the highway leads to the Lake Superior shoreline. Along the way, you'll be able to cross the Temperance River on a new catwalk bridge that affords a bird's-eye view of the river's confluence with Lake Superior.

White Sky Rock Trail (Map 18)

Length:	0.25 mile (one way)
Hiking time:	½ to ¾ hour
Difficulty:	Moderate
Highlights:	Scenic overlook
USGS map:	Lutsen

From the Tofte Ranger Station, drive 10.8 miles on Highway 61 to County Road 4 in Lutsen. Turn left and follow the Caribou Trail 4 miles north to the marked trailhead. All but the last 0.5 mile of road is blacktop. There is no designated parking area, so park well off to the side of the road.

The short trail climbs steadily uphill from the road to the top of White Sky Rock. Though undeveloped, it is well marked and easily followed. Panoramic overlooks are located on the edge of cliffs, and children should be kept under close supervision.

GUNFLINT DISTRICT

Thirteen trails in the Tip of the Arrowhead region, ranging from 0.25 mile to 4 miles, are ideally suited for day-hikers. Five enter the BWCA Wilderness, eight are entirely outside it. Day-hikers may also enjoy the southeast end of the Eagle Mountain Trail, from Forest Route 153 to the summit of Minnesota's highest peak (see the "Overnight Trails for Backpackers" section of this chapter). The Pincushion Ski Trail and parts of the Gunflint Ski Trail system also provide some good paths for hikers (see "Gunflint Trails" in Chapter 5). The Banadad Ski Trail, in particular, is also popular with hikers, especially grouse hunters in autumn. Furthermore, several resorts along the Gunflint Trail maintain their own networks of foot trails. And finally, two portages used by canoeists to enter the BWCAW also provide good foot trails for hikers (see BWCAW Entry Points 44 and 45 in Chapter 3).

Cascade River Trail (Map 18)

Length:	0.5 mile (loop)
Hiking time:	½ to 1 hour
Difficulty:	Easy to moderate
Highlights:	Outstanding scenery
USGS map:	Deer Yard Lake

Drive 8.5 miles southwest of the Gunflint ranger station in Grand Marais via Highway 61, to Cascade River State Park. This short trail offers some lovely scenery along the North Shore of Lake Superior. Maintained by the Minnesota DNR, it closely parallels the picturesque banks of the Cascade River, first on one side of the river and then looping back along the other side. In between, the rushing river plunges through a narrow gorge en route to its confluence with Lake Superior. A nearby campground accommodates overnight visitors.

The Upper Cascade River

Daniels Lake Trail (Map 10)

Length:	3.5 miles (one way)
Hiking time:	3 to 4 hours
Difficulty:	Easy
Highlights:	Access to the Border Route Trail
USGS map:	Hungry Jack Lake

This nearly level trail follows an old railroad grade along the southeast shore of Daniels Lake and intersects the Border Route Trail on the Long Portage connecting Daniels and Rose lakes. The right-of-way may be quite brushy in places, but the path is smooth and you can accomplish a fairly quick pace.

From the ranger station in Grand Marais, drive 27 miles north on County Road 12 to the Clearwater Lake Road (County Road 66). Turn right and proceed

4.2 miles northeast to the trailhead on the left side of the road, 0.1 mile beyond Clearwater Lodge. Parking is available at either the Bearskin Lake public access, 1 mile closer to the Gunflint Trail, or the Clearwater Lake landing, 0.9 mile farther on C.R. 66.

The trail starts along a one-lane, unimproved road that leads 1 mile west, loops around the west end of a small pond and enters the BWCA Wilderness near the south shore of Daniels Lake. The trail clings to the shoreline, passing three developed campsites. From the north end of the trail you can continue another 1.5 miles northwest along the Canadian border to the east end of Rose Lake, or you can hike 0.6 mile east to Rove Lake. Walking in either direction, you'll be on the Border Route Trail.

For a more ambitious day hike or for an overnight excursion, hike 4.1 miles west on the Border Route Trail to the Rose Lake Trail and then proceed 3 miles south to County Road 65. This outstanding 10.5-mile trek requires some exhausting climbs, but for seasoned hikers or for anyone with two days to spare, it's a loop worthy of consideration. You'll end up 8 miles from the trailhead, so be sure to have a car waiting (see directions to Rose Lake Trail in this section).

Devil Track Wild Flower Sanctuary (Map 18)

Length:	0.13 mile loop
Hiking time:	15 minutes
Difficulty:	Easy
Highlights:	Wildflowers
USGS map:	Grand Marais

Drive 5.5 miles north of Grand Marais via County Road 12, to a small parking area southwest of the Devil Track River, near Hedstrom Lumber Company.

Maintained by the Grand Marais Garden Club, the Devil Track Wild Flower Sanctuary is a good place for a leisurely walk in a lovely setting. Each flower is labeled for easy identification, and a brochure is available at the Visitor Information Center in Grand Marais.

Gunflint High Cliffs Trail (Map 9)

Length:	0.5 mile (one way)
Hiking time:	1 hour
Difficulty:	Moderately difficult
Highlights:	Dramatic view
USGS maps:	Gunflint Lake, Long Island Lake

From the ranger station in Grand Marais, drive 42 miles north and west on County Road 12 to a signed turnoff on the right that leads 0.25 mile to the "Loon Lake" landing.

This short trail begins at the boat landing and climbs 160 feet in a northwesterly direction. At the top of a sheer cliff is a breathtaking view across the west end of Gunflint Lake, more than 350 feet below, and the Canadian wilderness beyond. Part of the Gunflint Ski Trail system, the trail continues along the crest of this high ridge for about 2 miles, before descending abruptly to the south shore of Gunflint Lake. A loop is possible by returning via the Lonely Lake Trail (part of the upper Gunflint Ski Trail system—see Chapter 5) at the base of the palisade.

Honeymoon Bluff Trail (Map 10)

Length:	0.13 mile (one way)
Hiking time:	15 minutes
Difficulty:	Moderate (steep, but with steps)
Highlights:	Panoramic overlook
USGS map:	Hungry Jack Lake

From the ranger station in Grand Marais, drive 27 miles north on County Road 12. Turn right onto Clearwater lake Road (County Road 66) and follow it 2.2 miles northeast to a small parking area on the left side of the gravel road, about 100 feet beyond the entrance to the Flour Lake Campground.

This short, steep trail leads to a beautiful overlook above the east end of Hungry Jack Lake, especially nice at sunset and during the colorful autumn season. The trail forms a loop around the top of the bluff, affording vistas across Wampus Lake to the east, Hungry Jack Lake to the west and Bearskin Lake to the north. The Hungry Jack Burn of 1967 is visible to the southwest. The trail is well maintained, has steps on the steepest slopes and receives a good deal of use.

Kekekabic Trail (Map 8)

Length:	3 miles (one way)
Hiking time:	3 to 4 hours
Difficulty:	Easy
Highlights:	Paulson Mine, Bingshick Lake
USGS map:	Long Island Lake

Drive 46.5 miles northwest from the Gunflint ranger station in Grand Marais on County Road 12, to a small parking lot on the left side of the road, where there is a sign marking the trailhead.

This is the east end of the 38-mile route described in the "Overnight Trails for Backpackers" section of this chapter. The trail leads almost straight west, skirts the north shores of several ponds and Mine Lake and passes the historic site of the old Paulson Mine, about 2 miles from the trailhead. The land here is still privately owned and hikers are advised, for their own safety, not to wander from the trail.

Beyond the north shore of Mine Lake, the trail continues west to the north shore of Bingshick Lake, where there are two developed campsites. The first 2.5 miles of this trail fall outside the BWCA Wilderness, but Bingshick Lake is inside the Boundary Waters and campers must have permits (Entry Point 56).

Lima Mountain Trail (Map 10)

Length:	1 mile (one way)
Hiking time:	1 to 2 hours
Difficulty:	Moderate
Highlights:	Panoramic view
USGS map:	Lima Mountain

From the ranger station in Grand Marais, drive 20.8 miles north on County Road 12. Turn left onto Forest Route 152 and proceed 2 miles west to the junction of Forest Route 315, where there is a parking space large enough for only one vehicle. The trail begins at the junction.

This route leads to the summit of Lima Mountain (elevation 2,238 feet), where there is a panoramic view west toward the Misquah Hills. It was formerly the site of a fire lookout tower (removed in 1978), it's a good destination for hikers on a cool, crisp autumn day.

Magnetic Rock Trail (Map 8)

Length:	1.5 miles (one way)
Hiking time:	1½ to 2 hours
Difficulty:	Moderate
Highlights:	Huge rock with magnetic attraction
USGS map:	Long Island Lake

Drive 46.7 miles northwest of the Gunflint ranger station in Grand Marais via County Road 12, to the signed trailhead on the right side of the road. About 200 feet beyond it is the parking lot, which is adequate for about 10 vehicles.

This interesting trail leads to a huge rock, left stranded by the glaciers, that has a strong magnetic attraction. Relatively easy to hike, the path passes over bare rock for much of its length. One quarter mile from the trailhead, you might see signs of moose and beaver as you cross Larch Creek. The route then cuts through the Magnetic Burn of 1974—a good place to find blueberries in midsummer. Magnetic Rock is marked with a sign; be sure to bring along a compass to test the magnetic attraction.

Backtrack from here, or continue on the ski trail that goes on to the northwest corner of Gunflint Lake (see "Gunflint Trails" in Chapter 5).

Mucker Lake Trail (Map 9)

Length:	3.5 miles (one way)
Hiking time:	3 to 4 hours
Difficulty:	Moderate to difficult
Highlights:	Access to the Border Route Trail and South Lake
USGS map:	South Lake

From the ranger station in Grand Marais, drive 33.8 miles north and west on County Road 12 to Forest Route 317. Turn right and drive 0.5 mile to the east shore of Mayhew Lake, where there is pull-over parking space along the road. From there, the trail continues along the same road, but the road isn't suitable for driving in this section.

The Mucker Lake Trail follows an old logging road from Mayhew Lake east to Hoat Lake, then north to the south shore of South Lake. En route, you skirt the north shore of Hoat Lake and the west end of Dunn Lake, and then intersect the Border Route Trail 0.5 mile south of South Lake. The junction lies in a grassy opening near a pile of sawdust that was once the site of a portable sawmill used during the early 1900s. From that point, the trail descends 250 feet to a campsite on the shore of South Lake.

The easiest way back to the trailhead is to backtrack. Seasoned hikers, however, can loop west on the Border Route Trail, then turn at a spur trail that intersects the Mucker Lake Trail at the edge of the BWCA Wilderness. After skirting the north shore of Mucker Lake, the trail climbs more than 250 feet to a scenic overlook that affords a splendid view across Mucker and Dunn lakes.

Isolated campsites, like this one on Whiskey Jack Lake, are accessible only to hikers.

After following the crest of a high ridge for about 0.5 mile, watch for the spur trail that leads south and descends 150 feet to its junction with the Mucker Lake Trail.

Developed campsites are located at Hoat, Mucker and South lakes, for those who would rather stretch this loop over two days.

Northern Light Lake Trail (Map 10)

Length:	0.25 mile (one way)
Hiking time:	½ hour
Difficulty:	Moderate
Highlights:	Moose habitat
USGS map:	Pine Mountain

Drive 12.8 miles north of the Gunflint ranger station in Grand Marais via County Road 12. Watch for the signed trailhead on the right side of the road.

From the trailhead, one short trail leads down to the Brule River, which flows into Northern Light Lake. The main trail leads south and climbs to the top of Blueberry Hill, with good views in several directions. There is a wealth of wildlife in this area.

Rose Lake Trail (Map 9)

Length:	3 miles (one way)
Hiking time:	3 to 4 hours
Difficulty:	Moderate to difficult
Highlights:	Rose Lake cliffs and Stairway Portage
USGS map:	Hungry Jack Lake

Caribou Rock, a popular tourist attraction, is an easily accessible overlook that affords a beautiful vista across Bearskin Lake, less than 0.25 mile from the County Road. Recently, the Forest Service added a new trail that continues on from Caribou Rock and leads north to intersect the Border Route Trail at the famed Stairway Portage connecting Duncan and Rose lakes, formerly accessible only to day visitors using canoes.

From the ranger station in Grand Marais, follow County Road 12 north 28.7 miles to County Road 65 at Trail Center. Turn right and drive 2 miles northeast to the signed trailhead marked Caribou Rock Trail on the left side of the road.

Beyond Caribou Rock, the trail parallels the east shore of Duncan Lake along a high ridge above the water. It affords some nice overviews of Moss and Duncan lakes, and includes some steep sections that require strenuous climbing. At the Border Route Trail intersection, dramatic palisades tower more than 350 feet above the southwest shore of Rose Lake to provide an impressive view across the lake and the Canadian wilderness beyond. Nearby, at Stairway Portage, a lovely waterfall cascades next to the portage trail.

South Lake Trail (Map 9)

Length:	4 miles (one way)
Hiking time:	4 to 6 hours
Difficulty:	Moderate to difficult
Highlights:	Old pines, access to the Border Route Trail
USGS map:	South Lake

Drive 31 miles northwest of the ranger station in Grand Marais on Country Road 12, to the Laurentian Divide Overlook.

This interesting trail leads north to the southeast corner of South Lake. Along the way, you skirt the south side of Birch Lake, the east end of East Otter Lake and the southwest shore of Partridge Lake. The north half of the trail lies in the BWCA Wilderness, with impressive stands of old-growth red and white pines.

Most of the trail crosses a gently rolling landscape, ranging from forested hills to beaver ponds and lakes. After intersecting the Border Route Trail, the final 0.5 mile drops 350 feet to the shore of South Lake, where there is a campsite nestled in a lovely, small bay.

You can extend this trail to a 9-mile loop by hiking west on the Border Route Trail to the Mucker Lake Trail, and walking the final 2 miles along County Road 12 back to the trailhead. If you plan to overnight, campsites are located at Partridge and Hoat lakes, as well as two along the shore of South Lake.

Sweetheart's Bluff Trail (Map 18)

Length:	1 mile (one way)
Hiking time:	1 hour
Difficulty:	Easy
Highlights:	Views of Lake Superior
USGS map:	Good Harbor Bay

The trailhead is located in Grand Marais. From Highway 61, three blocks west of the ranger station, turn south onto Eighth Avenue West and drive until you reach the baseball field. The signed trail begins at the far west end of the cleared area.

This 1-mile nature trail affords beautiful views of the Grand Marais harbor and the Lake Superior shoreline—especially scenic in autumn, when all the trees are in full color. There are three Adirondack-type shelters along the trail.

TRAILS INDEX

The following alphabetical list is a summary of all the foot trails for hikers and skiers in Superior National Forest.

Table 10 — Trails Index

Name	District	Miles	Type	G Map	Name	District	Miles	Type	G Map
Angleworm	K	13.7	H,s	6	Big Lake	L	2	H		15
Arrowhead Creek	I	5	H,s	16	Big Moose	LC	2	H,s		5
Ashawa	LC	15	S,h	X 4	Birch Lake	K	3.8	S,h	X	15
Astrid Lake	LC	7	H,s	4,5	Bird Lake	L	18	S,h	X	14
Bass Lake	K	5.5	H	6	Blandin	LC	2.7	H,s		5
Big Aspen	L	20	S,h	X 13	Border Route	G	55	H,s		9,10,11

* The North Arm Trail was designed for cross-country skiers, but it is not machine groomed.

DISTRICT: G = Gunflint, I = Isabella, K = Kawishiwi, L = Laurentian, LC = La Croix, T = Tofte
MILES: Length in miles
TYPE: h = hikers, s = cross-country skiers; capital letter denotes primary use
GROOMED (G): Machine-groomed ski trails are marked with an X

Table 10 cont'd — Trails Index

Name	District	Miles	Type	G	Map	Name	District	Miles	Type	G	Map
Britton Peak	T	0.25	H		17	McDougal Lake	I	1	H		16
Cascade River	G	0.5	H		18	Mucker Lake	G	3.5	H,s		9
Crane Lake	LC	5	S,h	X	1,2	Ninemile Lake	T	2.5	H,s		17
Cummings Lake	K	5.8	H,s		5	North Arm	K	34.4	S,h	*	5
Daniels Lake	G	3.5	H,s		10	Northern Light	G	0.25	H		10
Dark River North	L	1.3	H,s		12	North Shore Mtns.	T	135	S,h	X	17,18
Dark River South	L	0.8	H,s		12	Norway	LC	2.5	H,s		5
Devil Track	G	0.13	H		18	Oberg Mountain	T	2.3	H		18
Divide Lake	I	2	H		16	Onion River	T	0.5	H		18
Eagle Mountain	G	9	H		9	Otto-Harris	L	11.2	H,s		19
Eighteen Lake	I	2.5	H		16	Pfeiffer Lake	L	3	H		13
Flash Lake	K	8	S,h	X	7	Pincushion Mtn.	G	15.6	S,h	X	18
Flathorn-Gegoka	I	15	S	X	16	Pine Lake	LC	2.5	H,s		5
Flathorn Lake	I	2	H,s		16	Powwow (2)	I	29.5	H		7,16
Giants Ridge	L	31	S,h	X	13	Rose Lake	G	3	H		9
Gunflint	G	86	S,h	X	9,10	St. Louis River	L	4	H,s		14
Hegman Lakes	K	1	H,S		6	Secret-Blackstone	K	3	H		7
Herriman Lake	LC	14.7	H,s		2,4	Sioux-Hustler	LC	35	H,s		2,5
Hidden Valley	K	11.2	S,h	X	6	Slim Lake	K	1	H		5
High Cliffs	G	0.5	H,s		9	Snowbank/Old Pines	K	40.5	H		7
Hogback	I	5	H		17	South Lake	G	4	H,s		9
Honeymoon Bluff	G	0.13	H		10	Stuart Lake	LC	8	H,s		5
Jasper Hills	K	22	S	X	6,7	Sturgeon Grouse	L	3.5	H,s		12
Kane Lake	I	4	H,s		20	Sturgeon River	L	22.2	H,S	X	12
Kekekabic (2)	K	38	H		7,8	Superior	T	50	H		17,18
Leveaux Mountain	T	3.5	H		18	Sweetheart Bluff	G	1	H		18
Lima Mountain	G	1	H		10	Temperance R.	T	1	H		17
Longyear	L	0.25	H		14	Whiteface	L	2.5	H		19
Lookout Mountain	L	15	S,h	X	13	White Pine	I	0.25	H		20
Magnetic Rock	G	1.5	H,S	X	8	White Sky Rock	T	0.25	H		18

FOR MORE INFORMATION

Fletcher, Colin, *The Complete Walker III.* New York: Knopf, 1984 (3rd Ed.).

Hart, John, *Walking Softly in the Wilderness.* San Francisco: Sierra Club Books, 1977.

Manning, Harvey, *Backpacking One Step At A Time.* New York: Random House, 1980 (3rd Ed.).

All three of the books listed above are comprehensive guides to backpacking, from A to Z.

Silverman, Goldie, *Backpacking With Babies and Small Children.* Berkeley: Wilderness Press, 1988. Good advice for parents who aren't about to give up the sport when the family expands.

Winnett, Thomas, *Backpacking Basics.* Berkeley: Wilderness Press, 1988. A basic primer for people who know absolutely nothing about the sport and are starting from scratch.

CROSS-COUNTRY SKIING AND OTHER WINTER SPORTS

White-frosted conifers against a blue, cloudless sky, uncrowded trails, crisp temperatures, abundant snow, a rolling landscape of pine-covered hills, spruce bogs, beaver ponds and frozen lakes, and lots of wildlife all combine to make Superior National Forest one of the finest Nordic ski regions in America. Sixteen separate cross-country ski areas with more than 450 miles of nicely groomed trails offer something for every type of skier, from thrill-seeking expert to nervous neophyte. There are also many more "natural environment trails" that are not machine-groomed and track-set, as well as hundreds of miles of lake routes and unplowed forest roads for the ski-touring enthusiast who prefers to escape from the "beaten path."

You are never likely to feel crowded—certainly not if you're accustomed to skiing on trails in metropolitan areas. Nevertheless, the winter resort and motel accommodations in this region are limited and often booked up early (sometimes a *year* in advance) for holidays and for prime weekends in January and February, so make your reservation as early as possible (see Appendix). The best option is to come midweek, when many lodges offer lower rates and there are even fewer people on the trails.

CLOTHING AND EQUIPMENT

Lovely as this corner of the world is, however, you *must* prepare yourself to confront the wilderness on *its* terms. Wearing several layers of clothing allows you to adjust to varying temperatures and levels of exertion. Wear long underwear made of silk or synthetics to "wick" moisture away from your skin. Cover it with one or more layers of wool, synthetic fleece or goose down for warmth. And protect yourself from wind by wearing a lightweight nylon windbreaker. Avoid tight-fitting clothes and boots that may restrict circulation.

For both comfort and safety, always carry extra socks and gloves or mittens, a warm cap, a spare ski tip, matches in a waterproof container, a candle, nylon cord, a pocket knife, a compass and a large-scale map of the area you plan to visit (and know how to use them!), a plastic tarp or space blanket, a first-aid kit, duct tape for repairs and a metal container for melting snow.

FOOD AND WATER

In winter, active people burn calories and dehydrate more quickly than at other times of year. Even when planning only a short day trip, carry plenty of high-energy snacks, extra food in case of emergency and a water bottle. The only available water may be what you carry with you or melt from snow. The body loses as much as 2 to 4 quarts of fluid per day under exertion. Replacement of fluid loss is imperative for maintaining good physical condition. Eating snow provides only limited water (10–20%), while draining energy and cooling the body temperature.

WINTER SAFETY

Knowledge of the area, weather, route, and the limitations of your body and equipment, along with some common sense, can help you have a safe and enjoyable outing. Consider these hints:
• Check the forecast, and don't venture out if a major storm is coming.
• Don't ski alone.
• Let someone back home (or at the resort) know where you are going and what time you expect to return.
• Guard against hypothermia (see Chapter 2, "Clothing")
• Check your companions periodically for frostbite, caused by the exposure of inadequately protected flesh to cold and wind.
• Use extreme caution when crossing lakes and rivers—layers of snow can insulate still water enough to prevent it from freezing solid. Running water and springs can also weaken ice.
• Boil, filter or treat all water before drinking.
• Make sure at least one member of your party is carrying a first-aid kit.

SPECIAL REGULATIONS

Minnesota state law requires that cross-country skiers between the ages of 16 and 64 who use non-federal public trails designated for cross-country skiing must purchase a state ski pass. Although Superior National Forest trails are on federal lands, state funds may have been used for trail development, so check with local officials or resort operators to see if a pass is needed. Passes may be purchased for a day, a year or for three years.

If you plan on ski touring within the Boundary Waters Canoe Area Wilderness, be prepared to camp overnight, and always carry emergency food rations. Most BWCAW rules apply to winter visitors (see "The Boundary Waters Canoe Area Wilderness" in Chapter 2). You may, however, camp at locations other than designated sites and build fires outside of fire grates. Although a BWCAW travel permit is not required from October 1 through April 30, it is recommended that all campers make use of the Forest Service's voluntary registration form.

SKI-SKATING

Reflecting a worldwide trend, ski-skating is growing in popularity in northern Minnesota. Many of the trails in Superior National Forest, however, are narrow,

Flathorn-Gegoka Ski Trail

tree-lined, single-tracked corridors that simply are not suitable for this type of skiing. Very few ski areas cater to skating, and some even discourage it. Many of the trails are maintained and groomed by resorts and private ski associations, working in cooperation with the Forest Service and the DNR. As a matter of courtesy, always inquire whether or not skating is permitted on any trail system before striking out.

Giants Ridge is perhaps the only ski area in northeastern Minnesota that actually encourages skating by maintaining a course that will accommodate both skaters and traditional skiers. Part of the North Shore Mountains Ski Trail is also designated for skaters. The Taconite State Trail and the North Shore State Trail provide good skating surfaces, too, but use extreme caution on them. Although designated as multiple-use trails, they were, in fact, designed for, and are primarily used by, snowmobiles. On weekends, they bear a considerable amount of traffic.

In midwinter, the hard-packed, windswept surface of a large lake provides an ideal route for ski-skaters. Similarly, in late winter and early spring, morning skiers are able to skate across the crusty snow until the sun rises high enough to transform it into soggy slush.

ALPINE SKIING

Although northeastern Minnesota has not been regarded as a mecca for downhill skiers, two excellent alpine ski areas in Superior National Forest have done much to alter that attitude.

Lutsen Mountain Ski Area is one of the Midwest's premier slopes. Located 9 miles northeast of Tofte via Highway 61 to County Road 36 and nestled among the peaks of the Sawtooth Mountains are 27 slopes and trails on four different mountains. With ski runs over a mile long, an 800-foot vertical drop and 105 inches of annual snowfall, Lutsen offers some of the best downhill skiing east of the Rockies.

Lutsen's Poplar River Trail

The Giants Ridge Ski Area (see below) also boasts some popular and exciting alpine slopes—over 60 acres, with almost half running through Superior National Forest. With a vertical drop of 450 feet, it offers skiers a choice of nine runs for all skill levels. Three high-capacity chair lifts service the slopes, and the runs are lighted for night skiing.

The Hidden Valley Ski Area is not in the same league with either Lutsen or Giants Ridge. Owned and operated by the city of Ely, and located on the east edge of town, its eight downhill runs are serviced by two rope-tows and a J-bar. The longest run is 1800 feet, with a vertical drop of 165 feet.

MUSHING

It's not yet on a par with skiing, but dogsledding is growing in popularity in northeastern Minnesota, and is more accessible to the public at large. Dogsleds are capable of negotiating the winding course of any ski trail; unfortunately, the dogs do as much damage to groomed trails as do snowmobiles. Consequently, if you're looking for a route, do *not* use the trails described below.

There are still many good routes in Superior National Forest for mushers. Unplowed forest roads are the most accessible, the least likely to cause conflicts with other winter recreationalists and they furnish an almost unlimited supply of route options. Many of the roads recommended for mountain bikers in Chapter 7 are also ideal for mushing. Use the maps in Chapter 2 to select an area that looks interesting, then contact the appropriate district office to find out which roads are currently being plowed. They vary from year to year, depending on where the active logging operations are taking place.

Most of the districts have other dogsled routes too. In the Laurentian District, the Seven Beaver Snowmobile Trail is probably the best route for mushers. The northern part of the network is used primarily by ice-fishing snowmobilers; the southern part may be abandoned if use does not increase. The northern part of the Sturgeon River Ski Trail may also be used by mushers (but the southern loop is reserved strictly for skiers). The Thomas Lake Trail, in the Kawishiwi District, leads to a popular trout lake deep in the BWCA Wilderness. For mushers who really want to escape from other people, the Forest Service recommends the Knife-Kekekabic lakes area in the central part of the BWCAW. In the Tofte and Gunflint districts, the North Shore State Trail provides a good route for dog teams, but be alert for snowmobiles.

WINTER CAMPING

Many folks who camp regard winter as the best of all seasons to enjoy the wilderness: no people, no biting insects, no bears. For anglers interested in lake trout, northern pike and crappies, winter camping is a necessary part of ice fishing. Some of the most productive lakes, particularly those with lake trout, are located far from the closest plowed road (see Chapter 8).

Even though camping is allowed anywhere in the BWCA Wilderness during the winter, and fires are not restricted to the grates, the Forest Service recommends that people camp well away from designated campsites, to avoid leaving charred logs where they might be seen by summertime visitors. Cedar swamps and black spruce bogs are among the best winter camping sites: they offer protection from icy north winds, and are inaccessible to summertime hikers and paddlers.

All other Wilderness regulations do apply to winter campers (see Chapter 2). And don't think for a moment that sleeping on frozen ground justifies cutting pine boughs for bedding. It does not! You'll be a whole lot more comfortable with a thick foam pad.

Destinations for winter campers are virtually unlimited. You're limited only by your imagination and sense of adventure. Winter is not a time for mistakes, however. Poor judgment and accidents, which might result in nothing more than inconvenience in summer, could be deadly in winter. Winter camping requires special techniques, special gear and special clothing. Do your homework before slipping on your snowshoes, or find someone with experience to accompany you on your first winter expedition (see "For More Information" at the end of this chapter).

RECOMMENDED SKI TRAILS

The trails listed below were designed for skiers. They are groomed by machines and track-set (with one exception). Other trails, ungroomed skiing trails, hiking trails (see Chapter 4), portages and unplowed logging roads also provide routes for ski-touring enthusiasts (see Table 10 for specific suggestions). Furthermore, when ice conditions are safe, there is unlimited potential for ski touring in and out of the BWCA Wilderness on the routes used by canoeists (see Chapter 3).

The map numbers following the trail names refer to the maps in Chapter 2 on which the trails are shown. These maps, however, are not meant to be used for route finding. For that purpose, use the maps supplied by the Forest Service or by the resorts associated with individual trails.

LAURENTIAN DISTRICT

Five ski areas with 167 kilometers of groomed trails lie in the Laurentian District. Except for Giants Ridge, they are used mostly by local residents. Traffic is rather heavy on weekends, but light during the week. Ski-skaters may enjoy parts of the extensive snowmobile trail network in the district, including the Seven Beavers Trail, the Laurentian Trail and the Taconite State Trail. Contact the district office for details (see Chapter 2).

Big Aspen Trails (Map 13)

> **Length:**   20 miles
> **Difficulty:** Easy, moderate, and difficult

Big Aspen offers a maze of interconnected loops that begin at the north end of County Road 405. To get there, drive 7 miles north from Virginia on Highway 53 to County Road 302. Turn right and follow C.R. 302 1 mile to County Road 68. Turn left and drive 0.3 mile to County Road 405, which leads north (right) 2 miles to the trailhead at a parking area on the left side of the road.

A large map at the trailhead enables you to plan an outing that conforms to your expertise. The landscape is decorated with Norway pines and aspen; a vast logged-over region affords a panoramic view. Part of the system utilizes old logging roads with easy grades, but there are also some steep, curving slopes that require both skill and caution. The trails are maintained by the Forest Service and

Snowshoeing on Lake Gegoka

grooming is provided by the Iron Range Resources and Rehabilitation Board (IRRRB).

Bird Lake Trails (Map 14)

Length:	18 miles
Difficulty:	Easy and moderate

Known by few people outside of Hoyt Lakes and Aurora, the Bird Lake Trail system offers something for every kind of skier. To reach it from Aurora, drive 4.4 miles east on County Road 110 to the stop sign in downtown Hoyt Lakes. Continue straight ahead on County Road 565 for 1.5 miles to Country Road 569. Turn right and proceed 4 miles southeast to the signed trailhead at a small parking area in a wide spot in the road.

Groomed and set with a single track as needed, the trail winds through both upland and lowland regions, passes through dense stands of black spruce, across flat, open bogs and undulates across birch- and aspen-covered hills. A relatively flat loop is provided for beginning skiers; another loop offers a challenge to more experienced skiers. Birch Run penetrates a pure stand of paper birch trees.

Giants Ridge Ski Area (Map 13)

Length: 31 miles
Difficulty: Easy, moderate and difficult

One of the finest cross-country ski centers in the Midwest, Giants Ridge was designed for both competitive and recreational skiers, and has hosted such notable events as the World Cup. It is located 17 miles northeast of Virginia. Drive 2 miles southeast on Highway 53 to the Highway 135 exit for Gilbert. Proceed 12 miles on Highway 135 through Biwabik to County Road 416. Turn left and drive 3 miles north on C.R. 416 to the ski area, where there is a large parking area next to the main chalet.

Trails are immaculately groomed and arranged in loops that will delight most skiers. Chair lifts to the top of the ridge enable "norpine" skiing—the luxury of skiing long downhill runs without first having to climb. A daily trail fee is charged, and rental equipment is available.

Lookout Mountain Trails (Map 13)

Length: 15 miles
Difficulty: Moderate and difficult

Straddling the scenic Laurentian Divide, this challenging trail network is composed of many short loops that interconnect to enable outings of almost any duration. The trailhead is located at the Laurentian Divide Picnic Area (see directions to Lookout Mountain Physical Fitness Trail in "Day Hikes" in Chapter 4).

A large color-coded map at the trailhead will help you plan a route. The trails traverse a variety of landscapes and lead to occasional scenic overlooks. A three-sided log shelter at the east end of the system offers a good destination for experienced skiers. The trails are maintained and groomed by the Laurentian Nordic Ski Club.

Sturgeon River Ski Trail (Map 12)

Length: 20 miles
Difficulty: Moderate and difficult

This long, scenic trail parallels the steep banks of the Sturgeon River and uses the same trailhead as the Sturgeon River Hiking Trail (see "Overnight Trails for Backpackers" in Chapter 4). For the most part, the trail is gently rolling, but the loop around Jean Lake is steep and long, and recommended only for experienced skiers. The trail is groomed by the Forest Service. Because it receives very light use, however, it ranks low in grooming priority and you might have to break trail during the first few days after a snowstorm. The 8-mile trail section that lies south of County Road 65 is exclusively for skiers, while the northern loop may be shared with mushers.

LA CROIX DISTRICT

Currently there are only 32 kilometers of groomed trails in the La Croix District, but that number will increase when the Ashawa Trail is completed. The Forest Service also recommends the Astrid Lake Trails, the Big Moose Trail, the Stuart Lake Trail and the Herriman Lake Trails. For an extended overnight winter-camping trek, you might also consider the Sioux-Hustler Trail (see "Overnight Trails for Backpackers" in Chapter 4 for details). One popular winter outing in this part of the Forest is the trek north from the Echo Trail along the Little Indian Sioux River to Devil's Cascade (see Entry Point 14 in Chapter 3). For ski-skaters, there are 110 miles of groomed snowmobile trails in the district, but use them with caution.

Ashawa Trail (Map 4)

Length: 15 miles (and growing)
Difficulty: Moderate

Parking and trail access is available at Pehrson's Lodge at the west end of Lake Vermilion and at Elbow Lake Lodge on Elbow Lake. To get to either of these trailheads, drive north from Cook on County Road 24. Pehrson's Lodge is on the right side of the road, 5 miles north of Cook, while the turnoff to Elbow Lake Lodge (left) is 13 miles north of town.

Skirting the west shore of Lake Vermilion, the Ashawa Trail is already the longest groomed trail in the La Croix District. When complete, it will consist of a 65-kilometer corridor trail around the hilly west end of Lake Vermilion with spur trails and loops adding up to a total network of 100 miles through gently rolling terrain, challenging hills and flat black spruce swamps.

The trail is groomed by volunteers from the Ashawa Trail Ski Club.

Crane Lake Neighborhood Trails (Maps 1, 2)

Length: 5 miles
Difficulty: Easy and moderate

To reach these trails, drive 9 miles north on County Road 24 from the Echo Trail junction (see the directions in "Paddling the Boundary Waters" in Chapter 3). Three different trails, ranging in length from 1 to 2 miles, connect the tiny lakeside village of Crane Lake with outlying points of interest, including the scenic Vermilion River gorge. Groomed by the local snowmobile club, the trails are generally easy enough for skiers with little or no previous experience. With prior arrangements, the club may also set a track on the nearby Herriman Lake Trails (see the "Overnight Trails for Backpackers" section in Chapter 4). Contact the Crane Lake Commercial Club (see the Appendix) for details.

KAWISHIWI DISTRICT

The five ski areas described below provide 127 kilometers of trails in the Kawishiwi District. All receive a fair amount of use on weekends, but very little through the week. Two other trails are also maintained by the Forest Service—the Angleworm Trail (*not* the hiking trail described in Chapter 4) and the Thomas Lake Trail, which leads to a popular source of lake trout. Perhaps the most popular winter trail in this district is the canoe route to the Hegman Lake pictographs (see Entry Point 77 in Chapter 3) since winter is the best time to get close to those ancient Indian rock paintings. Maps and brochures for any of these trails are available from the Forest Service in Ely. Ski-skaters might also enjoy the Taconite State Trail, which is used mostly by snowmobilers.

Birch Lake Plantation (Map 15)

Length: 4 miles
Difficulty: Easy

To reach the trail, drive 17 miles south from Ely on Highway 21 to County Road 70. Turn left there and continue 3 miles east to the signed trailhead on the left side of the road.

This easy trail meanders through the oldest plantation in Superior National Forest. Planted in 1915, the tall pines provide a lovely setting for skiers who need very little skill to negotiate the maze of interconnected loops. The trails are marked and occasionally groomed with a single track.

Flash Lake Trails (Map 7)

Length: 8 miles
Difficulty: Easy and moderate

The trailhead is located at the Charles L. Sommers National High Adventure Base, adjacent to the Moose Lake public access (see Entry Point 25 in Chapter 3).

The Flash Lake trails network is one of the busiest in the Kawishiwi District, especially on weekends. Designed for and maintained by the Boy Scout base, it is used throughout the winter for winter camping and survival training exercises. The system consists of several loops that extend from Moose Lake to Flash and Snowbank lakes and connect with the Secret–Blackstone (see "Day Hikes" in Chapter 4) and Snowbank (see "Overnight Trails" in Chapter 4) trails. The terrain is generally level to gently rolling, with a few short, steep hills for excitement. Don't count on nicely groomed trails—skiers share the network with hikers and snowshoers, who sometimes drag sleds behind them.

Hidden Valley Recreation Area (Map 6)

Length: 11 miles
Difficulty: Moderate

Hidden Valley is on the east edge of Ely, 1.5 miles east of the Chamber of Commerce via Highway 169.

Owned and operated by the city of Ely, this municipal recreation area includes a world-class 60-meter ski jump and a small alpine ski hill, in addition to the cross-country trails. The hilly terrain is a deterrent to beginning skiers, but for more experienced skiers, this easily accessible trail system should provide plenty of challenge and excitement. To help maintain and groom the system, donations are sought from trail users.

Jasper Hills Ski Area (Maps 6, 7)

Length: 22 miles
Difficulty: Moderate

Wolf tracks beside a ski trail on the Kawishiwi River

The trailhead is located at Northwind Lodge, 15 miles east of the Ely Chamber of Commerce via Highway 169 and the Fernberg Road (County Road 18). Watch for the turnoff on the left side of the road.

Started in 1984, the Jasper Hills has already become popular with experienced skiers. The trails cross a hilly woodlands, creekside marshes, cedar swamps

Dog sledding on Lake Gegoka

and frozen lake surfaces. Some exciting downhill runs will thrill an expert, but the entire network is suitable for intermediate skiers. To accommodate beginners, construction of a new 10-kilometer network of shorter, easier loops was begun in 1987. Eventually, the system will extend all the way east to the Flash Lake Trails.

The North Arm Trails (Map 5)

> **Length:** 34 miles
> **Difficulty:** Moderate and difficult

Use the trailhead for the Slim Lake Trail (see "Day Hikes" in Chapter 4).

This trail is *not* groomed and tracked by a machine, but it's simply too nice to omit. Three-hundred-year-old white pines, panoramic overlooks from high bald ridges, secluded lakes and rolling pine-covered hills add up to a memorable skiing experience for skiers with at least moderate experience. The trails are usually skier-tracked and always well maintained.

ISABELLA DISTRICT

There is only one groomed ski trail in the south-central part of Superior National Forest, but it's a fine one and you can pretty much have it all to yourself on weekdays. The Isabella District is also blessed with a plethora of unplowed logging roads that make excellent routes for ski-tourists who don't mind breaking trail (see "Isabella District" in Chapter 7 for some suggestions).

Flathorn-Gegoka Ski Touring Area (Map 16)

Length: 15 miles
Difficulty: Easy and moderate

Use the trailhead at the Lake Gegoka public access. From the Isabella ranger station, drive 6.4 miles west on Highway 1 to the access (right).

This is one of the best ski areas in northern Minnesota for beginning skiers. Made up of wide, smooth, level to gently rolling trails that, in large part, overlay old logging roads, the main corridor trail is double-tracked, while single-tracked trails veer off from it. Skiers have a choice of many loops, and all intersections are well marked. The area is blanketed by a forest that varies from tall pines to young aspen to spruce bogs, and blessed with an abundance of wildlife, including whitetailed deer and timber wolves.

TOFTE DISTRICT

The North Shore Mountains Ski Trail, the granddaddy of all cross-country ski trails in Minnesota, meanders 134 miles through the Sawtooth Mountains, paralleling Lake Superior's beautiful North Shore. Although it does extend into the southwest corner of the Gunflint District, most of it lies in the Tofte District and it falls under the auspices of the Lutsen-Tofte Tourism Association (see Ap-

Trailside shelter

pendix). Skiers are also welcome to use the North Shore State Trail, a multiple-use trail designed for and used primarily by snowmobiles. In particular, it offers a wide, smooth path for ski-skaters.

North Shore Mountains Ski Trail (Maps 17, 18)

Length:　　134 miles
Difficulty:　Easy, moderate and difficult

Access to this trail extends along a 22-mile stretch of Highway 61, from Schroeder at the southwest (3 miles southwest of the Tofte Ranger Station) end to Cascade River State Park at the northeast end (19 miles northeast of the ranger station). The best central accesses are at the Britton Peak and Onion River trailheads for the Superior Hiking Trail (see "Day Hikes" in Chapter 4).

This spectacular network is composed of several individual systems that are joined by a corridor trail roughly paralleling Lake Superior's North Shore. Several small villages along Highway 61 accommodate skiers using these trails, and numerous resorts are connected to the corridor by short spur trails from the coast to the Sawtooth Mountain highlands.

This trail system lends itself well to the concept of "norpine" skiing: with road access to the upper elevations, as much as 1000 feet above Lake Superior, you can start at one of the highest points and ski back down to the coast.

Because of the moderating effects of Lake Superior on the coastal climate, snow conditions are often poor at the lower elevations, right along the coast. At the same time, however, the Sawtooth Mountain highlands—only 3 or 4 miles inland from Lake Superior—are often blanketed with the deepest and best snow of the entire Arrowhead region.

GUNFLINT DISTRICT

The hilly region accessed by the Gunflint Trail (County Road 12) is usually blessed with an abundance of snow. In addition to the two outstanding ski areas described below, there is a nice trail for novice skiers at the George Washington Memorial Pine Plantation, 6 miles north of Grand Marais. Although the trail is not groomed, it is frequently used and almost always has a set of tracks on it. Ski-skaters might also be attracted to a snowmobile trail that parallels the Gunflint Trail. Of course, there are also many miles of lake routes that penetrate the BWCA Wilderness (see "Gunflint District" in Chapter 3), as well as unplowed logging roads adjacent to the Wilderness (see Chapter 7).

Pincushion Mountain Trails (Map 18)

Length:　　15 miles
Difficulty:　Easy, moderate and difficult

The trailhead is located 2 miles north of Grand Marais via County Road 12 at the Sawtooth Mountain overlook on the right side of the road.

This nicely groomed trail system consists of several loops that penetrate a rather hilly region overlooking Grand Marais harbor. The trails wind through a beautiful hardwood forest with some nice views of Lake Superior, distant ridges and the Devil's Track River valley. Loops vary in length from 1 to 6.8 kilometers. Though a few are suitable for beginners, most are geared to intermediate and advanced skiers. A steep trail connects the system with the village of Grand Marais below.

An incredible panorama across Gunflint Lake is the reward for experienced skiers who climb the steep trail to High Cliffs.

Gunflint Trails (Maps 9, 10)

Length: 85 miles
Difficulty: Easy, moderate and difficult

You can start from one of several trailheads along County Road 12, from East Bearskin Lake to Gunflint Lake, including Bearskin Lodge (26 miles up the Gunflint Trail from the Grand Marais ranger station), Golden Eagle Lodge (29 miles), Young's Island (30 miles), Gunflint Lodge (44 miles), Heston's County Store (46 miles) and Borderland Lodge (46 miles)—all but Young's on the right side of County Road 12.

This network consists of two major ski trail systems that are served by several fine resorts and joined by a corridor trail. Skiers may enjoy either end, or ski "lodge-to-lodge" from one end of the system to the other.

Although the Central Gunflint Trails were designed for intermediate-level skiers, there are also loops for beginners and experts. Winding through rolling hills and frozen bogs, the trail system is sandwiched, for the most part, between East Bearskin and Flour lakes, just east of the Gunflint Trail, 26 miles north of Grand Marais. Scenic overlooks, beaver ponds and some virgin white pines highlight the area.

Penetrating a corner of the BWCA Wilderness with abundant moose, the Banadad Trail is the connecting link between the Central and Upper Gunflint trail networks. Designed for lodge-to-lodge "ski-through" guests, primitive wilderness huts and a bed-and-breakfast establishment dot the route.

Snow shelter protects campers in the coldest winter weather.

Intermediate-level skiers will feel comfortable on most of the trails in the hilly region surrounding Gunflint Lake, but experts will find plenty of challenge on the steeper slopes. From atop high ridges, skiers may gaze across Gunflint Lake to the Canadian wilderness beyond. You may see moose in the western part of the network.

FOR MORE INFORMATION

Beymer, Robert, *Ski Country: Nordic Skiers' Guide to the Minnesota Arrowhead.* Virginia, MN: W.A. Fisher Company, 1986. A comprehensive guide to the entire Minnesota Arrowhead region, including winter resorts.

Brady, Michael, *Cross-Country Ski Gear.* Seattle: The Mountaineers, 1987. Good reading for anyone planning to buy his or her own equipment.

———, *Nordic Touring and Cross-Country Skiing.* Berkeley: Wilderness Press, 1979. All you need to know about skiing, from the easiest way to learn to the latest in waxing.

———, *Waxing and Care of Cross-Country Skis.* Berkeley: Wilderness Press, 1986. An essential primer on how to get the most out of your skis.

Cary, Bob, *Winter Camping.* Brattleboro, Vermont: The Stephen Greene Press, 1979.

Drabik, Harry, *The Spirit of Winter Camping.* Minneapolis: Nodin Press, 1985.

Gillette, Ned and John Dostal, *Cross-Country Skiing.* Seattle: The Mountaineers, 1986. Good information about equipment and techniques for skiing everything from tracks to backcountry.

The White Pines Picnic Area

6

CAMPING, PICNICKING AND SIGHTSEEING

The Boundary Waters Canoe Area Wilderness (BWCAW) attracts rugged, adventuresome folks who prefer to leave their amenities at home and face Mother Nature on her own terms. But not everyone enjoys carrying a 75-pound canoe across rocky portage trails to find a campsite that may not have been occupied since the Ojibway left the region. For many folks—families with small children, the physically disabled, camping neophytes and anglers who can't part with a six-pack—the "fringe" offers a much more enjoyable experience than roughing it in the wilds.

Sixty percent of the visitors to Superior National Forest do *not* enter the Boundary Waters. Of these, 37 percent use "dispersed campsites" that provide campers with BWCAW-*type* experiences, but without the regulations and isolation. To accommodate visitors who prefer to camp in comfort, the Forest Service also maintains 27 campgrounds and seven other less-developed camping areas adjacent to the most popular fishing lakes. In addition, the state of Minnesota administers six state forest campgrounds and three state parks that fall within the boundaries of Superior National Forest. All together 811 campsites are available to Forest visitors. Most are accessible by automobile, many are suitable for recreational vehicles, and unlike the campsites on the inside fringe of the BWCAW, the supply is much greater than the demand.

Every developed campsite outside the BWCAW provides acces to a wealth of recreational opportunities, including some found only in the Boundary Waters, making it possible for you to experience the best of both wilderness recreation and comfortable camping accommodations. Since you won't have to portage gear, you can bring along as many creature comforts and recreational toys as you wish.

From the security and comfort of your base camp, you can then explore different areas and enjoy different activities each day. Since permits are not required for daytime visits to the Boundary Waters, you'll have the freedom to go anywhere you wish any time you want. If the fish aren't biting or the wind is too strong for paddling, don your packsack and head for the nearest trail, or mount

McDougal Campground

your bicycle and explore the endless network of old logging roads, or pick berries. Each evening, just return to your base camp.

If you decide to venture into the Boundary Waters for a daytime outing, remember to abide by all the special regulations that apply to Wilderness visitors. For instance, even if you're not camping in the BWCAW, your group size still may not exceed 10 people, and you may not carry food or beverages in cans or bottles.

REGULATIONS

While camping in Superior National Forest outside the BWCAW, please observe the following regulations.

• Don't leave camping equipment unattended for more than 24 hours without permission by the Forest Ranger. You must pay a fee to use certain developed campsites and facilities. Such areas are clearly signed, and the fee must be paid prior to using the site, facility, equipment or service furnished.

• Within campgrounds and other recreation sites, cars, motorcycles and other motor vehicles may be used only for entering or leaving, unless areas or trails are specifically designated for them. Parking is restricted to marked parking areas.

• Picnic sites, swimming beaches and other day-use areas may be used only between the hours of 6:00 A.M. and 10:00 P.M. You may build a fire at campgrounds and other recreation sites without a permit, but only in fire grates, fire rings, stoves, grills or fireplaces provided for that purpose. Use only deadfall for fires; cutting standing timber, shrubs and other vegetation is prohibited.

• Use the water faucets only for drawing water; wash food and personal items away from drinking water supplies. Most campgrounds have wells and hand pumps that are tested periodically by Forest Service personnel for purity. Dispersed campsites do not. Always treat surface water before using it. Water from lakes and streams should not be considered safe, regardless of its clarity.

• Pets on leashes are welcome, except in swimming areas. Saddle, pack or draft animals are permitted only in authorized areas.

• Watch for special orders from the Forest Supervisor that may close or restrict certain areas when the need arises. These orders are posted in conspicuous locations.

• Camping is not restricted to developed sites outside the BWCA Wilderness. You may also camp at locations without facilities such as toilets and firegrates. To ensure a quality experience for yourself and other visitors, and to protect the environment and minimize the evidence of your visit, make sure you camp at least a quarter mile from developed sites or other groups and at least 100 feet from trails, portages, lakeshores and streams; dispose of wastes at least 150 feet from lakes and streams; and pack out all trash. Use a gas stove for cooking to minimize fire hazards.

CAMPGROUNDS

Campgrounds range from as few as two sites to as many as 67 sites. Designed for privacy, individual sites are spaced generously and separated by trees and shrubs. Some campsites have lakeside settings, others are tucked away in the woods. Each has a steel fire grate and a tent pad (a flat, smooth area that has been cleared to accommodate a large tent), nearby trash containers (usually) and separate outhouses for men and women. Most campgrounds also have hand pumps for potable well water. None has electrical hookups. Many of the sites and toilet facilities were designed specifically for wheelchair accessibility. All are situated adjacent to lakes or rivers, and most have public boat ramps. Eight have swimming beaches. The National Forest campgrounds and state parks have picnic tables, as do some of the state forest campgrounds.

A few camping areas are free, but most charge from $5 to $8 per site per night, higher for premium and large-group sites. The state parks that offer showers and modern toilet facilities also charge more. Fees are not charged during the off-season.

The main camping season runs from mid-May through September. Although most campgrounds remain open throughout the year, water pumps are shut down and garbage collection is discontinued after the regular season. The only National Forest campgrounds closed during the winter are at Birch Lake, the South Kawishiwi River, Cadotte Lake and Whiteface Reservoir (they are open from early May through mid-November).

Campsites are generally available only on a first-come, first-served basis. The exceptions are those National Forest campgrounds operated by concessionaires who are willing to take reservations, and at the state parks. All campgrounds limit campers to a 14-day stay in one campground, unless special permission has been secured.

Although many of the campgrounds have suitable space for RVs, water, electricity and sewage connections are available only at two state parks, and waste

Table 11

Campgrounds

Name	D	Type	Sites	Occ.	Use	Fee	Res	BL	SW	DW	HF	FT	BT	PA	LG	MAP	Comments
Baker Lake	T	NFC	5	56	L	no	no	X		X		X				8	Direct access to BWCAW; better arrive early
Big Rice Lake	L	NFA	5	n/a	L	no	no	X								13	A popular ricing site for more than 2000 years
Birch Lake	K	NFC	16	32	M	yes	no	X		X						15	20 miles of navigable waters available to boaters
Cadotte Lake	L	NFC	27	33	M	yes	yes	X	X	X	X			X		19	Reservation may be necessary for summer weekend
Cascade River S.P.	G	MSP	42	n/a	H	yes	yes		X	X	X	X	X			18	Reservation may be necessary during the summer
Cascade River	G	NFC	3	44	L	no	no			X		X	X			9	EZ access to Eagle Mountain, MN's highest peak
Clara, Lake	T	NFA	3	n/a	L	no	no	X								18	Good place to escape from summer crowds by car
Crescent Lake	T	NFC	33	51	H	yes	no	X	X	X	X	X			X	18	Can accommodate 2 large groups of up to 24 each
Devil Track Lake	G	NFC	16	46	M	yes	no	X	X	X	X		X			9	Busy lake with an airport at the east end
Divide Lake	I	NFC	3	43	L	yes	no		X	X		X				16	Very popular among stream trout anglers
East Bearskin Lake	G	NFC	33	20	M	yes	no	X	X	X	X	X	X			10	Direct access to BWCAW; usually a vacancy here
Echo Lake	LC	NFC	25	26	M	yes	no	X	X	X	X			X	X	4	Can accommodate large group of up to 21 people

Table 11 cont'd — Campgrounds

Name	D	TYPE	SIZE	OCC	USE	FEE	RES	BL	SW	DW	HF	FT	BT	PA	DW	LG	MAP	Notes
Eighteen Lake	I	NFA	3	n/a	L	no	no					X			X		16	Good place to escape from summer crowds by car
Esther Lake	G	SFC	3	n/a	L	no	no					X					10	A good base camp for trout anglers
Fall Lake	K	NFC	67	36	H	yes	yes	X	X	X	X	X		X			6	Direct access to BWCAW; largest campground in SNF
Fenske Lake	K	NFC	15	33	M	yes	no	X	X	X	X	X					6	Entertains fewest visitors in Kawishiwi District
Flour Lake	G	NFC	35	12	L	yes	no	X	X			X					10	A vacant site is nearly always available here
Four Mile Lake	T	NFA	4	n/a	L	no	no					X					17	Rated one of MN's top 100 walleye lakes
Hinsdale Island	LC	SFC	11	n/a	M	yes	no	X				X					4	You'll need a boat to camp at this island campground
Iron Lake	G	NFC	7	52	M	yes	yes	X				X					9	Direct access to seldom visited part of BWCAW
Jeanette, Lake	LC	NFC	9	77	M	yes	no	X				X					5	Plan to arrive early to ensure a vacancy

DISTRICT (D): G = Gunflint, I = Isabella, K = Kawishiwi, L = Laurentian, LC = La Croix, T = Tofte
TYPE: NFC = National Forest campground, NFA = National Forest area, SFC = state forest campground, MSP = Minnesota state park
SIZE: Number of campsites
OCCUPANCY (OCC): Occupancy rate percentage
USE: H = heavy, M = moderate, L = light
FEE: Whether or not a fee is charged
RESERVATIONS (RES): Whether or not reservations are accepted

BL: Boat landing
SW: Swimming beach
DW: Potable drinking water
HF: Facilities for the handicapped
FT: Foot trails
BT: Bike trails
PA: Picnic area
DW: Potable drinking water
LG: Facilities for large groups
MAP: Numbers refer to maps in this book.

Table 11 cont'd

Campgrounds

Campground															Notes
Judge C.R. Magney S.P.	G	MSP	42	n/a	M	yes	yes	X			X	X		11	Primitive sites near lovely Brule River rapids & falls
Kawishiwi Lake	T	NFC	5	49	L	no	no	X			X	X		8	Direct access to BWCAW; good moose-viewing area
Kimball Lake	G	NFC	8	47	L	yes	no	X			X	X		10	Good base camp for stream trout anglers
Little Isabella River	I	NFC	11	13	L	yes	no	X			X	X		16	Good place to escape from the summer crowds
McDougal Lake	I	NFC	21	15	M	yes	no	X	X	X	X	X		16	Great base camp for mountain bikers
McFarland Lake	G	SFC	2	n/a	L	no	no	X			X	X		10	Direct access to BWCAW and Border Route Trail
Ninemile Lake	T	NFC	24	44	M	yes	no	X	X		X	X		17	Your best bet for a vacancy in the Tofte District
Pfeiffer Lake	L	NFC	21	21	L	yes	no	X	X		X	X		13	An often overlooked but lovely campground
Poplar River	T	NFC	4	77	M	no	no			X				18	Must arrive early in summer to get a campsite
Rocky Shores	I	SFC	4	n/a	L	no	no				X	X		15	Boat needed to reach this isolated campground
Sawbill Lake	T	NFC	50	63	H	yes	no	X	X		X	X		8	Direct BWCAW access; busiest campground in Forest
South Kawishiwi River	K	NFC	32	19	M	yes	no	X	X		X	X		15	Direct access to BWCAW; nice log pavilion for rent

Table 11 cont'd

Campgrounds

Campgrounds	L													
Sullivan Lake	L	SFC	10	n/a	M	yes	no	X		X	X	X	20	Site of a Civilian Conservation Corps camp in 1930s
Temperance River	T	NFC	9	76	M	yes	no		X	X	X	X	17	Must arrive early in summer to get a campsite
Temperance River S.P.	T	MSP	50	n/a	H	yes	yes	X	X	X	X	X	17	Reservation may be necessary during the summer
Trail's End	G	NFC	33	32	H	yes	yes	X	X	X	X	X	8	Direct access to two BWCAW entry points
Two Island	G	NFC	36	16	M	yes	no	X	X	X	X		9	Nearly always a vacant site here
Wakemup Bay	LC	SFC	21	n/a	H	yes	no	X	X	X		X	4	On one of northern Minnesota's most popular lakes
Whiteface Reservoir	L	NFC	53	42	H	yes	no	X	X	X	X	X	19	2nd busiest campground in the Forest
Whitefish Lake	T	NFA	3	n/a	L	no	no	X					17	Good place to escape from summer crowds by car
White Pine Lake	T	NFA	3	n/a	L	no	no	X					18	Good place to escape from summer crowds by car
Wilson Lake	T	NFA	4	n/a	L	no	no	X					17	Rated one of MN's top 100 walleye lakes

Fall Lake Beach

water is not permitted to drain onto the ground. The possibility of modernizing some National Forest campgrounds to fully accommodate RVs is currently under consideration.

The following table includes information about the 43 campgrounds and camping areas within the boundaries of Superior National Forest.

DISPERSED CAMPSITES

Most visitors to Superior National Forest camp either in the BWCA Wilderness or in the developed campgrounds. Nevertheless, 229 dispersed campsites have been constructed and designated for people who want a more remote camping experience than is available in the campgrounds, but one that is not quite as isolated as in the Wilderness.

These partially developed sites are equipped with steel fire grates or fire rings and tent pads. Toilet facilities are either outhouses or wilderness-type box latrines. Trash containers are not provided, and picnic tables are available only at some of the more developed sites. All sites are free of charge.

Most dispersed campsites sit by themselves; most are on lakeshores or next to streams. Although many are accessible only by canoe or boat, others are adjacent to public landings and you can drive right to them, although some require high-clearance vehicles—even four-wheel-drive. A few campsites are accessible only to backpackers.

Although most of the sites are primitive and the facilities are similar to what is available in the BWCAW, visitors are not subjected to BWCAW regulations: permits are not required, bottles and cans are permitted and, of course, motorboats are not prohibited from the lakes and rivers on which the campsites are located. (See "Regulations" at the beginning of this chapter for a summary of the rules and regulations.)

The following table lists all 229 dispersed campsite locations in Superior National Forest.

Table 12 — Dispersed Campsites

Laurentian District

Location	Sites	Access	Map	Location	Sites	Access	Map
Big Lake	3	W	15	Otto Lake	2	W,T	19
Big Lake	2	W,T	15	Pfeiffer Lake	2	W,T	13
Deepwater Lake	1	T	12	Pine Lake	2	W	15
Harris Lake	1	R,T	19	Round Lake	2	W	15
Jean Lake	1	R	12	St. Louis River	1	W	14
Little Sandy Lake	1	R	13	Seven Beaver Lake	1	W	15
Long Lake	1	W	15	Whiteface Reservoir	3	W,T	19

La Croix District

Location	Sites	Access	Map	Location	Sites	Access	Map
Astrid Lake	2	W,T	4	Maude Lake	2	W	4
Crane Lake	3	W	2	Meander Lake	2	W	5
Echo Lake	3	W	4	Myrtle Lake	3	W	4
Franklin Lake	2	W	1	Nigh Lake	1	W,T	4
Lake Jeanette	6	W	5	Picket Lake	3	W	4
Little Johnson Lake	1	W	1	Lake Vermilion	8	W	4,5
Johnson Lake	6	W	1	Vermilion River	4	W	4

Kawishiwi District

Location	Sites	Access	Map	Location	Sites	Access	Map
Agassa Lake	1	W	5	Johnson Lake	1	W	15
August Lake	1	W	15	Little Sletten Lake	1	W	6
Bass Lake	2	W	6	Low Lake	2	W	6
Bear Island Lake	2	W	14	Nels Lake	3	W	6
Big Lake	4	W	5	Perch Lake	1	W	15
Birch Lake	16	W	15	Pickerel Lake	2	W	6
Blackstone Lake	1	T	7	Picket Lake	1	W	6
Burntside Lake	5	W	5,6	Sletten Lake	1	W	6

ACCESS: W = water, T = trail, R = road
SITES: Number of sites
MAP: Numbers refer to maps in this book.

Table 12 cont'd — Dispersed Campsites

Kawishiwi District cont'd

Location	Sites	Access	Map	Location	Sites	Access	Map
Everett Lake	1	W	6	Snowbank Lake	2	W,T	7
Grassy Lake	2	W	6	Tee Lake	1	W	6
Greenstone Lake	1	W	6	Tofte Lake	3	W	6
Harris Lake	2	W	15	Twin Lakes	5	W	5,6
High Lake	4	W	6	Whisper Lake	1	W	15

Isabella District

Location	Sites	Access	Map	Location	Sites	Access	Map
Cloquet Lake	2	R	16	Lupus Lake	1	T	17
Comfort Lake	1	W	16	Scarp Lake	2	W,T	17
Dam Five Lake	2	R	17	Section 29 Lake	2	R	16
Dragon Lake	2	R	16	Silver Island Lake	5	W	17
Harriet Lake	2	R	17	Steer Lake	1	T	17
Island River	4	W	16	T Lake	2	W	17

Tofte District

Location	Sites	Access	Map	Location	Sites	Access	Map
Cascade Lake	2	W	9	Lichen Lake	1	W	9
Crescent Lake	2	W	18	Rice Lake	2	W	18
Elbow Lake	2	W	17	Superior Hiking Trail	3	T	17,18
Finger Lake	1	W	17	Timber Lake	1	W	17
Four Mile Lake	2	W	17	Whitefish Lake	2	W	17
Frear Lake	2	W	17	Windy Lake	3	W	17
Homer Lake	1	W	9	Wilson Lake	1	W	17

Gunflint District

Location	Sites	Access	Map	Location	Sites	Access	Map
Ball Club Lake	1	W	9	Little Iron Lake	2	W	9
Bath Lake	1	W	9	Loon Lake	1	W	9
Bearskin Lake	3	W	10	Mayhew Lake	1	W	9
Birch Lake	1	W	9	Moss Lake	1	W	10
Carrot Lake	1	W	10	North Lake	2	W	9
Deer Yard Lake	1	W	18	Northern Light Lake	1	W	10
Devilfish Lake	2	W	10	Pine Lake	1	W	10
East Twin Lake	2	W	10	Round Lake	1	W	8
Elbow Lake	2	W	10	Sunfish Lake	1	W	10
Greenwood Lake	2	W	10	Trout Lake	1	W	10
Gunflint Lake	7	W	9	West Twin Lake	1	W	10
Ham Lake	4	W	8				
Kemo Lake	1	W	10				
Little Gunflint Lake	2	W	9				

Exploring the Gabbro rock quarry

PICNICKING

The wonderful thing about Superior National Forest is that you don't have to be a camper to enjoy it. Nor must you be a canoeist, a biker, or a skier. There is a whole lot to see and do outside the Wilderness that doesn't require "roughing it." Consider a picnic, for instance. There are 29 designated picnic sites in Superior

National Forest, all accessible to passenger cars. Facilities are not fancy, but they are comfortable. Each has picnic tables and fire grates, and there are outdoor biffies nearby. Most have well water. Besides the scenery, other attractions, like interpretive hiking trails or historical points of interest, are usually nearby. Camping is not permitted at any of the designated picnic areas, though some are adjacent to campgrounds.

The following table provides information about the 16 picnic areas that are not associated with any campground (see the campground table for those that are).

| Table 13 | | Picnic Areas | | | | | | | | |

Name	D	Size	Use	BL	SW	DW	HF	FT	BT	Map
Bassett Lake	L	2	M	X	X					19
Birch Lake Wayside	K	2	M	X					X	15
Bird Lake	L	2	L					X		14
Dumbbell Lake	I	4	L	X		X				16
Echo River	LC	1	L					X		4
Fisherman's Point Rec.	L	n/a	H	X	X	X				14
Flathorn Lake	I	5	M		X	X		X		16
Hogback Lake	I	5	M	X				X		17
Kjostad Lake	LC	1	L	X						4
Laurentian Divide	L	7	M					X	X	13
Leander, Lake	L	28	H		X	X				12
Meander Lake	LC	3	L					X		5
Norway Point	L	2	L	X						14
Salo Lake	L	2	L	X						19
Vermilion Falls	LC	5	L					X		1
White Pines	I	2	L					X		20

DISTRICT (D): L = Laurentian, LC = La Croix, K = Kawishiwi, I = Isabella, T = Tofte, G = Gunflint
SIZE: Number of picnic tables   USE: H = heavy, M = moderate, L = light
BL: Boat landing   BT: Bike trails
SW: Swimming beach   PA: Picnic area
DW: Potable drinking water   LG: Facilities for large groups
HF: Facilities for the handicapped   MAP: Numbers refer to maps in this book
FT: Foot trails

SIGHTSEEING

The Forest also contains an assortment of good, old-fashioned tourist attractions. There simply isn't enough space here to provide *all* the sightseeing information that's available, so this chapter will simply describe some of the lesser-known sights. For more information, contact the appropriate district office (see Chapter 2) or tourism association (see Appendix).

LAURENTIAN DISTRICT

Longyear Drill Site (Map 14)

On June 3, 1890, Edmund J. Longyear was the first person to use a diamond-bitted drill on the Mesabi Range to explore for iron ore. Driven by a steam engine, it bored to a depth of 1,293 feet but failed to show evidence of recoverable ore. Undaunted by this first failure, Longyear went on to direct the exploration of over 7,000 test pits and diamond drill holes across the iron ranges of northeastern Minnesota.

Longyear's first diamond drill site is located about 7.5 miles east of Aurora (see directions for Longyear Physical Fitness Trail in "Day Hikes" in Chapter 4). An information booth next to the parking lot directs visitors along a 0.25-mile trail to the actual site. The trail is easy, with benches along the route.

Taconite Iron Mines (Maps 12, 13, 14)

Iron ore mining has been the economic lifeblood of this region for more than a hundred years: nearly all the towns in and around the Laurentian District owe their very existence to this industry. After the high-grade ore was exhausted, the companies turned to taconite and millions of tons of taconite pellets are now extracted here each year. Visitors can view the operation of the Inland Steel Company from parts of the Lookout Mountain Ski Trails (see Chapter 5), but the best place to learn about this industry and the effect it has had on northeastern Minnesota is at Iron World, located 18 miles west of Virginia on Highway 53. This "living" museum is operated by the Iron Range Resources and Rehabilitation Board.

Fall Color Tour (Map 19)

The Laurentian District is not well known for its spectacular autumn colors but Forest Route 416 (the Otto Lake Road) is a lovely woodland route that winds through a region with considerable maple, birch and aspen. From Aurora, drive 6 miles east on County Roads 110 and 565 (through the town of Hoyt Lakes) to County Road 569. Turn right and follow C.R. 569 1.2 miles southeast to Forest Route 130. Turn right again and proceed 10.5 miles south on this narrow, winding road to County Road 16. Turn left and drive another 10.5 miles east to F.R. 416. With a high-clearance vehicle, you can continue south to County Road 4. In a normal passenger car, however, you'll have to stop soon after the Otto Lake portage (5 miles) and backtrack to County Road 16.

LA CROIX DISTRICT

Little Indian Sioux Fire Area (Map 5)

In the spring of 1971, nearly 15,000 acres of Superior National Forest were destroyed by a raging fire just north of the Echo Trail (County Road 116), between the Little Indian Sioux and Nina-Moose rivers. Although most of the area has been regenerated with jack pine, aspen, spruce and fir, you can still see evidence of the devastation at several points along the road. One of the best vantage points is the Meander Lake picnic grounds. You can also hike across the burned over region via the Sioux-Hustler Trail (see Chapter 4).

Lookout Mountain Overlook (Map 4)

A 0.25-mile user-developed trail climbs up 100 feet from the Echo Trail to a high flat rock that once held a fire tower. It's located near Camp 97 Creek, 5 miles east of County Road 24 (see "Paddling the Boundary Waters" in Chapter 3). There are still remnants of the tower lying around. The district plans to construct a 1.5-mile loop trail soon.

A station on the Lookout Mountain Fitness Trail

"High point" of the Laurentian Divide Picnic Area

The Rock (Map 5)

A 200-foot trail leads to a very large erratic on the northeast side of County Road 116, near Range Line Creek, 17.5 miles east of County Road 24 (see "Paddling the Boundary Waters" in Chapter 3). The rock is dangerous to climb. The district plans to construct an interpretive trail that will lead to it.

Winston City (Map 13)

In 1865, high-grade gold ore was discovered along the south shore of Lake Vermilion by the state's chief geologist. When his first assays indicated that the lode might be wealthier than California's, the anouncement spawned the Vermilion Gold Rush, which brought 300 people there by the spring of 1866. The town of Winston City was created, consisting of 14 homes, a sawmill, a general store and a blacksmith shop. A hotel, a post office and four saloons were planned, but the boom was short-lived. Very little gold was actually found and, within a year wild-eyed enthusiasm had turned to despair. The town was completely gone by the 1880s, and Winston City earned the distinction of being the oldest ghost town on the Vermilion Range. Today, the only reminder of that short period is a plaque on the north side of Highway 1 near the town of Tower, 24 miles west of Ely.

KAWISHIWI DISTRICT

Birch Lake Plantation (Map 15)

The Birch Lake Plantation, 1 mile northeast of Babbitt, was the first plantation in Superior National Forest. Planted in 1915 and 1917, the lovely grove of pine trees now provides a scenic setting for a cross-country ski trail (see directions to the Birch Lake Plantation ski trail in Chapter 5).

Young deer "yard" together during the long, hard winter months.

Highway 1 (Maps 6, 15)

Between 1900 and 1914, Highway 1 from Ely to County Road 2 was a supply road for the St. Croix Lumber Company. A logging camp at the intersection of those two roads was the headquarters for the company. The Stony River drainage to the Kawishiwi River was the route for logs en route to Winston. The Baird ranger station, at the junction of Highway 1 and Forest Route 1461, 18 miles southeast of Ely, was the first ranger station in Superior National Forest, built in the early 1900s.

Rock Quarry (Map 15)

Drive south 16 miles from the Ely Chamber of Commerce on Highway 1 to an unmarked, obscure turnoff on the east (left) side of the road. Immediately after turning off the highway, you'll come to a Y in this primitive forest road. Take the right fork and drive 0.1 mile to a grassy area where you can park and turn around. A short trail from there leads to a granite quarry that operated from the 1920s to the late 1930s. In an area about 200 yards in circumference, there are piles of large rectangular rocks with three-inch drill marks in them. Rumor has it that a chunk from this quarry is in the Brooklyn Bridge. It's a fascinating site that you could explore for hours, or for just a few minutes.

Fall Color Tour (Maps 6, 15, 5)

Like the other western districts in Superior National Forest, the Kawishiwi District is not well known for its spectacular fall colors. Nevertheless, two major routes reward travelers with a lovely display in September. One is Highway 1, which leads southeast to the Isabella District and eventually to the North Shore of Lake Superior. The other is the Echo Trail (County Road 116), which leads northwest to the La Croix District. Along the way, you should take a short detour on the Passi Road (Forest Route 803; see directions to the Burntside Lake–Dead River Canoe Route in Chapter 3).

ISABELLA DISTRICT

While in this district, be alert for moose: this part of the Forest is thick with the big, burly beasts. This is also one of the best areas in the Forest to see timber wolves along the roads.

Forest Center Landing (Map 16)

To most of its visitors, Forest Center is only a small parking lot near the south shore of Isabella Lake (see Entry Point 35 in Chapter 3 for directions). From 1949 to 1964, however, it was known as Logging Camp 3 of the Tomahawk Timber Company and it was home for 250 people. Fifty-three homes, a two-room schoolhouse, a recreation center and a restaurant, a sawmill, barracks and a mess hall all existed here at one time. The timber was hauled away on a railroad, and there were several rows of tracks at the landing. Today, the entire area is covered by a forest of young pines, except for the parking lot.

Gaseau Homestead (Map 17)

Near the Harriet Lake boat landing is a large, open meadow that is currently maintained as a grassy wildlife opening. From about 1900 to 1935, this was the site of the Gaseau Homestead, a farm with 10 buildings, fences and a root cellar, among other things. It produced food for logging crews in the area. Today, it's a marvelous campsite for large groups.

To drive there from Isabella, follow Forest Route 172 13.5 miles east to County Road 7. Turn left and proceed 0.4 mile to a turnoff on the right that leads 0.5 mile through the clearing to Harriet Lake.

Jackpine Mountain (Map 16)

The cement base of a fire lookout tower is all that remains on the top of this 1,655-foot bald knob, but you can still enjoy a panoramic view across the Forest in every direction. You can get to it by driving 7 miles west from Highway 1 on the Tomahawk Road (see directions on page 91). An unmarked turnoff on the right leads to the summit, which is not maintained. No facilities are provided.

Jackpot Forest Fire Area (Map 15)

Along County Road 2, about 15 miles west of Isabella, is a stretch of rocky, open hills on the west side of the road. They mark the edge of the 1200-acre Jackpot Fire of 1980. The hot fire burned a cigar-shaped pattern across the landscape, skipping from treetop to treetop. The area was replanted in 1981 and has quickly recovered.

To get there from the Isabella ranger station, drive 13 miles west on Highway 1 to County Road 2. Turn left and continue 1.5 miles south to the fire site.

Old Stony Lookout (Map 16)

Once the site of a fire lookout tower, this knob now has only the cement foundation, but there is still a fine view in every direction. From mid-September to mid-October, you can enjoy a beautiful blend of colors across the landscape. The lookout is accessible from Forest Route 103 (the Stony Loop). From the Isabella ranger station, drive 0.4 mile west to Forest Route 103. Turn left onto this one-lane road and proceed 3 miles southwest. Watch for the unmarked turnoff on the right, which leads north to the site. It is not maintained, and no facilities are provided.

TOFTE DISTRICT

Fall Color Tour (Maps 17, 18)

Many folks seem to associate fall colors only with leaf-bearing trees, but it is the contrasting dark green color of the conifers that make the autumn show in this region *extra*-special. The rich greens of pine, spruce and balsam fir provide a magnificent backdrop for the red maples, yellow birch and the golden aspens of Superior National Forest. And there is no better place to witness this spectacle than the Sawtooth Mountains.

The Tofte District has made it easy to find the very best scenes by designating certain forest roads as part of a Sawtooth Mountain Fall Color Tour. In cooperation with the Lutsen-Tofte Tourism Association (see Appendix), the district has produced a pamphlet with a map that shows the various loops that originate along Highway 61 and penetrate the Sawtooth Mountain highlands. The routes range in length from 6 to 31 miles and require driving times ranging from 30 minutes to nearly two hours. Along the way, you can stop and hike to the summits

The Stony Loop, Isabella District

of some notable peaks, like Oberg and Leveaux mountains and Britton and Carleton peaks (see "Day Hikes" in Chapter 4 for details). Of course, you can also enjoy any of these loops on a mountain bike, but watch out for automobiles. The peak weekends of autumn are the busiest times of the entire year along the North Shore.

Heartbreak Hill (Map 17)

One historic point of interest on the Fall Color Tour is found along Forest Route 166, just east of Forest Route 343. One legend relates how this steep hill broke many a logger's heart because, during the winter, he could not haul logs up or down the slope with teams of horses. After driving up the hill (or, better yet, riding on a bicycle), you can understand why so many folks believe this myth. According to the Forest archaeologist, however, Heartbreak Hill derives its name from a smallpox epidemic that killed many members of the nearby Anderson homestead.

Marsh Lake Road (Maps 9, 17)

Forest Route 165—the Marsh Lake Road—between the Sawbill Trail (County Road 2) and the Caribou Trail (County Road 4), is lovely at *any* time of year. Closely paralleling the southern border of the BWCAW, this good gravel road skirts eight lovely lakes and the Temperance River in the short span of only 15 miles. All of the lakes have pullover access points or developed boat landings (see Chapter 3). If you make the drive in early morning or in the evening, you'll probably see at least one moose. Be alert and drive carefully! There are two National Forest campgrounds along the route (Crescent Lake and Baker Lake), so you can spend the night and explore the road at dawn.

GUNFLINT DISTRICT

Although there is only one designated picnic area in the Gunflint District, picnicking is permitted without charge in all of the National Forest campgrounds in this district.

Artist's Point (Map 18)

This small peninsula jutting into Lake Superior is a favorite refuge for locals seeking respite from the stresses of modern living. Located straight south of the Visitor Information Center in Grand Marais, which is 5 blocks east of the ranger station and 0.25 mile south on Broadway Avenue, the point is especially beautiful in autumn, with its scenic views of the Sawtooth Mountains to the west and the lake in all other directions. Artist's Point is named for the dozens of artists who spend time sketching or painting there. You'll surely enjoy the rock formations along the shore, the view of the old lighthouse (see "Lighthouse" below) and the seagulls. Parking space is available just before the entrance to the U.S. Coast Guard Station.

Fall Color Tours (Maps 8, 10, 11)

Thanks to the Sawtooth Mountains and the North Shore of Lake Superior, you'll find a lovely, colorful blend of hardwoods and conifers that can be enjoyed from many scenic viewpoints. Drop by the ranger station in Grand Marais and ask for their Fall Color Tour brochures, a selection of four maps with directions to the best places in the district. One tour goes west to the Pike Lake area, with its large stands of maples, birch, aspens and white spruce. Another leads north to the Maple Hill cemetery, in a beautiful setting with the Maple Hill church in the foreground. A third tour stretches east to the Hovland Lookout (see "Hovland Lookout," below). The fourth stays right in Grand Marais, visiting Artist's Point,

Bikers enjoy a panoramic view toward Lake Superior at the Grand Marais Overlook.

the lighthouse and Sweetheart Bluff. All of the tours employ good gravel roads that any passenger car can negotiate.

Grand Marais Overlook (Map 18)

Two miles north of the Gunflint ranger station on County Road 12 is a turnoff that leads 0.25 mile east (right) to a large parking area and a scenic overlook. From there you can view Grand Marais, the harbor and the lighthouse piers below. On a clear day, the North Shore of Lake Superior can be seen curving off to the west. You can also see why the Sawtooth Mountains received their name. The overlook is also the trailhead for the Pincushion Mountain Cross-Country Ski Trail, and you can hike from the parking lot to the summit of the mountain.

Gunflint Lake Overlook (Map 9)

If you continue driving north on County Road 12 to a point 43 miles north of Grand Marais, you can enjoy a scenic overlook located high above Gunflint Lake. The view is obscured somewhat by the dense forest around the small parking lot, but you can see a corner of the lake and the Canadian wilderness beyond. The site is intersected by one of the upper Gunflint ski trails (see Chapter 5), which leads southeast to the High Cliffs (see "Gunflint High Cliffs" in "Day Hike" in Chapter 4).

Hovland Lookout (Map 11)

The site of an old lookout station looms over beautiful stands of sugar maples, aspens and evergreens that blend to create a spectacular array of colors in autumn. Many types of wildlife are also frequently seen in this area. Drive 18 miles east of Grand Marais on Highway 61 to the village of Hovland. Turn left onto County Road 16 (the Arrowhead Trail) and proceed 2.5 miles north to the Hovland Tower Road. The tower site is about 1.5 miles north on this dirt road.

Laurentian Divide Overlook (Map 9)

Thirty-four miles north of Grand Marais via County Road 12, a small parking lot lies above the south shore of Birch Lake. At this point, the Gunflint Trail straddles the Laurentian Divide, the ridge that separates the Lake Superior and Hudson Bay watersheds. Rain falling south of the Divide ultimately drains into the Atlantic Ocean, while water on the north side eventually ends up in Hudson Bay. The Divide winds across Superior National Forest, from the Canadian border at South Lake to the Laurentian Divide Picnic Area, just north of Virginia, crossing the Gunflint, Tofte, Isabella and Laurentian districts en route.

The Lighthouse (Map 18)

Located adjacent to Artist's Point in Grand Marais (see "Artist's Point," above), the historic lighthouse in Grand Marais was lit each day by hand for many years, until automation took over. The lighthouse keeper lived in what is now the Cook County Historical Museum. A 200-yard walk on a wide cement pier takes you to the entrance of Grand Marais harbor, a scenic place for photographers and anyone else who appreciates Minnesota's inland coast.

The Pines (Map 10)

Eight miles north of Grand Marais, along County Road 12, a group of white pines lines the road. Towering above the other trees in the forest, these majestic trees are close to 200 years old. Extensive logging and fires have reduced the white pine forests to a few sparsely scattered stands similar to this. The few remaining trees are now being killed by blister rust, a disease that causes the tops of older trees to die and fall off. Because of the epidemic, the Forest Service no longer plants white pine seedlings, although there are hopes that a new, disease-resistant strain will be developed. Eventually The Pines will no longer be standing—this is your opportunity to see the Forest as the Native Americans and voyageurs of the 18th century saw it.

MOUNTAIN BIKING

In 1988, there were approximately 2700 miles of USFS roads in Superior National Forest. New roads are built every year to accommodate new logging operations. As new ones are opened, old ones are "closed" to keep the road mileage to a minimum. Because of that, perhaps no place in the Midwest is more suited to safe backcountry bicycling than Superior National Forest.

MOUNTAIN BIKES

Until recently, the only vehicles that could successfully challenge the back roads of Superior National Forest were four-wheel-drive trucks and other motorized off-road vehicles (ORVs).

Now there's a means for silent-sports enthusiasts to enjoy the Forest roads. All-terrain bicycles (ATBs), or mountain bikes, as they are known out West, where they were invented only a few years ago, have quickly taken the country by storm. They look like a cross between old-fashioned fat-tire bicycles and the popular 10-speeds. Most have 15 to 18 gear ratios, no fenders, straight handlebars and extraordinarily wide tires.

ATBs are tough bikes for rugged terrain. You can pedal across loose gravel, scale the barren slope of a rocky ridge, splash through deep puddles on forest roads flooded by beaver dams, climb over the trunks of fallen trees, and cruise comfortably along a black-topped highway at 20 mph—all with the same bike on the same outing.

ENVIRONMENTAL IMPACT

Like other off-road vehicles, mountain bikes can have an adverse environmental impact on certain types of trails and soil. For that reason, ATBs are not permitted on some trails.

Because interest in all-terrain bicycles is so new to the Arrowhead region, Forest Service officials have not yet officially identified the best routes for bikers.

Mountain bikers on the North Shore State Trail

In fact, authorities don't yet agree on how to deal with the subject. Should bikes be allowed on foot trails? On portages? The BWCA Wilderness Act of 1978 restricted the use of mechanized equipment in the Boundary Waters. Bicycles are mechanized: hence, they are not permitted in the Wilderness. To date, this is the *only* categorical restriction on the use of ATBs in Superior National Forest. Outside the BWCAW, bike riding is permitted anywhere it is not specifically prohibited. (It *is* restricted in some districts, such as Tofte, where the Oberg Mountain Trail is off-limits to ATBs.)

Until a sound policy is established, it's important for fat-tire enthusiasts to be sensitive to the potential impact they might have—both on the environment through which they are riding and on other visitors to the Forest. Just as most cross-country skiers prefer not to share their trails with snowmobiles, many hikers also prefer not to share their trails with mountain bikes. Furthermore, some Forest ecologists prefer to restrict the use of ATBs to existing roads, at least until the effects of off-road riding can be determined. These concerns are understandable and should be respected by visiting bikers.

The best way to avoid potential conflicts with other Forest visitors and with USFS ecologists is either to drop by the district office to inquire about the attitudes in that particular district *before* attempting any off-road tours, or to stick to the Forest roads. Frankly, with over 2700 miles of fascinating roads from which to choose, there is no reason to look elsewhere.

BE PREPARED

Regardless of where you ride, do not leave home without a compass and a good map of the region. Old abandoned logging roads are usually not signed, nor are the intersections of many currently used, numbered roadways. And if you strike out cross-country, it is *very* easy to get lost.

For that reason and others, like hikers and canoeists in the Wilderness, bikers should also be prepared for emergencies (see Chapter 2 for tips). Most of these back roads see far fewer people than do the canoe routes of the Boundary Waters. An accident, sudden illness, mechanical breakdown or dramatic change in the weather could render a bike rider helpless, miles from the nearest highway with darkness fast approaching.

PLANNING A ROUTE

Rather than describe all of the potentially good routes in Superior National Forest, which would be an entire book by itself, this chapter has been designed to assist you in planning your own route. The maps in this book show "official" USFS roads, county roads and state and federal highways that cross Superior National Forest. The appropriate map number for each trip in this chapter follows the trip name (if more than one map applies, they are listed "in order of appearance" along the route). Choose your bike tour based on your riding skill, ambition, physical condition and sense of adventure. To lessen the chance of getting disoriented or lost, stick to the numbered roads that are shown on the map.

Figure on an average riding speed of no more than 10 mph on the gravel roads and no more than 5 mph on the native surface roads. That's *riding* time! For most folks, riding time is interspersed with walking time going up steep hills, panting time at the tops of those hills, drinking time, wildlife observation time, swimming time, photograph-taking time and lunch time. Allow plenty of time for rest stops.

While pedaling along the back roads of Superior National Forest, you'll see many primitive road spurs, perhaps even some downright decent roads, gravelled and signed, that are not indicated on the map. As mentioned earlier, new roads are built every year. Enter the "spirit of adventure." With map, compass and emergency gear firmly affixed to your bike or person, feel free to explore these uncharted territories.

One word of warning: avoid roads where active logging operations are taking place. Loggers don't like to slow down for bikers. Besides the inherent dangers, the dust created by truck traffic is a nuisance. These roads are usually signed "Heavy truck traffic ahead." USFS officials recommend that you stop by the district office first to get an update on where the logging operations are taking place.

ROADS AND NON-ROADS

No federal highways penetrate the central part of the Forest. Highway 53 skirts the western edge of the Laurentian and La Croix districts, and Highway 61 parallels the North Shore of Lake Superior along the eastern perimeter of the Tofte and Gunflint districts. State Highways 1 and 169 slice right through the

Lunch break along the North Shore State Trail

middle of the Forest. All of the other roads fall under the jurisdiction of either the counties (Cook, Lake or St. Louis), the Forest Service or, occasionally, the Minnesota DNR. The county roads are either blacktop or gravel. USFS and DNR roads are either gravel or "native surface." (Native surfaces can be anything from natural sand and gravel to dirt and mud, or even ledge rock. Some are good enough for normal passenger cars to negotiate, but most require vehicles with high clearance.) The gravel county roads are usually wider and have broader right-of-ways than forest routes. County roads are often rougher, too. USFS routes are normally more "intimate," with narrower right-of-ways and thinner road surfaces—more interesting for bikers.

"Closing" a road is usually done by simply scratching it from the official USFS map and, without any further maintainance, leaving it to the inevitable reclamation forces of Mother Nature. Sometimes barriers are added to prevent motor vehicles from using the closed roads.

These "non-roads," often little more than two ruts with grass growing between them, are the best of all possible routes for mountain bikers. There is no truck traffic, no automobiles, only an occasional motorized ORV with which to contend. The only tracks on the roadway are those of moose, timber wolves, whitetailed deer and, perhaps an occasional black bear, pine marten or red fox.

To locate some of these non-roads, drop by one of the district offices and ask for suggestions. Mention right away that you are a *bicycle* rider. Some receptionists don't understand what a mountain bike or an ATB is. They conjure up images of motorized ORVs and may be reluctant to discuss roads that have been closed to motorized traffic. If they understand that all you want to do is ride a bicycle through the woods, they are more likely to share some of their "secret" roads with you.

Whether or not that tactic works, there is one other good source for information about "non-roads" (roads in fact if not in name). Pick almost any USGS map for Superior National Forest (see Appendix). Compare it with the maps in this book or with any official USFS map. You'll see many more miles of unimproved roads on the USGS map. That's because the USGS maps show the *physical* characteristics of a region, including abandoned roads. USFS maps, however, show only those roads officially in use.

Unfortunately, most logging roads are not circle routes. Many spur trails branch out from a single corridor and penetrate the woods, but they don't connect with one another. You might ride for an hour or more on a route that simply comes to an end. All you can do is turn around and backtrack.

As you plan your route, watch for dashed lines on the map that are labeled "winter trail" or "winter road." If you look closely at a topographic map, you'll see that these roads pass through swamps and bogs. In winter, they are fine for truck traffic or snowmobiles; in summer, however, you would likely sink up to your axles.

USFS personnel have recently been given directives to develop recreational opportunity guides for off-road vehicles, including mountain bikes. They are eager to hear from bikers: user feedback is imperative for the development and maintainance of recreational trails in Superior National Forest. If you "discover" a route that is ideal for mountain bikers, share your discovery with the appropriate district office. Furthermore, if you'd like to see more routes developed— routes that are not open to motorized vehicles—let the USFS know how you feel.

WHERE TO GO

The following routes are merely suggestions and barely hint at the numerous fine excursions awaiting bike riders. See Chapter 6 for information about camping in the vicinities of these routes; see Table 11 for campground locations and Table 12 for dispersed-campsite locations.

LAURENTIAN DISTRICT

Taconite Trail (Maps 6, 5, 14, 13, 12)

Length:	165 miles (one way)
Riding time:	5–6 days
Difficulty:	Moderate
Highlights:	Scenic variety and historic sites
USGS Maps:	Ely, Shagawa, Bear Island, Eagles Nest, Soudan, Tower, Sassas Creek, Britt, Idington, Dark Lake, Dewey Lake NW, and others west of Superior National Forest

Administered by the Minnesota DNR, this multiple-use trail stretches all the way from Ely at the east end to Grand Rapids at the west end, slicing through the western part of the Laurentian District. Closed to motorized use (except snowmobiles in winter), the trail winds through picturesque forests, crosses many

streams and skirts numerous lakes. Wayside rests and picnic facilities are scattered along the trail. Parts of the trail follow old logging roads that allow relatively
easy riding. Other parts, however, are rough and a few places may be wet. For
more information and/or a free map of the trail, contact the Minnesota Department of Natural Resources, Trails and Waterways Unit, Information Center, Box
40, 500 Lafayette Road, St. Paul, MN 55146.

Big Aspen Ski Area (Map 13)

Length:	20 miles of loops
Riding time:	1–5 hours
Difficulty:	Moderate
Highlights:	Variety of forest habitats
USGS Map:	Britt

This maze of interconnected loops passes through Norway pines, aspen and a
vast logged-over region that affords a panoramic view. Part of the system utilizes
old logging roads with easy grades, but there are also some challenging, steep
hills. Though designed and maintained for cross-country skiers, USFS officials
don't mind if the trails are used during the "off-season" (see Chapter 5 for
directions).

Langley Truck Trail (Maps 19, 22)

Length:	8.7 miles (one way)
Riding time:	3 hours (round trip)
Difficulty:	Easy
Highlights:	Stands of pine
USGS Maps:	Kane Lake, Brimson SE

Originally built by the CCC in 1937–38, this narrow, winding, single-lane
road has a good gravel surface for easy riding. Paralleling the Langley River, it
runs from County Highway 2 at the east end to Forest Route 412 at the west end.
There are nice stands of red pine along the road, alternating with a younger forest
of birch, aspen, spruce and balsam fir. You'll also pass through a jack pine plantation planted in 1940. The road crosses the Cloquet River at a point 0.8 mile from
its west end.

LA CROIX DISTRICT

Crane Lake Loops (Maps 1, 4)

Length:	2 loops of 7 and 12 miles each
Riding time:	2–3 hours
Difficulty:	Moderate to challenging
Highlights:	Vermilion Falls, Crane Lake lookout tower
USGS Maps:	Crane Lake, Johnson Lake, Kabustasa Lake

Near the village of Crane Lake, 45 miles north of Cook, is a small network of
routes that incorporates Forest Roads 491 and 207 and part of the Voyageur
Snowmobile Trail between Crane Lake and the Vermilion River. Two loops of 7
miles or 12 miles are possible, and the route includes gravel roads, rocky ledges
and narrow woodland corridors through tall grasses and shrubs. Highlights in-

An old forest road in the Laurentian District

clude lovely Vermilion Falls at one end of the system and the Crane Lake lookout tower at the intersection of the two loops.

Big Moose Loop (Map 5)

Length:	9.5 miles (loop)
Riding time:	2–3 hours
Difficulty:	Easy
Highlights:	Moose country
USGS Maps:	Lapond Lake, Bootleg Lake

Located about midway between Ely and Crane Lake, Forest Route 464 loops south from the Echo Trail to skirt the edge of the Wilderness. The mostly level, one-lane roadway has a fine-gravel surface. It passes through a recently logged-over region where there is now young growth of red pine—a good region in which to see moose. A 1.7-mile spur leads north from County Road 116 to the Meander Lake picnic grounds, a lovely place for a swim or for mere relaxation. You can also stretch your legs there by hiking a ways on the Sioux-Hustler Trail (see "Overnight Trails for Backpackers" in Chapter 4).

Nigh Creek Road (Map 5)

Length:	6 miles (one way)
Riding time:	2–3 hours (round trip)
Difficulty:	Easy
Highlights:	Recent logging activity; moose
USGS Maps:	Astrid Lake, Bootleg Lake

Just east of the Lake Jeanette Campground, Forest Route 471 (the Nigh Creek Road) leads south to a point just north of the BWCA Wilderness, where the Norway Trail begins (see Chapter 4). The road winds through mixed forest and a vast area that has been recently logged over. Beyond the road's end, high rocky ridges afford bikers an excellent opportunity to explore cross-country. The ancient weathered granite provides a relatively smooth riding surface for bicycles, and trees are more sparse on the high ridges. With a good topographic map and a compass, mountain bikers can test their skill and stamina in a true wilderness setting. Be careful to not enter the Boundary Waters, however, where bikes are illegal. Spur roads from logging activity also provide side trips. Milepost markers along the route help you judge your time.

KAWISHIWI DISTRICT

August Lake Loop (Map 15)

Length:	13.5 miles (round trip)
Riding time:	3–4 hours
Difficulty:	Easy to rugged
Highlights:	Rock quarry, August Lake
USGS Maps:	Bogberry Lake, Gabbro Lake, Slate Lake West, Slate Lake East

This delightful route around August Lake includes 5.3 miles of gravel forest routes, 4.5 miles of native-surface non-roads and 3.7 miles along Highway 1, which has a blacktop surface. The easiest access is at an old granite quarry adjacent to Highway 1, 16 miles south of the Ely Chamber of Commerce (see "Rock Quarry" in Chapter 6). The most challenging and interesting part of the loop is the 4.5-mile stretch between the quarry and August Lake. The old, single-lane logging road crosses some hilly terrain and skirts a beaver pond. Watch for moose and wolf tracks.

Kawishiwi River Loop (Maps 6, 15)

Length:	26 miles (one way)
Riding time:	7–8 hours

Resting on the shore of Birch Lake

Difficulty:	Challenging
Highlights:	Wildlife potential
USGS Maps:	Kangas Bay, Ely, Farm Lake, Bogberry Lake

Accessible from State Highway 1, 8 miles south of Ely, or from Lake County Road 16, 7 miles east of Ely, this big loop gives bikers a taste of everything. Most of the loop is a snowmobile route, built and maintained by Timber Trail Resort on Farm Lake, that skirts the southern edge of the BWCA Wilderness. It crosses some wet terrain that could cause trouble in spring and early summer. The rest of the loop requires a 4-mile jaunt on the county Spruce Road (gravel) and a 2.4-mile stretch of State Highway 1 (blacktop).

ISABELLA DISTRICT

Stony Loop (Map 16)

Length:	9.3 miles (one way)
Riding time:	3–4 hours (round trip)
Difficulty:	Easy
Highlights:	Old Stony Lookout
USGS Maps:	Isabella Station, Greenwood Lake East, Slate Lake East

Forest Road 103 makes a partial loop south from Highway 1 through the region just east of the McDougal Lake Campground. The east end of the loop intersects Highway 1 0.5 mile west of the Isabella ranger station, while the west end emerges just 0.75 mile from the campground turnoff. The native-surface road, two smooth, sandy lanes with grass growing between them, provides bikers with a ride past some large pine, aspen and considerable birch. Watch for the turnoff to the Old Stony Lookout about 3 miles from the east end of the loop (see "Sightseeing" in Chapter 6). It offers a good side trip, especially in autumn. About midway through the loop, an intersection with Forest Route 393 leads 100 yards south to a one-lane bridge across the Stony River, both a scenic area and a source of drinking water. A complete loop of 18 miles can be made from the campground by riding on Highway 1. Watch out for motor traffic.

Pike Lake Loop (Maps 15, 16)

Length:	13 miles (one way)
Riding time:	2–3 hours
Difficulty:	Moderate
Highlights:	Several small lakes
USGS Map:	Slate Lake East

Although this route does not have as good a road surface for bikers as the Stony Loop, it does have several lake accesses and campsites along the way. It begins at the intersection of the Bandana Lake Road (Forest Road 383) and Highway 1, just 1 mile north of the McDougal Lake Campground, loops through a woodland region north of Highway 1, and finally ends back at Highway 1 only 1.4 miles west of the intersection. It can be combined with the South Kelly Road (Forest Route 386 just to the north) and the Tomahawk Road (Forest Route 173) for a large loop of 31 miles round-trip from the campground. Along the way, you'll have access to 8 lovely lakes and several nice campsites. The road surfaces include gravel, native surface and a short stretch of blacktop on Highway 1. You might also enjoy a short side trip from the Tomahawk Road to Jackpine Mountain (see "Sightseeing" in Chapter 6).

Forest Route 172 (Maps 16, 17)

Length:	13.5 miles (one way)
Riding time:	3–5 hours (round trip)
Difficulty:	Easy
Highlights:	Passes several lakes
USGS Maps:	Isabella, Cabin Lake, Silver Island Lake

This hilly, winding gravel road leads east from "downtown" Isabella to County Road 7. It's considered a "one-lane road with turnouts," but it is plenty wide to accommodate passing traffic. The road skirts the shores of several lakes, crosses several creeks and also passes the Dumbbell Lake and Hogback Lake picnic grounds and the Divide Lake campground. Unfortunately, short loops are not possible. By turning either north or south onto County Road 7, however, you can make a large loop back to Highway 1 at Isabella.

Flathorn—Gegoka Ski Area (Map 16)

Length:	15 miles of loops
Riding time:	2–3 hours
Difficulty:	Easy
Highlights:	Marked intersections
USGS Map:	Mitiwan Lake

This has recently been designated as a mountain bike touring area. National Forest Lodge, located 6.5 miles west of the Isabella ranger station on Highway 1, serves as the trailhead. For more information, contact Bob Hunger, 3226 Highway 1, Isabella, MN 55607.

TOFTE DISTRICT

Fall Color Tour (Maps 17, 18)

Length:	60 miles of loops
Riding time:	2–10 hours
Difficulty:	Challenging
Highlights:	Panoramic views
USGS Maps:	Schroeder, Tofte SE, Tofte NE, Lutsen

To help visitors find the most colorful scenes, the Tofte District has signed the forest roads that are the most beautiful in autumn and prepared a map to illustrate the routes (see "Fall Color Tour" in Tofte District section of Chapter 6). All the roads are gravel and they receive a great deal of automobile traffic on peak weekends, but, for breathtaking scenery, you can't beat it! Routes range in length from the 6-mile Mountain View Drive to the 31-mile Beaver Dam Drive. Starting at Highway 61, you'll climb several hundred feet en route to the Sawtooth Mountain highlands. Don't attempt it unless you're in good physical condition. If you're not, you can always shuttle cars and start in the highlands, working your way down to the coast.

North Shore State Trail (Maps 17, 18)

Length:	70 miles (one way)
Riding time:	2–3 days
Difficulty:	Rugged
Highlights:	Panoramic views
USGS Maps:	Cramer, Schroeder, Tofte SE, Tofte NE, Lutsen, Deer Yard Lake, Mark Lake, Devil Track Lake, Finland, Little Marais

Winding its woodland way from Duluth to Grand Marais, this multiple-use trail crosses 60 rivers and creeks, skirts several lakes and affords some terrific scenic overlooks. The entire trail is 153 miles long, but only the section between the town of Finland and County Road 6 near Grand Marais is suitable for summer use. Trail shelters along the route can be used for camping and picnicking.

Though much of this part of the trail falls on Superior National Forest land (both the Tofte and Gunflint districts), the trail is administered by the Minnesota Department of Natural Resources. For more information and/or a map of the trail, contact the DNR, Trails and Waterways Unit, Information Center, Box 40, 500 Lafayette Road, St. Paul, MN 55146.

Timber and Frear Lakes Loop (Map 17)

Length:	25 miles
Riding time:	3–5 hours
Difficulty:	Easy
Highlights:	Access to several lakes
USGS Maps:	Wilson Lake, Kawishi Lake, Beth Lake, Tofte NW

The Timber–Frear Lakes canoe route (see Chapter 3) uses the Whitefish Lake public landing as the trailhead. You can pedal through a scenic region on primitive, native-surface roads that pass several lovely lakes, including Organ, Four Mile, Cross River, Wigwam and Besho, as well as Whitefish. Short side trips provide access to Lost, Finger, Elbow and Toohey lakes. Allow a full day to explore the options along this fascinating route.

Biking the North Shore Trail

GUNFLINT DISTRICT

For years, the Gunflint District, thanks largely to efforts by the private sector, has been in the forefront of developing recreational trails in Superior National Forest. Now, it is also the first to acknowledge mountain biking as a genuine form of outdoor recreation.

The North Superior Ski and Run Club mapped out nearly 200 miles of bike routes in the Grand Marais area. Most loops can be completed easily in half a day, or they can be combined with other loops for a full day—or more—of biking. Most of the roads lie above the ridge line (1000 feet above Lake Superior), and use graded gravel roads. The most primitive roads are in the northeastern part of the district (toward the Arrowhead Trail), where some old, native-surface logging roads are used.

For experienced bikers who want off-road challenges, there are some snowmobile and ski trails in the area (including the North Shore State Trail described in the Tofte District section above). A good trail map is available for anyone interested in riding on the Pincushion Mountain Cross-Country Ski Trail, which is mowed regularly to accommodate both hikers and bikers. Contact the Pincushion Inn and Cross-Country Ski Center, Gunflint Trail, P.O. Box 181, Grand Marais, MN 55604, or call (218) 387-1276.

FISHING

On the opening day of the Minnesota fishing season, about 1 million Minnesotans—a quarter of the state's population—head for the lakes. Not all of them drive to Superior National Forest; but a lot of them do, and they are joined by thousands of people from other states.

Nearly all of the Forest's 2000 lakes larger than 10 acres contain fish. The most popular game fish are walleyes, smallmouth bass, lake trout and northern pike, but stream trout and pan fish also attract a good many anglers. Muskies are found in a few isolated lakes, largemouth bass are in some, and salmon can be found along the Lake Superior coastline. The state's largest recorded walleye (17 lbs. 8 oz.), northern pike (45 lbs. 12 oz.), lake trout (43 lbs. 8 oz.), rainbow trout (17 lbs. 6 oz.), brook trout (6 lbs. 2 oz.), splake (9 lbs. 6 oz.), coho salmon (10 lbs. 6.5 oz.), Chinook (25 lbs. 8 oz.), pink salmon (3 lbs. 14 oz.), Atlantic salmon (12 lbs. 8 oz.) and whitefish (10 lbs. 6 oz.) all came from the lakes and streams of northeastern Minnesota.

Walleyes are the favorite of most Minnesota anglers. These lazy, unaggressive fish thrive in lakes with rocky or sandy bottoms. They are most easily caught with live bait, including minnows, leeches and night crawlers. Under the right conditions, however, they can also be caught on slow-moving small spoons, artificial minnows, jigs and deep-diving, bottom-bumping plugs. Walleyes prefer the safety of deeper water, but when they start feeding, the shallows off the tips of sand bars and rocky points are the places to start looking for them, especially in the twilight hours. Walleyes are schooling fish. If you catch one, a few more are usually around. Sizes range from less than a pound to more than 17 pounds. (The tastiest are between one and three pounds.) The catch limit is six (in combination with saugers).

Most out-of-state folks are more interested in smallmouth bass, pound for pound, the feistiest fish in the water. Not native to these northern lakes, bass have, nevertheless, adapted nicely to clear lakes with rocky bottoms and uneven shorelines. They weigh up to six and a half pounds, with lots of three- to five-pounders caught each year. They congregate at windswept points where waves stir up food for minnows and crayfish, their two favorite foods. Fallen trees and other structures that are above or slightly below the surface of the water also attract them. Dawn and dusk are the prime times to catch them, but you can be successful at almost any time of day by fishing the shoreline. Smallmouth bass can be caught with a variety of small plugs, spoons, spinners and flies. Minnows, leeches, crayfish and night crawlers can also be effective. The possession limit is six (in combination with largemouth bass), and the season may start later than for other fish.

Northern pike are probably sought less than any other game fish. Many folks consider them a nuisance, because they bite off lures aimed at walleyes and bass. But scrappy, smaller pike are fun to catch and, when filleted properly, they are as tasty as any other fish. They feed almost exclusively on other fish, primarily during the day, and they are much easier to catch than walleyes or bass. They'll attack almost any lure, but large bucktail spinners, spoons and plugs are best. Four- to eight-inch sucker minnows are also effective. A steel leader is imperative, since the razor-sharp teeth of northern pike can cut monofilament line. The possession limit is three (except in certain Canadian border waters, where the limit is six).

Lake trout are probably the species least known to summertime visitors. That's because, as the lakes warm up, lake trout retreat deeper and deeper, preferring water temperatures between 45°F and 55°F. In July and August, lake trout may be resting on the bottom of cold, clear lakes that are more than a hundred feet deep. In midsummer, the most successful anglers are those who know the lakes they're fishing. In spring, however, soon after the ice leaves, almost anyone can catch trout by casting with artificial lures or by still fishing with dead minnows. The limit is three, and there are separate seasons for summer and winter fishing.

REGULATIONS

Each year, the Minnesota Department of Natural Resources publishes a free fishing regulations booklet that is available from any county auditor or any place of business that is authorized to sell fishing licenses. You may also obtain one by writing to License Bureau, Box 26, 500 Lafayette Road, St. Paul, MN 55155-4026.

WHERE THE FISH ARE

LAURENTIAN DISTRICT

The Laurentian District is not generally known for its outstanding fishing, but several lakes contain nice populations of walleye, northern pike and panfish, and there are also some state-managed trout streams. You won't find any lake trout, however, and bass populations are scarce.

For big northern pike, try Dark Lake in the western part of the district. Big Rice Lake can also be good in spring and early summer, before the wild rice gets too thick. Just about all of the lakes in the eastern part of the district harbor northerns, and most also contain walleyes. A few have bass.

Stream trout inhabit Murphy Creek, Breda Creek, Berry Creek, Weinman Creek, Sullivan Creek and Trapper Creek in the southeastern part of the district. The Dark River and Johnson Creek are also good sources of trout in the northwestern part of the district.

LA CROIX DISTRICT

Walleyes, northern pike, smallmouth bass and lake trout are all found in the lakes of the La Croix District.

The best sources of walleyes are Vermilion, Black Duck, Elephant, Johnson, Crane, Jeanette, Big Moose, Little Trout and Trout lakes. Trout Lake is usually best at the shallower northern end in the early part of the season. Trout Lake is also a good source for northern pike, as are Picket Lake and the Pelican River. Your best bets for smallmouth bass are Trout Lake and the Vermilion River. Cold-water lakes that contain lake trout are Trout, Gun, Little Trout, Oyster and Takumich, all of which are inside the BWCA Wilderness. Trout is the easiest lake to access.

The North Arm of Trout Lake is popular with winter campers in search of lake trout. It can be reached by skiing north from Vermilion Lake (see directions to "1—Trout Lake" in Chapter 3) or by following the Norway Trail south from the Echo Trail to the lake (see "Day Hikes" in Chapter 4). Ice fishermen may also want to ski up to Ramshead Lake via the Blandin Trail for some good northern pike fishing (see "Day Hikes" in Chapter 4 for directions to the Blandin Trail).

The single best lake in the district—one "designed" for the angler who wants it all—is Lac La Croix, a big, beautiful lake that lies in the BWCAW and stretches more than 20 miles along the U.S.–Canadian border. It's one of the best lakes in the area for both walleyes and northern pike, but you can also find lake trout and smallmouth bass. Unfortunately, if you're paddling a canoe, you can't get to and from it in just one day. Still, it's a lovely place to spend a night—or two.

KAWISHIWI DISTRICT

The only choice missing in this district is the opportunity to fish trout streams. Nevertheless, stream trout have been stocked in several area lakes.

If lake trout fishing is your main interest, you won't be disappointed. The best lakes in the area are Thomas, Fraser, Ima, Knife, Kekekabic and Basswood, all in the BWCAW. Closer to civilization are Burntside and Snowbank lakes. Some 10-pound-plus monsters are pulled out of Burntside every year, and one pulled from Snowbank Lake weighed over 20 pounds.

The most dependable sources of northern pike are Hoist Bay and Wind Bay of Basswood Lake, Ramshead, Mud, Wind, Wood, Disappointment, Birch, Crooked, Farm and Insula lakes and the Numbered Lakes chain. Early spring anglers are attracted to the Canadian border waters, where the northern pike season is continuous and the limit is double that of other lakes in the area. The biggest northern ever caught in Minnesota came from Basswood Lake, a 45 lb.–12 oz. monster recorded back in 1929.

One of the best lakes in northern Minnesota for smallmouth bass is Crooked Lake, a beautiful, winding lake that forms part of the U.S.-Canadian boundary. More accessible lakes are Basswood, Big, Ojibway, Shagawa and the Moose Lake chain.

Divide Lake is a popular stop for trout anglers.

Big, Fall, Basswood and Shagawa lakes are rated among the top 100 walleye lakes in Minnesota. Other good sources of this scrumptious fish are Alice, Crooked, Insula, Gabbro, Moosecamp, Ima, Horse and Angleworm lakes.

ISABELLA DISTRICT

Dumbbell Lake, one of only two state-managed muskie lakes in Superior National Forest, is found here along with several state-managed stream trout lakes, but this is not a good area for smallmouth bass or lake trout.

Forest Service officials say that the three best walleye lakes in the district are Greenwood, Dumbbell and Silver Island; all have good roads leading right to them. Greenwood is also good for northern pike, as are Sylvania, Two Deer, Pike and Comfort lakes and the Island River. Stream trout enthusiastics should try Arrowhead and Trappers lakes and the Little Isabella River between Highway 1 and the Arrowhead Road.

TOFTE DISTRICT

The southeastern corner of Superior National Forest boasts some fine trout streams along the Lake Superior coastline. But, like the other southern districts in the Forest, this is not the place to look for lake trout or smallmouth bass.

The Minnesota Department of Tourism rates Wilson, Four Mile, Caribou and Crescent lakes among the best 100 walleye lakes in Minnesota. All lie outside the BWCA Wilderness. Within the Wilderness, Brule Lake and the upper flowage of the Kawishiwi River, including Polly, Koma and Malberg lakes, are also good sources of walleyes.

Northern pike can be found in White Pine, Little Wilson, Little Cascade and Four Mile lakes. Cross River Lake is also a good source in the spring. Stream trout are stocked in Hare, Goldeneye and Echo lakes, but most of the stream trout are in streams, where they belong.

GUNFLINT DISTRICT

Good populations of walleyes, northern pike, lake trout and smallmouth bass are all found in the northeastern corner of Superior National Forest.

The Minnesota Department of Tourism includes five lakes here among the top 100 walleye lakes in the state: Devil Track, Gunflint and Pike lakes lie outside the BWCAW; Saganaga and Sea Gull lakes are inside. All are easily accessible, with good roads leading to all of them. The state-record walleye (17 lbs. 8 oz.) was taken from the Seagull River at the south end of Saganaga Lake. Pine and North lakes are also outstanding sources of walleyes.

Minnesota DNR officials consider Davis, Gordon and Saganaga among the best lakes in the district for northern pike, while Saganaga and Tuscarora lakes are among the best for lake trout within the BWCA Wilderness. Gunflint Lake is a good source of lake trout outside the BWCAW. Daniels, Pine and East Pike lakes are three of the most dependable sources of smallmouth bass.

ANGLER'S GUIDE TO LAKES AND STREAMS

The following table lists 355 accessible lakes and streams in Superior National Forest and the species of game fish that are found in them. It does *not* include:
• Many of the remote, interior lakes in the BWCAW
It includes:
• All of the lakes and streams *outside* the BWCAW that are readily accessible to Forest visitors
• Lakes and streams *inside* the BWCAW that constitute day-route possibilities from all entry points, and
• Lakes in the BWCAW that are accessible to hikers.

The locations of these lakes and streams are shown on the maps in Chapter 2. The number of the appropriate map for each body of water is listed in the map column. The fish column lists the most prevalent species first.

> ## Table 14 — Lakes, Streams, and Fish

Name of Lake	Dis	Fish	Acc	Map	Name of Lake	Dis	Fish	Acc	Map
Agassa	K	W	H	5	Big	K	W NP B	D	5
Ahsub *	K	BT S	B,H	7	Big	L	W NP	D	15
Alder *	G	W NP LT B	B	10	Big Moose *	LC	NP W B	B	5
Alpine *	G	LT NP W B	B	8	Big Rice	L	NP	D	13
Alton *	T	LT NP B W	B	8	Binagami	G	W RB	H	10
Alworth *	K	W NP	B,H	7	Bingshick *	G	BT	H,B	8
Angleworm *	K	W NP	H	6	Birch	G	RT S LT	H	9
Astrid	LC	NP PF	H	4	Birch	K	W NP PF	D	15
Arrowhead	L	W PF	D	13	Bird	L	NP	D	14
August	K	W NP	D	15	Black Duck	LC	W	D	3
Baker *	T	NP P	D	8	Blackstone	K	NP	H	7
Bald Eagle *	K	W NP	B	16	Bog *	I	W	H	16
Ball Club	G	W NP	D	9	Bogus	G	BT S	D	10
Banadad *	G	NP	B	9	Bootleg *	LC	B	B	5
Barker	T	W BC NP	H	18	Bower Trout *	G	W NP PF	D	9
Bass	K	NP B PF	H	6	Boys	G	BT RT	H	10
Bassett	L	W NP	D	19	Brant *	G	NP P	B	8
Basswood *	K	W NP LT B	B	6,7	Breda	L	NP	D	19
Bath	G	BT	D	9	Brule *	T	W NP B	D	9
Bear Island	K	W NP B	D	14	Bulge	T	W NP P	B	18
Bearskin	G	B LT NP W	D	10	Burnt *	T	W NP	B	8
Beetle	I	RT	D	16	Burntside	K	W LT B NP	D	5,6

DIS (District): I = Isabella, K = Kawishiwi, L = Laurentian, LC = La Croix, G = Gunflint, T = Tofte
FISH: B = bass, BC = black crappie, BG = bluegill, BT = brook trout, LT = lake trout, M = muskellunge, NP = northern pike, P = perch, PF = panfish, RB = rock bass, RT = rainbow trout, S = splake, ST = stream trout varieties, W = walleyes, WF = whitefish
ACC (Access): B = boat, D = driving, H = hiking
MAP: Numbers refer to maps in this guide. Note: somes are too small to show clearly on the maps; to find them, refer to the corresponding Fisher or McKenzie maps (see page 74).
An asterisk (*) next to the name indicates that it is located in the BWCAW.

Table 14 cont'd	Lakes, Streams, and Fish

Name of Lake	Dis	Fish	Acc	Map	Name of Lake	Dis	Fish	Acc	Map
Cadotte	L	W NP	D	19	Dunnigan	I	W B BG	D	15
Camp Four	L	RT	H	12	East Bearskin	G	W B NP	D	10
Canal	I	RT	B,H	17	East Chub	I	N W BG	D	15
Canoe *	G	W NP B	B	10	East Pike *	G	B WF M	B	10
Caribou *	G	WF NP B W	B	10	East Twin	G	W	D	10
Caribou *	G	W NP	B	9	Echo	LC	NP W	D	4
Caribou	T	ST	D	18	Echo	T	RT BT S	D	17
Carl *	G	ST	B	9	Edith *	G	NP P	B	8
Carrot	G	BT	D	10	Eighteen	I	W B	D	16
Cascade	T	W NP P	D	9	Eikela	I	BT	D	15
Chester	G	ST	D	10	Elbow	G	W NP P BG	D	10
Chow	L	NP	D	15	Elbow	LC	W	D	4
Christine	T	NP W PF	D	18	Elbow	T	NP	B	17
Clara	T	W NP PF	D	18	Elephant	LC	W NP BC	D	3
Clear	L	PF B	D	12	Elixir	I	NP	D	17
Clear *	K	W NP	B	6	Ella Hall *	K	BG NP W B	B	6
Clearwater *	G	LT B	D	10	Emerald *	LC	PF	B,H	5
Clove *	G	W B NP	B	8,9	Ennis	K	BT S	H	7
Cloquet	I	NP W	D	16,20	Ensign *	K	W NP B	B	7
Cloquet River	L	W NP	D	19	Esther	G	ST	D	10
Colby	L	W NP B	D	14	Everett	K	W NP PF	H	6
Comfort	I	W NP	D	16	Fall *	K	W NP BC	D	6
Cones *	T	W NP B	B	9	Farm	K	W NP BC	D	6
Crab	G	W NP BG B	B,H	9	Fenske	K	W NP B PF	D	6
Crab *	K	B NP	B	5	Finger	T	W NP	D	17
Crane	LC	W	D	2	Flash	K	W NP	H,B	7
Crocodile *	G	B W	B	10	Flathorn	I	W NP BG B	D	16
Crescent	T	W M NP P	D	9,18	Fleck	T	W NP P	B	18
Crooked	T	W B M	D	17	Flour	G	W B NP P	D	10
Cross River	T	W NP	D	17	Found *	K	RT S	B	7
Dam Five	I	NP B W	D	17	Four, *	K	NP W	B	10
Daniels *	G	LT B	B,H	10	Four Mile	T	W NP PF	D	17
Dark	L	NP W	D	12	Fourtown *	K	W NP B	B	6
Dark River	L	ST	H	12	Fowls	G	W NP B P	B	11
Deepwater	L	RT	H	12	Fran	L	NP	B	15
Deeryard	G	W	D	18	Franklin	LC	W	H	1
Devilfish	G	LT W	D	10	Frear	T	NP	B	17
Devil Track	G	W NP WF P	D	18	Gabbro *	K	W NP	B	6
Disappointment*	K	W NP B	7		Garden	K	NP W B PF	D	6
Divide	I	BT	D	16	Gegoka	I	W NP P	D	16
Dogtrot	T	NP	B	18	Gogebic *	G	BT	H	10
Dovre *	LC	NP W	H	2	Goldeneye	T	BT	D	17
Dragon	I	NP BC W	D	16	Good *	K	NP W B PF	B	6
Dry	K	BT S	B,H	6	Grace *	T	W NP	B	8
Dumbbell	I	W B M	D	16	Grassy	K	NP B PF	B	6
Duncan *	G	LT W NP B	B,H	9	Greenwood	G	LT W B WF	D	10

Table 14 cont'd

Lakes, Streams, and Fish

Name of Lake	Dis	Fish	Acc	Map	Name of Lake	Dis	Fish	Acc	Map
Greenwood	I	W NP	D	15	Knute *	LC	NP B	H	2,4
Grub *	K	B	H	7	Korb *	K	B NP BG	B	5
Gunflint	G	LT W NP B	D	9	Lamb *	LC	NP	H,B	5
Ham	G	W P NP	B	8,9	La Pond *	K	NP	B	5
Hand	G	NP P	H	9	Larch *	G	NP P	B	8
Hare	T	ST	D	17	Lichen	T	W NP P M	D	9
Harriet	I	W NP BC	D	17	Lily *	T	NP	B	9
Harris	K	M B PF	D	15	Little Cascade	T	NP P	H	9
Harris	L	W NP B	H	19	Little Dry	K	BT	B	6
Hay	L	NP	B	13	Little Gabbro *	K	W NP	H	6
Hegmans *	K	W NP B	H,B	6	Little Gunflint	G	W NP B	B	9
High	K	RT S	B	6	Little Long	K	PF NP B W	B	6
Hogback	I	RT	D	17	Little North	G	W NP LT B	B	9
Holly	T	NP BG P	D	18	Little Iron	G	W NP PF	D	9
Home *	K	W NP	B,H	6	Little John	G	W NP B P	D	10,11
Homer *	T	W NP P	D	9	Little Rush *	G	W NP P	B	9
Homestead	I	B BC	D	16,17	Little Sletten	K	B	B	6
Horse *	K	W NP BG	B	6	Little Trout *	G	LT	B	5
Horseshoe *	G	W NP	B	9	Little Vermilion*	LC	W NP B P	B	2
Horseshoe *	K	NP W BG	B,H	7	Little Wilson	T	W NP	D	17
Hula *	K	NP	B	6	Lizz *	G	S	B	9
Hungry Jack	G	B W NP PF	D	9	Long	L	NP	B	15
Hustler *	LC	NP PF	B,H	5	Loon	G	LT B W NP	D	9
Indiana *	K	NP B	B	6	Loon *	LC	NP W B	B	2,5
Inga	I	NP	H	16	Low	K	W NP B PF	D	6
Iron	G	W NP P	D	9	Lux *	G	ST	B	9
Isabella *	I	W NP	H	16	Magnetic *	G	W NP LT B	B	9
Isabella River *	I	W NP	B	16	Marsh	T	NP P	D	17,18
Island River	I	W NP	D	16	Maude	LC	N	H	4
Jake *	G	ST	B	9	Mayhew	G	LT	D	9
Jammer	L	BT RT	D	13	McDonald	G	W NP B P	H	9
Jeanette	LC	NP W	D	5	McDougals	I	NP W	D,B	15,16
John *	G	W B NP P	B	10	McFarland	G	B W NP P	D	10
Johnson	K	PF W NP	D	15	Meander	LC	B W BG	D	5
Johnson	LC	W NP B	H	1	Meeds *	G	W	B	9
Junco	G	BT	H	10	Mink	G	RT BT S	D	10
Juno *	T	NP P	B	9	Misquah *	G	LT	B	9
Kawasachong *	T	NP W	B	8	Missing Link *	G	RT BT	B	8
Kawishiwi *	T	NP W	D	8	Moore	T	NP BG	D	18
Kawishiwi River *	K	W NP	D,B	6,7,8	Moose *	K	W B NP	D	7
Kelly *	T	W NP P	B	8,9	Morgan *	G	ST	H	9
Kelso *	T	NP	B	8	Moss	G	LT RT	H	10
Kemo	G	LT S	B	10	Mudro *	K	W NP B	B	6
Kimball	G	RT BT S	D	10	Mulligan *	T	BT RT	B	9
Kjostad	LC	W	D	4	Myrtle	LC	PF	D	4
Knuckey	L	NP	D	12	Nels	K	W NP	D	6

Table 14 cont'd — Lakes, Streams, and Fish

Name of Lake	Dis	Fish	Acc	Map	Name of Lake	Dis	Fish	Acc	Map
Newfound *	K	W B NP	B	7	Royal *	G	W	B	11
Newton *	K	W NP BC	B	6	Rush *	G	NP	B	9
Nigh	LC	None	H	4	Saganaga *	G	LT W NP B	D	8
Nina-Moose *	LC	W NP B	B	5	St. Louis River	L	W NP	D	14
Ninemile	T	W NP BC	D	17	Salo	L	W NP B	D	19
North	G	LT W NP B	B	9	Sand	L	W NP	D	15
Northern Light	G	NP W B P	D	10	Sawbill *	T	W NP B	D	8
Ojibway	K	B LT	D	7	Scarp	I	RT	H,B	17
One, *	K	W NP	D	7	Sea Gull *	G	LT NP W B	D	8
One Island *	G	NP P	B	9	Section 29	I	W NP	D	16
One Pine	K	W NP PF	D	15	Shagawa	K	W NP B	D	6
Otto	L	W NP	H	19	Shamrock	I	B	H	15
Parent *	K	W NP	B	7	Shoe Pack	L	PF	D	12
Parsnip	G	B	B	10	Seven Beaver	L	W NP	B	15
Partridge *	G	LT	H	9	Silver Island	I	W NP	D	17
Partridge River	L	W NP	D	14	Skipper *	G	W NP P	B	9
Pauline	LC	NP PF	H	4	Skull *	K	S BT	B	7
Paunesss *	LC	W NP	B	5	Slate	I	W NP	D	15
Perch	K	NP P	H	15	Sletten	K	B	B	6
Perent *	T	NP W	B	17	Slim *	K	W	H	5
Peterson *	T	W NP P	B	8	Slip	T	W NP P	B	18
Petrel Creek	L	NP	D	19	Smoke *	T	NP W B	B	8
Pfeiffer	L	W B PF	D	13	Snowbank *	K	LT NP W B	D	7
Phoebe *	T	W NP	B	8	South *	G	LT NP B	B,H	9
Picket	K	W NP	D	6	South Farm *	K	W NP BC	B	6
Picket	LC	NP BG	H	4	Square *	T	NP W	B	8
Pike	I	NP B	H	15,16	Star	T	NP P	D	9
Pine *	G	W B WF LT	B	10	Steer	I	BT	H	17
Pine	G	RT	D,B	10	Stone	L	NP	H	15
Pine	L	W NP	H	15	Stony River	L	W NP	D	15
Pine *	LC	W NP	H,B	5	Stuart *	LC	NP B	B	5
Pit	G	NP PF	D	9,10	Sullivan	L	ST	D	20
Poplar	G	W B NP WF	D,H	9	Sunfish	G	ST	H	10
Portage *	G	S	B	9	Surprise	I	NP W BC	H	16
Quadga *	I	NP W	B	16	Swallow	I	W NP	D	15
Ram *	G	RT LT	H	9	Swamp *	G	NP	B	9
Ramshead *	LC	NP W	H,B	5	Swan *	G	NP W WF	B	9
Range *	K	W NP PF	H	6	Sylvania	I	NP	D	16
Range Line *	LC	LT	H	5	Tait	T	NP W P	D	18
Red Rock *	G	W NP WF B	B	8	Talus	G	RT	B	10
Redskin	I	ST	D	16	Tee	I	W	H	17
Rice	L	NP	B	13	Tee	K	NP	B	6
Rice	T	W NP P	B	18	Thrasher	G	RT BT S	D	9
Rose *	G	B LT W WF	B,H	9,10	Three, *	K	NP W	B	7
Round	G	W B NP	D	8	Thunderbird	T	NP	B	17
Round	L	W NP	H	15	Timber	T	NP	B	17

Table 14 cont'd	Lakes, Streams, and Fish

Name of Lake	Dis	Fish	Acc	Map	Name of Lake	Dis	Fish	Acc	Map
Tin Can Mike *	K	W NP B BG	B	6	Ward	G	NP	D	18
Tofte	K	RT S	D	6	West Pike *	G	LT B	B,H	10
Toohey	T	W NP	D	17	West Twin	G	W	D	10
Topper *	G	BT	H	9	Whack *	T	NP	B	9
Trappers	I	BT	H	16	Whale *	G	NP P	H	9
Triangle	K	W NP B	B	7	Whisper	K	W B	H	15
Trout	G	RT LT P	D	10	Whiteface Reser.	L	W NP	D	19
Trout *	LC	LT W B	B	4,5	White Feather *	K	NP	B	5
Tuscarora *	G	LT NP P	B	8	Whitefish	T	W NP	D	17
Twins	K	W NP B PF	B	5,6	White Iron	K	W NP B PF	D	6
Two, *	K	W NP	B	7	White Pine	T	NP W P	D	18
Two Deer	I	NP	D	15	Whitewater	L	W NP B	D	14
Two Island	G	W B NP	D	9	Wilson	T	W NP P	D	17
Vermilion	LC	W B PF	D	4,5	Wind *	K	NP	B	7
Vermilion River	LC	B W NP	D	4	Windy	I	W NP	D	17
Vern *	T	NP W	B	9	Wood *	K	W NP B	H	6
Vista *	G	NP W	B	9	Wye	I	NP	D	17
Wampus	G	PF B	D	10					

FOR MORE INFORMATION

Furtman, Michael, *A Boundary Waters Fishing Guide.* Duluth: Birch Portage Press, 1984. If you're interested in a general introduction to all of the northern fish, along with specific guidance to the lakes of the BWCA Wilderness, this is the only book currently on the market that does both. It also includes discussions of the equipment needed, cleaning and cooking techniques and a lake index that reveals what kinds of fish are found in the BWCAW lakes.

APPENDIX

For general information about all aspects of Superior National Forest, contact the Forest Supervisor, Superior National Forest, P.O. Box 338, Duluth, MN 55801; (218) 727-6692. For information on state parks and state forests, contact Regional Forest Supervisor—DNR, 1201 East Highway 2, Grand Rapids, MN 55744; (218) 327-1718.

MAP DISTRIBUTORS

Maps that cover all or parts of Superior National Forest are available from the following sources:
- Creative Consultants, 727 Board of Trade Bldg, Duluth, MN 55802.
- Denver Distribution Center, U.S.G.S., Denver Federal Center, Building 41, Denver, CO 80225.
- Forest Supervisor, Superior National Forest, P.O. Box 338, Duluth, MN 55801. Or call (218) 727-6692.
- W.A. Fisher Company, Box 1107, Virginia, MN 55792.

COMMERCIAL INFORMATION

For information about restaurants, lodging, outfitting services and private campgrounds in the Superior National Forest region, contact the following area chambers of commerce.

FOR ALL DISTRICTS

- Minnesota Arrowhead Association, Box 204, Duluth, MN 55801; (218) 722-0874.
- Minnesota Travel Information Center, 240 Bremer Building, 419 N. Robert Street, St. Paul, MN 55101; (612) 296-5029, or toll-free within Minnesota (800) 652-9747, or toll-free outside Minnesota (800) 328-1461.

LAURENTIAN DISTRICT

- Aurora Chamber of Commerce, Aurora, MN 55705.
- Virginia Chamber of Commerce, 233 Chestnut Street, Virginia, MN 55792.

LA CROIX DISTRICT

- Cook Chamber of Commerce, Cook, MN 55723; (218) 666-2366.
- Crane Lake Commercial Club, Crane Lake, MN 55725; (218) 993-2346.
- Tower-Soudan Chamber of Commerce, Tower, MN 55790; (218) 753-6550.

KAWISHIWI DISTRICT

- Babbitt Chamber of Commerce, Box 299, Babbitt, MN 55706; (218) 827-2410.
- Ely Chamber of Commerce, 1600 E. Sheridan, Ely, MN 55731; (218) 365-6123.

ISABELLA DISTRICT

- Ely Chamber of Commerce (see "Kawishiwi District," above).
- Heart of the Arrowhead Association, Box 578, Finland, MN 55603.

TOFTE DISTRICT

- Lutsen-Tofte Tourism Association, Box 115, Lutsen, MN 55612.

GUNFLINT DISTRICT

- Tip of the Arrowhead Association, Grand Marais, MN 55604; (218) 387-1330 or 387-2524.

INDEX

About the author:

Robert Beymer literally lives his subject — his lakeside home near Ely, Minnesota is surrounded by Superior National forest. Its roads and trails form his daily jogging paths, and he shares his yard with the Forest's native residents — deer, black bear, moose, timber wolves, pine martens, squirrels and birds.

Constantly exploring the trails and waterways of his own home region and other areas of North America, Beymer regularly writes articles and supplies photographs for both regional and national outdoor magazines. He is the author of four previous books: *A Paddler's Guide to Quetico Provincial Park* and *Ski Country: Nordic Skiers Guide to the Minnesota Arrowhead* (both published by W.A. Fisher Co.) and the two-volume guidebook series *Boundary Waters Canoe Area* (Wilderness Press).

Beymer is a graduate of the University of Northern Iowa in sociology and history, with further study at the University of Minnesota. He is a member of Friends of the Boundary Waters, the Superior Hiking Trail Association, and the Isle Royale Natural History Association.